home

space, community and marginality in sydney's...

home/world

space, community and marginality in sydney's west

helen grace

ghassan hage

lesley johnson

julie langsworth

michael symonds

Pluto Press

First published in 1997 by Pluto Press Australia Limited
Locked Bag 199, Annandale, NSW 2038
www.socialchange.net.au/pluto/

© Helen Grace, Ghassan Hage, Lesley Johnson, Julie Langsworth, Michael Symonds

Cover and book design: Ulla Korgaard
Index: Neale Towart

Text typeset by Chapter 8 Pty Ltd.
Printed and bound by Southwood Press, 80 Chapel St, Marrickville, NSW 2204

Acknowledgements
Thanks to Yolanda Gill, Research Officer, WESTIR, for permission to reproduce Figure 1 on page 5, and to Geraldine Star, Manager, Information Branch, Department of Urban Affairs and Planning to reproduce photographs on pages 49–51.

Australian National Library Cataloguing-in-Publication data
Home/World: Space, community and marginality in Sydney's west.

Includes index.
ISBN 1 86403 036 4.

1. Suburbs — New South Wales — Western Sydney — Public opinion.
2. Western Sydney (N.S.W.) — Social conditions. I. Grace, Helen, 1949–.

307.7609941

contents

preface ix

1. introduction 1
lesley johnson, julie langsworth and michael symonds

    The politics of defining western Sydney
    Mapping western Sydney
    Aboriginal people in western Sydney
    Locating western Sydney; locating ourselves
    Suburbia and Australian debates about the city and modernity
    The city, space and modernity
    Readings of the landscape

2. feral suburbia? 31
    western sydney and the 'problem of urban sprawl'
lesley johnson
    Imagining the city
    'Urban ... What's that word mean?'
    'A people's plan'
    Private dreams and the 'public interest'
    'When one flies over the County ...'

3. outside the spaces of modernity: 66
    western sydney and the logic of the european city
michael symonds

    I The logic of the city
    The city-as-cultural-centre
    Early origins of the modern city
    The city-as-secular-centre

    II Home and modernity
    City and nature
    Modernity and loss
    The logic of home

    III Understanding the western suburbs
    The western suburbs' relationship to nature
    The end of the 'westie'?

4. at home in the entrails of the west: 99
multiculturalism, 'ethnic food' and migrant home-building

ghassan hage

I Migrant home-building
Multiculturalism, food and migrant home-building
On the nature of homes and home-building
Migrant home-building: the fostering of positive intimations
Migrant home-building and food
Migrant home-building, food and the dominant culture

II Cosmo-multiculturalism
The field of culinary cosmo-multiculturalism
Cosmo-multiculturalism and class
Cosmo-multiculturalism, class and western Sydney

III Multiculturalism without migrants
Cosmo-multiculturalism, ethnic 'authenticity' and power
Cabra-multiculturalism
For a multiculturalism of inhabitance

5. 'icon house':   154
towards a suburban topophilia

helen grace

I Utopian dreaming
The socialist garden suburb
'The Australian with his clay hut'
Everyman's 'instinctive desire'

II Displacement and disorientation
'House famine'
'House hunger'

III At homeworld
Dreamscapes
'Icon House'
The real and the fake home

IV 'The lost paradise of the body'
The centrality of the girl's room
The marital bedspread
The nursery
The absence of the boy's room
Kitchen and bathroom utopias
The veneer of the father

Index **196**

preface

This book began as a project on the politics of defining 'western Sydney'. Four of the authors were at that time employed at the University of Western Sydney, Nepean. As the introduction to the book explains, the project fairly quickly became much broader in its concerns. While the region known as 'western Sydney' continues to provide the empirical grounding for the book, it focuses on questions of home, belonging, marginality and space in the modern world. As the various essays that shape this book make clear, the term 'western Sydney' is a slippery and contested one. But we are not interested in providing a clear definition of this region; on the contrary, central to our concerns is the way in which various groups and agencies have set out to represent this region as marginalised.

This book is the result of an Australian Research Council funded project awarded to researchers at the University of Western Sydney, Nepean. Julie Langsworth joined the project soon after it started as research assistant and she has played a major role in the book's conception and writing. Michael Symonds is a lecturer in the Faculty of Humanities and Social Sciences at the University of Western Sydney, Nepean and was trained as a philosopher. Helen Grace is a Senior Lecturer in the Faculty of Visual and Performing Arts at the University of Western Sydney, Nepean, a film-maker and was trained in visual and film theory. Ghassan Hage is a Senior Lecturer in Anthropology at the University of Sydney and was trained as a sociologist. Lesley Johnson is Pro-Vice-Chancellor (Research) and Professor of Cultural Studies at the University of Technology, Sydney and was trained as a sociologist.

We would like to acknowledge the following organisations which have assisted us in this project: the Australian Research Council for the major grant that enabled us to undertake this project; the Urban Research Program of the Research School of Social Sciences at the Australian National University, which provided a three-month secondment to Lesley Johnson during the course of her work on chapter 2; and the University of Western Sydney, Nepean for its support of the project. We are indebted to Justine Lloyd for her highly professional assistance during various stages and to Gar Jones, Director of the Research Office at the University of Western Sydney, Nepean, for his generous help and goodwill throughout. Patricia Bower too has been supportive and assisted in various ways. Finally, we would like to express our appreciation to our publishers, Maria Nugent and Penny O'Donnell, for their enthusiasm for the project, their advice and their assistance in making it into a book. Maria, in particular, has made an enormous contribution to the final polishing of the chapters of the book for which we are deeply grateful.

1. introduction

lesley johnson, julie langsworth and michael symonds

In December 1816, Governor Macquarie began an annual feast-day ritual at Parramatta for the Aboriginal peoples of Sydney and surrounding regions. One hundred and seventy-nine Aboriginal people turned up on this occasion (as many as three hundred came in 1818 at the height of the success of this initiative). Officials of the colony and 'leading citizens' were also in attendance and large quantities of food and beverages were provided. The site of these occasions was said to be a major meeting place of Aboriginal tribes before white settlement, a place for corroborees. Macquarie would use the meetings over the next few years to hand out 'chieftaincies' and other honours to those individual Aboriginal men he favoured and to those that had assisted the military campaigns against 'refractory natives'.

As a precursor to these events, a similar feast had occurred in December 1814. On this earlier occasion, Macquarie 'persuaded' Aboriginal parents to provide six boys and six girls for instruction at a new institution he was to establish the following month, the Native Institution at Parramatta. In the 1816 ceremony, children from this school were paraded before the gathering to demonstrate the benefits of 'civilisation', a practice that was to continue until 1822. The following year the Native Institution was moved to what became known as Black Town, a reserve 19 kilometres from Parramatta. The Reverend Robert Cartwright had proposed to Macquarie that a 'native establishment' be developed at such a site. The Native Institution for children was envisaged as the beginning of what the Reverend Cartwright hoped would eventually become a series of Aboriginal villages and towns. A number of Aboriginal people were granted land for cultivation, but the project as a whole, including the Native Institution itself, was abandoned in 1828.[1]

In 1835 the feast-days were also abandoned. Attendances had declined considerably in the 1830s as the numbers of Aboriginal people living in and around Sydney diminished. The ceremonies had also come under increasing criticism as they were seen to encourage drunken and obscene behaviour among the Aboriginal population. Macquarie had initiated these contacts with Aboriginal people in the Sydney region, according to historian Keith Willey, as a way of pacifying — civilising — the Aboriginal populations and as an attempt to eliminate the conflicts and often deadly clashes that continued to erupt between white settlers and Aboriginal people, particularly at this time in the regions of the Nepean and Hawkesbury rivers.[2] By the middle of the nineteenth century, this 'problem' had disappeared: white settlement had almost totally obliterated any obvious signs of an Aboriginal presence from the landscape of Sydney and surrounding areas.

These stories of invasion, bloodshed, political struggle, colonialism and the almost total decimation of a people, only very briefly sketched in here, scarcely seem to register today on the landscapes of outer-urban regions, such as the one now known as 'western Sydney'. 'Blacktown', as the name of one of the suburbs in this region, has remained, as have the Aboriginal names of places such as Parramatta, but rarely are there any public reminders of where such names came from, of the history they signify. In 1989 the *Sydney Morning Herald* carried a feature article on the work done by a number of Aboriginal people, and the historian Jim Kohen, on recovering the history of Aboriginal peoples — the Dharuk[3] — who had lived in this region before and since white invasion.[4] But this was a rare reminder of the traces of these previous generations of indigenous peoples, of their continuing presence in this region, and of the way this landscape had been shaped by their activities before white settlement and then by their subsequent struggles with the colonial government and white people.

For the most part, however, the news media read the landscape of 'western Sydney' from within a quite different frame of reference. According to Diane Powell, the media are preoccupied with presenting this region as some kind of 'third world' space in relation to the rest of Sydney. Media audiences, she argues, are positioned as observers of this space, which is represented as foreign and disconnected from them; and its inhabitants are stigmatised, made 'other' — victims perhaps of disadvantage, but passive and often hopeless. Such representations in the past have certainly dominated the metropolitan media's accounts of this region of Sydney (although there is at least now some awareness of these issues). And they have served to obliterate the history of the making of this space; they have constituted a denial and marginalisation

introduction

of the everyday lives of the diverse population that now lives in the region: their sufferings, struggles, hopes and desires as played out in and actively shaping this urban landscape.

the politics of defining western Sydney

In 1973 Peter Weir, the now famous Australian film director, made a film *Whatever Happened to Green Valley?*, in which he sought to take up precisely these issues. Green Valley was a site in western Sydney, developed by the New South Wales Housing Commission between 1961 and 1964 for 6000 families. By 1973, 28 000 people were living there, some in home units, but most in suburban houses. Mocking media representations of this area as a 'valley of despair', Weir began his film with a satire of its portrayal by television and ended it by staging an 'evacuation' of the valley, moving its families by train to the peaceful, leafy streets of Sydney's northern suburb, Killara. Much of the remainder of the film is made up of brief documentaries produced by the residents themselves, with Weir's assistance, in which they tell stories of the hopes, desires, concerns and struggles they live out in this suburban space.[5]

This book began as a project on the politics of defining 'western Sydney' and concern with how the region had been represented in various contexts since the Second World War. Four of us were working at the University of Western Sydney, Nepean at the time we first began to discuss the project. None of the four was born in the region and we did not live there, but we travelled each day to work in this new university that had emerged out of the federal Labor government's moves in the late 1980s to establish a mass higher education system. The project was initially conceived as a way of analysing why at that time the region of western Sydney was consistently defined in the popular press in negative terms; the extent to which attempts to establish a positive sense of identity, as exemplified in local campaigns such as the one to establish a university 'in the West' in the mid-1980s, were successful or marginalised; and the way dominant representations of 'western Sydney' constituted this region as a grim and monotonous landscape in which the diversity of the lives and histories of populations of this vast area was repressed and denied.

Analyses of the predominantly negative media representations of this region had already been carried out before we began our project. Peter

Weir's film was just one example.[6] In the course of our undertaking the project, Diane Powell's major study of this issue, *Out West: Perceptions of Sydney's suburbs* (1993), was also published. But while seeking to be part of the moves to establish a positive sense of identity for the region that had increasingly emerged in the 1980s and 1990s,[7] Powell's book was also brutally recruited by the popular media to continue the very stereotypes she sought to challenge.[8] Thus we have seen some changes in public discourses about the region since we first began the project in 1992, but evidence still emerges frequently of how powerful the stereotypes are. A furore erupted in May 1996, for example, when Paul Whelan, New South Wales State Minister for Police, compared the people of western Sydney, 'westies', to English soccer hooligans in his attempt to cast a slur on a Liberal member of parliament; the incident provided evidence of how prevalent, and convenient, the negative definitions of this region and its residents remain.[9]

This issue, then, constitutes at least part of the context for our study and the background to some of our concerns. But rather than engage with the issue specifically, we have sought to provide a number of reflections on the production of this particular urban landscape that will address in part the politics of defining 'western Sydney', but in a way that links it to broader questions of the problems and possibilities of home, community, belonging and identity in the space of modern urban environments. These latter broader concerns emerge out of the more local issues of how people live in a region such as western Sydney, which is both materially disadvantaged and struggling to assert a positive sense of identity for those who live in the region. In this book, we have focused on both the local and more general issues as we have sought to understand what is at stake for those who live in the region, for ourselves as intellectuals working in a particular setting, and for the broader community.

mapping western Sydney

To the extent that we talk about western Sydney or the western suburbs of Sydney, for convenience we use the definition of this region produced by WESTIR.[10] According to this agency, it is a region located west and south-west of the city of Sydney along the Cumberland Plain. The region is described by WESTIR as 'The Greater West', and covers

introduction

Local Government Areas In Greater West

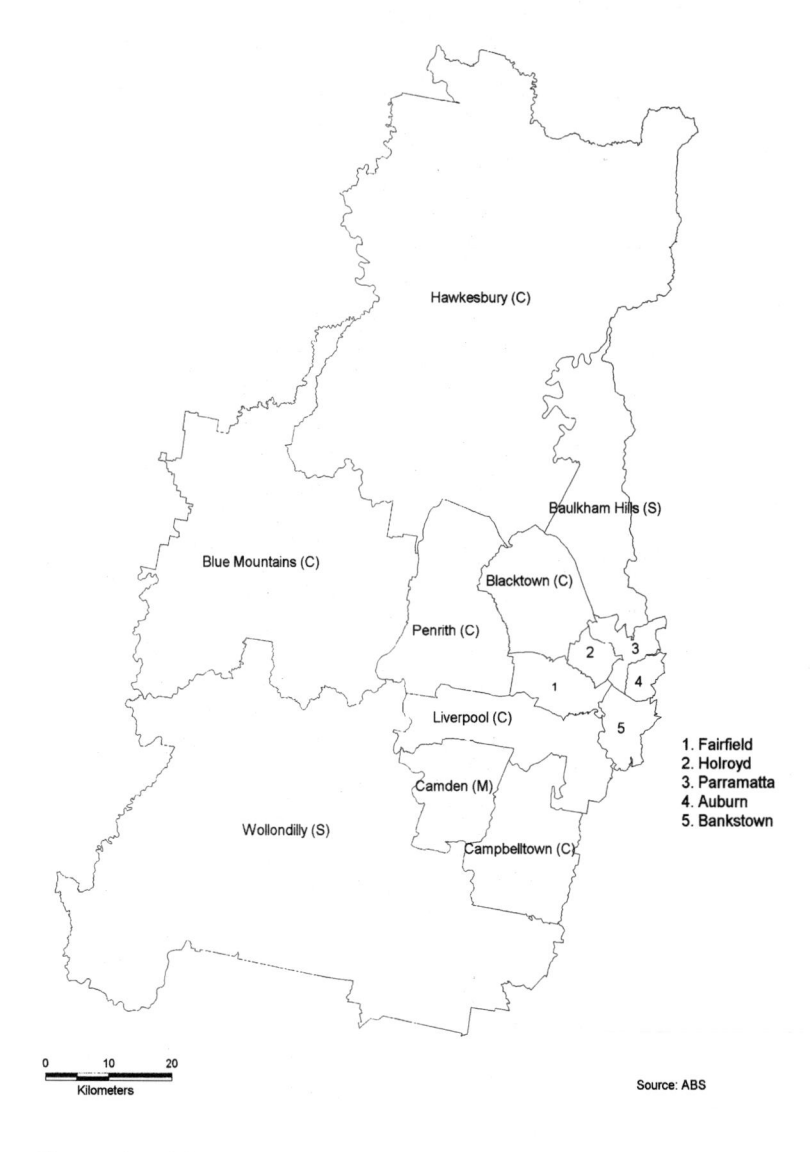

Figure 1 Local Government Areas in Greater West.
Compiled by WESTIR. Used with permission.

8 950.63 square kilometres, 72 per cent of metropolitan Sydney.[11] In 1995 it had a population of close to 2 million, and a population size of 2.25 million is expected by the year 2011. As defined by WESTIR, it has fourteen Local Government Areas (LGAs) as indicated on the Figure 1.[12] The city of Parramatta is considered the central business district of the region, although the LGA of Blacktown has the largest population. The region of western Sydney has both pockets of high population density (such as Blacktown and Fairfield) and large rural areas of very low population density (such as Hawkesbury). The Blue Mountains LGA is noted for its extensive National Park lands.

The Gross Domestic Product (GDP) of the region in 1996 was $A34 billion, the equivalent of Singapore's GDP. Western Sydney contributes one of Australia's largest markets for goods and services.[13] It has one major university, the University of Western Sydney (UWS), which is a federation of three separate networks: Hawkesbury, Macarthur, and Nepean. With a total student population of 25 699 in 1996, the university is the largest employer in the western suburbs.

The greatest changes to the region occurred in the years after the Second World War. Between 1966 and 1971 there was a 21 per cent increase in the population in the area, with large numbers coming from overseas. A significant proportion of new migrants chose to live in the outer suburbs of Sydney. A majority of these came from non-English-speaking (NESB) countries such as Malta, Vietnam, Philippines, Poland, Lebanon, the former Yugoslavia, Germany and India. At the 1991 Census, 43.9 per cent of Sydney's NESB population lived in western Sydney. The Aboriginal and Torres Strait Islander population is estimated to be 13 341 although many of the Aboriginal organisations in the region believe the figure to be much higher. Some say the numbers of Aboriginal people alone may be as high as 20 000.[14] While Redfern is well-known as the location of Sydney's largest Aboriginal community, 60 per cent of Sydney's Aboriginal and Torres Strait Islander population live in western Sydney, with the majority of these living in the LGA of Blacktown.

Since 1945 western Sydney has been portrayed as a region with vast stretches of suburban housing lacking services and facilities. Urban planning is seen to have failed the region, leaving the site a subdivided wasteland.[15] In an attempt to accommodate the post-war population, homes were rapidly erected by what M. T. Daly calls the 'hooligan developer', without the provision of public transport, roads, schools or recreational and cultural facilities.[16] In 1973 the federal Labor government initiated the Area Improvement Program to provide these necessary services and facilities. As some commentators have noted, it was not until this time that western Sydney was officially designated a region.[17] The action of the Whitlam government brought together councils and residents under the common cause of improving the western region of Sydney. As outlined in the Department of Urban and Regional Development publication *Community*, they sought to 'improve [the] regions (sic) environment so that it is a fairer, more interesting, and gentle place to live and work'.[18]

Despite this, the western suburbs of Sydney continue to be mythologised in terms of lack — lack of resources, lack of beauty, lack of taste.[19] The media describe the region to the west as 'Sydney's poor cousin',[20] and, as already noted, politicians refer to each other as 'westies' when searching for the ultimate insult.[21] Meanwhile residents attempt to defend the image of western Sydney, and politicians are forced to apologise and newspapers receive letters of protest about their claims.

Since the 1970s a number of political structures as well as community organisations and lobby groups have sought to create opportunities for residents in western Sydney, including the Western Sydney Regional Organisation of Councils (WSROC), Western Sydney Area Assistance Scheme (WSAAS), Creative Cultures, Greater Western Sydney Economic Development Board, radio station 2WS, and the University of Western Sydney. All express a need to understand and utilise the diversity of the region.

Aboriginal people in western Sydney[22]

While the focus of the book is on the post-war period, it must be remembered that Aboriginal associations with the site now known as western Sydney can be traced back to pre-invasion times and through the ensuing two centuries of colonial rule. Recent revisionist historical work in the area has begun to provide evidence of the survival of the descendants of Aboriginal families from the early nineteenth century well into the twentieth century.[23]

The arrival of white invaders in 1788 led to a significant decrease in the members of the Dharuk people who occupied this region. The accounts of early colonists testify to the devastating impact of smallpox on these people even before they had seen a white person. The spread of disease was like a calling card warning of the disaster that was imminent. Within the first few years of white settlement it was estimated that half the Aboriginal people in the western Sydney area were dead.[24]

As the newcomers moved out westwards from the settlement of Sydney, coveting the rich fertile soils around the Hawkesbury River, they established farms on Dharuk land causing the dispossession of Aboriginal people from their country. Many Aboriginal families and groups who had managed to stay on or close to their lands throughout the nineteenth century were only later to experience alienation from their country through continued pressure from white landholders. In the early part of the twentieth century, government agencies such as the Lands Department were complicit in aiding white people's desire for land by extending and granting leases over Crown land for farming purposes. The impact of the dispersal policies of the early twentieth century also had a significant impact on the surviving Dharuk people; as in most other parts of the state, Aboriginal people were herded into missions, government reserves and institutions.

In the late 1950s and early 1960s, however, a significant movement of Aboriginal people into western Sydney began. The migration of Aboriginal people from rural areas of New South Wales into Sydney was not a new phenomenon, but it was not until this time that they began to take residence in the western Sydney region. During this period, the Aborigines' Welfare Board was exerting pressure on Aboriginal people to move away from the government-run reserves in rural areas throughout the state. The board had adopted the policy of assimilation in the 1950s, but by the early 1960s it had become frustrated by the slowness with which Aboriginal people seemed to be assimilating into 'white' society. To speed up the assimilation process, the board began to apply pressure to individuals and families to move away from 'segregated' rural communities and into cities.

The offer of better housing was one way in which the board sought to attract Aboriginal people into urban areas.[25] In 1963, as part of their

introduction

assimilation program, the Aborigines' Welfare Board bought four houses in the western suburbs of Sydney: two in Green Valley and two in St Marys. The purchase of these houses and their subsequent occupation by the McLeod, Morris, Lovelock and Dixon families from Nowra and Armidale in rural New South Wales was marked by a small ceremony in which a wattle tree was planted by the chief secretary of the board.[26] This appeared to signal the beginning of what the board hoped would be a new phase of assimilation whereby Aboriginal people would become indistinguishable from other Australians.

The event made the front page of the *Sydney Morning Herald*. The headline to the article, 'Four keys to racial integration', clearly promoted the Aborigines' Welfare Board's view that a house in Sydney's west would facilitate the assimilation of Aboriginal families into white society. Among the elements the newspaper article outlined for successful assimilation were urban (as opposed to rural) living, employment for the male breadwinner, education and other opportunities for children, and the 'civilising' influence of white neighbours.

In moving Aboriginal families into densely populated housing estates, the Aborigines' Welfare Board (with the cooperation of the Housing Commission) hoped to break down Aboriginal people's desire to 'cling together' which the board interpreted as a major obstacle to assimilation.[27] It is clear that the policies of the Welfare Board to relocate Aboriginal people from segregated rural communities into urban areas like the western suburbs of Sydney, were partly about erasing the visible differences between blacks and whites which had previously been reinforced by racially segregated patterns of residence.

However it was not only Aboriginal people from rural areas who were moving into the region. By this time many Aboriginal people from throughout New South Wales had already settled in the inner-city suburbs of Sydney such as Surry Hills, Darlinghurst, Alexandria and Redfern. In search of better housing and employment opportunities, they had also perceived the city as providing better educational opportunities for themselves and their children as well as freedom from government control over their lives on the reserves and stations and the unceasing racism to which they were subjected in rural areas.[28] Some

Aboriginal families with young children who had been living in the inner-city suburbs began to move into the western suburbs in the 1960s. And many Aboriginal people from La Perouse in Sydney's south also moved to the western suburbs at this time where housing was being made increasingly available for them. In 1966 the Aborigines' Welfare Board had plans to close down the Aboriginal reserve there, arguing that 'reserves in the metropolitan area were incongruous'.[29] As in rural areas, the board sought to disperse young Aboriginal people throughout the wider community. In this way, displacement not only from rural areas but from other parts of the city characterised the 'first generation' of Aboriginal people relocating to the new housing estates of western Sydney.

In the early 1970s the movement of Aboriginal people into the region continued to increase. With the dismantling of the Aborigines' Welfare Board in 1969, the 'rehousing' programs were taken over by the newly formed Directorate of Aboriginal Welfare which instructed the Housing Commission of New South Wales to build housing for Aboriginal families in the high employment areas of Newcastle and Sydney, rather than in rural towns and cities. The directorate also established the Aboriginal Family Resettlement Scheme in 1971, a program of support designed to help Aboriginal families 'adjust' to urban living and which counselled them about how to 'stabilise' their families in the resettlement suburbs.[30] This practice reflected the prevailing view of government agencies that the regular return of Aboriginal people from urban areas back to their own country was caused by their 'failure' to make the changes necessary to assimilate into white society.

By the late 1980s and early 1990s the pattern of movement had changed. Aboriginal people from rural areas were more likely to relocate straight into the western suburbs of Sydney, rather than initially spending time in the inner-city areas. Although there were a number of reasons for this shift, the two main ones appear to have been that Aboriginal people moving into the region now had pre-existing kin networks in various areas and the cost of private rental accommodation in the inner-city suburbs had become prohibitive for many Aboriginal families. This period also witnessed the establishment of such agencies as Daruk Aboriginal Medical Service, Dharuk Local Aboriginal Land Council, Murrawina Child Care Centre, Mundara Youth Refuge, Gilgai

Centre for elderly and disabled Aboriginal people and Pittuma Resource Centre throughout the greater western Sydney region. Organisations like these provide a focal point for Aboriginal people dispersed throughout the western suburbs.

locating western Sydney; locating ourselves

Diane Powell has documented the extent to which western Sydney has become an object of social investigation. Research into 'problems' in this region of health, unemployment, transport, educational disadvantage, domestic violence, racial strife and so on has accelerated since the 1970s, particularly in the wake of perceived crises or events in that area.[31] Powell criticises these studies for creating an 'us and them' attitude about the people who live in this region, an attitude which the media then accentuate in their desire to create 'newsworthy' stories. Powell links these studies to a 'long tradition of writing about society's "low" classes', which began with investigations into 'the slums of Europe and America in the late nineteenth and early twentieth century'.[32]

Drawing on the work of Stallybrass and White in their book *The Politics and Poetics of Transgression* (1986), Powell suggests that media and research reports about the region of western Sydney function to create class distinctions. Stallybrass and White argue that literary writing as well as social reform texts of the eighteenth and nineteenth centuries set out to define and delineate the boundaries between the newly emerging middle classes and those from whom they wished to differentiate themselves — the 'lowly masses'. Cultural distinctions about taste, about the practices of everyday life, bodily comportment, morals and rituals were established to define that which was considered 'civilised' as opposed to the 'lowness' and 'immorality' of the masses. But, Stallybrass and White argue, in these various exclusions, the bourgeoisie not only defined itself but constituted the 'other' as an object of desire, of fascination:

> The bourgeois subject continuously defined and re-defined itself through the exclusion of what it marked out as 'low' — as dirty, repulsive, noisy, contaminating. Yet that very act of exclusion was constitutive of its identity. The low was internalized under the sign of negation and disgust. But

disgust always bears the imprint of desire. These low domains, apparently expelled as 'Other', return as the object of nostalgia, longing and fascination.[33]

Social researchers and media reporters today, Powell concludes, continue this tradition of providing the bourgeoisie with stories that define its 'other' — in this instance, those living in the urban outer-regions like 'western Sydney' — as those who are socially and geographically excluded. Issues associated with this perspective are explored in a number of chapters in this book and later in this introductory chapter, as is Powell's suggestion that the anti-suburbanism of writers such as Robin Boyd should be viewed as participating in this tradition. In exploring the latter concern in the following section of this chapter, we will be discussing further the question of our relation as intellectuals or 'knowledge workers' in a particular institution to the communities that live in the region of western Sydney and to other social groups, including to what Powell here refers to as the bourgeoisie.

Powell does not acknowledge, however, the extent to which social research has been carried out, and used, by groups within the region of western Sydney itself. Some of this work has been carried out by social welfare agencies operating in the region. Some has been conducted by organisations such as WSROC, set up as a collaborative venture in order to promote the interests of the region. Such organisations, particularly in the 1970s and early 1980s, have at times explicitly sought to use research to establish patterns of disadvantage on issues such as health and education, utilising this research as the basis for what Liz Fulop has analysed as specific kinds of 'needs talk' in order to make strategic interventions in government agendas.[34]

Such 'needs talk', for example, backed up with appropriate research data about educational disadvantage, was mobilised by groups who came together in the mid-1980s to argue for the establishment of a university in the region of western Sydney. Spearheaded by WSROC, this campaign produced figures about the number of higher education places in the region per head of population compared with the Sydney region as a whole and nationally, and argued a case for the spatial equity of such human services provision.[35]

introduction

The arguments of these groups were eventually overtaken by, but also to some extent, coalesced with, the reforms introduced by Education Minister John Dawkins of the federal Labor government in 1987 which set out to broaden participation in university education by creating a 'unified national system' in which former Colleges of Advanced Education became new universities, either in their own right or by amalgamations with other such colleges or with other universities. The University of Western Sydney was formed in 1989 out of two former Colleges of Advanced Education and one Agricultural College. These organisations were brought together into a 'federated' university (the University of Western Sydney, Nepean being one of the three campuses of this university).

As already indicated, four of the authors of this book were employed at the University of Western Sydney, Nepean when we received a government grant to undertake the project on which this book is based. One other joined the project at later stages, as explained in the preface to this book. It was initially conceived, then, by academics working in a university situated in the region we were wanting to investigate or think about. We saw our work in some ways as challenging the very tradition that Powell identified with the social research and media commentary that treated the region as an object of, at best, concern and, at worst, derision. As people working in the region we proposed our project be part of the struggle to develop a positive sense of identity for that region, rather than simply another study *of* the region.

However, this is to oversimplify the issue on a number of different levels. As intellectuals working in the particular location of a university, we inevitably participate in the very posture Pierre Bourdieu suggests is inherent in the scholarly gaze. That is, despite being part of 'western Sydney' to the extent that we worked there and were participating in the building up of a new university in that region, our training as academics meant that we necessarily retired from it, had to stand back and treat it as an object, as soon as we began to observe it, discuss it or study it. Our training in various forms of scholarship necessarily provide the means of constructing particular types of objects of study, the tools of analysis to then investigate those objects, and a specific relation to those objects, a specific subject position of observer-at-a-distance. As Bourdieu argues: 'As soon as we observe *(theorin)* the social world, we introduce in our perception of it a bias due to the fact that, to study it, to describe it, to talk about it, we must retire from it more or less completely.'[36] In this sense, we were and are not participating in the very practical problems that people living in the region experience and have to solve in their everyday lives in terms of its history of public denigration or negative definitions. And we cannot do so. Our view necessarily has to be 'off-side'. And our tools of analysis, drawing on various forms of scholarship, mean that we look for the general, for what we have seen, read or thought about before, in the particulars of this region.

While seeking to be aware of this 'bias' and hence the limits of our analysis, however, we do not claim to be able to avoid it. Nor do we claim to be able to narrow the gap between theory and practice by in some way bringing our personal biographies into the centre of our analysis. As Bourdieu argues, this form of 'reflexivity' risks becoming 'a form of thinly veiled nihilistic relativism', a form of narcissism that becomes an end in itself'.[37] Instead we have sought to use the very different tools of analysis that we each bring to this project to look at the constraints, double-binds and possibilities that constitute both the particularity and generality of this region. The tools of analysis that we bring to this study are very different from the demographic tools used by most studies of the region — those studies of the 'problems' of educational disadvantage, health, transport, domestic life and so on. We hope in this way to be reading the landscape of 'western Sydney' in ways that are quite at variance with those other studies — in a way that recognises 'disadvantage' and 'need', but produces a set of readable symptoms of the problems and possibilities of living in the modern world which are related to and yet at the same time unsettle our understandings of these issues as previously defined. We are reading the landscape of 'western Sydney' as a form of public history, as an articulation of the history and contemporary patterns of the politics of everyday life, colonisation, public policy and governmental action. But we do not claim any true or even better reading of the landscape of this region than has been provided by other authors. We are interested in the processes of re-visioning such spaces, but in providing five very different viewpoints on this space we deliberately seek to undermine the possibility of any claims our texts might make to the privilege or clear authority of our points of view.

introduction

In these terms, then, we make no general claim in this book to be able to represent the people of western Sydney. Indeed we want to point to the impossibility of doing so, while acknowledging the strategic importance of agencies or groups within the region seeking to give the people of 'western Sydney' a voice at various points in time. Each of us has written a very different analysis of questions concerned with the defining of western Sydney as a region and the experiences of populations living within such regions. This in itself undercuts any claim of the different types of scholarship we are trained in to be able to provide the definitive analysis of such a region. Our intention is to provide new perspectives on the region of western Sydney itself and on issues of identity, home and communality in the modern world, particularly as they are encountered in, or raised by, such outer-urban regions.

To understand the intellectual task in this way means that the assumption that one proposed theory can somehow lay claim to an objectively privileged truth cannot be maintained. We have deliberately sought to bring together a variety of disciplinary backgrounds in order to increase our understanding of the western suburbs beyond some unitary position from within a traditionally bound discipline. Our epistemological position is akin to what Adorno referred to as the provision of a *constellation* of theories. Instead of assuming a 'step-by-step progression' to a more abstract and 'supreme principle' or 'more general cover concept', the theoretical process 'enter[s] into a constellation'.[38]

> As a constellation, theoretical thought circles the concept it would like to unseal, hoping that it may fly open like the lock of a well-guarded safe-deposit box: in response, not to a single key or a single number, but to a combination of numbers.[39]

Adorno does not mean that objective truth is suddenly revealed by this multiplicity of theory. On the contrary, greater understanding *is* gained but it is achieved by maintaining the range of perhaps contradictory perspectives so that we are not seduced by the scientific myth of some unitary answer emerging triumphant and leaving all the previous attempted answers floundering in its wake of truth. However it is not just a position of relativist toleration of different theories. The concept being examined can be opened up and better understood because the various viewpoints are brought together and can feed off each other, thus generating new perspectives which can be added to the list of insights. Hence our attempt 'to unseal' the concept of the western suburbs relies on previous answers, like the one given by Powell, which we will criticise but still preserve as providing valuable insight. We wish to add to the previous work by using it, but our theories do not thereby transcend what has been done before.

This notion of constellation also applies to the chapters in this book. An overall unified theme or answer will not be found. Rather, each of us brings to bear a different outlook and disciplinary background to an aspect of 'the western suburbs' or 'western Sydney' and we hope we will help unseal this difficult concept by adopting such a heterogeneous approach. In writing this book we criticised each others' work, and our varying, conflicting positions helped shape each particular offering. But we did not move onto some more general, all-encompassing theory. The difference of our perspectives was never in question.

suburbia and Australian debates about the city and modernity

As a study of a major outer-urban region, this book could be seen to join the substantial body of Australian literature on suburbia. But for the most part, we wish to avoid the frame of reference within which suburbia has been constituted as an object of study by Australian social and cultural critics, academic or otherwise. We are neither 'for' suburbia nor 'against' it. But more than this, we wish to avoid, nor do we feel able to adopt, the position which would enable us to judge it one way or the other. A number of writers have set out to assess the issues arising from the way Australian intellectuals have constituted suburbia as an object of analysis in these terms.

Tim Rowse, writing in 1978, suggested that three phases can be identified in the development of Australian intellectuals' attitudes to suburbia. In the immediate post-Second World War period, particularly, he argued, intellectuals and literary figures claimed suburbia to be equated with a stifling materialism of outlook, against which they wanted to constitute themselves as representing a cosmopolitan civilisation. In the 1960s, Barry Humphries' satires on suburbia gave

introduction

intellectuals a certain sense of distance from suburbia, while facilitating a more sympathetic demeanour that begins to lead to a certain acceptance of suburbia as exemplifying certain values and attitudes that could be identified as Australian. Donald Horne in the 1960s was similarly ambivalent about suburbia. By the beginning of the 1970s, Hugh Stretton in his *Ideas for Australian Cities* (1970) signals a period of time in which suburbia is identified with all that is good about the 'Australian way of life'.[40]

Rowse argued that as the term 'suburbia' moved into a more sociological discourse in the late 1960s, early 1970s — apparently describing 'the Australian way of life' — issues of difference became increasingly obscured. In celebrating suburbia, for instance, Stretton refused to acknowledge the position of women in this form of domestic life and, in particular, the social division of labour between men and women assumed by this type of urban development.

In the 1980s and 1990s, however, issues of difference have been very much at the forefront of critiques of suburbia, particularly through the writings of feminist scholars. Sophie Watson, for example, focuses on both suburbia and the apparent preoccupation among all groups in Australia with 'owning a home of your own'. 'Housing in Australia', she declares, 'acts to both create and reproduce traditional family structures and the dependence of women'.[41] While home ownership has been associated with citizenship for men in Australian political discourse since the Second World War, women have always been depicted as dependent housewives. Suburbanisation of Australian cities and the associated urban sprawl — the outcome of what she refers to as 'the obsession with "a home of one's own" ' — Watson argues, 'may have provided a haven and a retreat for men from the hurly-burly of the inner-city world of work, but for women in many instances they may only have provided a prison'.[42]

In more recent work, Watson (with her co-author in this instance, Alec McGillivray) has further critiqued suburban housing developments in Australia as repressing ethnic differences. Migrant needs, such as spaces for worship, different kitchen needs and different preferences for the arrangement of rooms, are not recognised in the housing stock provided by developers. The assumption of the separation of public and private

17

spaces that goes with these suburban developments also imposes a particular way of life on the population that demands homogeneity, the suppression of difference. Yet Watson and McGillivray also note the way the dream of a 'home of one's own' becomes integrated into migrant narratives of success. Interviews they conducted with migrants in an area of western Sydney indicate that a suburban 'home of one's own', while clearly being the most secure form of housing stock available, has also come to represent a space in which different patterns of everyday life can be pursued in private, away from scrutiny and judgment, and also success to family and friends in their country of origin.

Diane Powell points out that Robin Boyd in his most famous text, *The Australian Ugliness* (1960), singled out western Sydney for criticism as exemplifying the 'dreary' suburbia that he claimed to exist on the outskirts of every Australian town with the 'same cold comfort conservatism of villa design'.[43] Powell suggests that Boyd's critique needs to be viewed in the context of that tradition of social investigation mentioned earlier in which the critics of modern life, Powell argues, are as much involved in defining class distinctions and class unity for themselves and their middle-class audiences as providing a clear analysis of the contradictions and problems of modern existence and urban life.

At first glance it would appear that these more recent critics of suburbia mentioned briefly here cannot be accused of defining a class unity for themselves and their middle-class audiences in the way that Powell argues we need to understand Boyd's work. But the issue is more complicated and points to a problem in Powell's argument in relation to this matter. It could be suggested, for example, that feminist critiques of suburbia depicting these urban developments as oppressive of women are addressed to a middle-class feminist audience and constitute women who live in the suburbs, 'the housewife' in particular, as 'other' to the feminist subject — the subject feminists want to emancipate and at the same time distance themselves from. While such an argument has some cogency and points to the importance of scholars scrutinising the way in which they set up their objects of analysis, what such a claim ignores is the inevitability of intellectuals setting up objects of analysis and of speaking to and creating a particular constituency and particular audiences. The important issue is the extent to which intellectuals are able to reflect on the way they constitute such an object of investigation and to be open to questions about both the terms in which that object is framed and their investment in the subject position it entails for the person who is doing the analysis, the observing.

Meaghan Morris pursues these issues in her discussion of what she considers should be the primary social role of cultural studies today. She argues that Donald Horne's text *The Lucky Country* (1964) could be seen to be speaking to and, at the same time, creating an 'institutionally mobile "new class"' of 'knowledge workers ... able to move between the media, policy-work and the academy'.[44] Morris points to various strategies in Horne's writing that both establish a sense of connection between his audiences and the culture of everyday life that he studies and of complicity in the ironic detachment that he establishes in relation to that phenomenon. This argument suggests an important qualification to claims such as those made by Powell. Morris is suggesting a far more specific and limited role for intellectuals like Horne than the claim that somehow critics of suburbia like Horne or Boyd are speaking for and constituting a general 'middle-class' audience.

Morris goes on to suggest, however, that the speaking position that Horne adopted in the 1960s of the public intellectual who, while speaking to a specific audience, could claim to be speaking to and of the 'nation' or 'culture' as a whole is no longer possible or desirable. Similarly, she argues, it is no longer possible to create the figure of everyman, as did Horne, as the object for both his analysis and desire. Intellectuals today are being forced to recognise that they speak not as subjects of culture but as subjects of particular forms of training or competencies about specific issues and that they speak to very particular audiences. In this context, intellectuals need to be self-conscious about the objects of analysis that they constitute, to be continually prepared to scrutinise the framework within which those objects have been established.

But these intellectuals, Meaghan Morris argues, also need to be 'mediating figures who translate between knowledges and negotiate between constituencies — thus changing the relations between them'. Learning to navigate differences in this way will ensure, she argues, a continuing social role for intellectuals in producing a new kind of general knowledge appropriate for a multicultural society.[45]

the city, space and modernity

These issues, among others, also arise in contemporary international debates about modernity and the city. The literature in this area served as a necessary background to our research, and it also threw up a series of problems for us as investigators of this particular space of the west of Sydney.

Most notably, once the city is recognised as the site of modernity, theory and values begin to lose their objective self-proclaimed status and need to be understood spatially. The pivotal work addressing these issues, which has gained enormous recognition in the last twenty years, is Walter Benjamin's incomplete study of Baudelaire's mid-nineteenth-century Paris written in the late 1930s.

A key figure for Benjamin's investigations (and a favourite topic for a significant volume of recent scholarship) is the 'flaneur'. The flaneurs were observers and artists of city life, who were at home in the crowd, and Baudelaire paid them great homage. Benjamin's descriptions of the flaneur are deceptively slight and charming. For example, he comments on how 'the flaneur... goes botanising on the asphalt'; and that: 'Around 1840 it was briefly fashionable to take turtles for a walk in the arcades. The flaneurs liked to have the turtles set the pace for them.'[46]

But what Benjamin provides in his exploration of the activities of the flaneur is an epistemology, aesthetics and ethics which are located in the crowds, shops and lights of the city. The flaneurs are like scientists (botanists) of their specific object of study — the city street — and have to maintain a certain anti-progressive relative autonomy of disposition (through the turtles) to enable their distinctive value sphere of aesthetic judgement and moral indifference. They are of a certain class, in a specific political regime, at a particular economic time (all this Benjamin recognises) but these standard historical understandings are given a detailed and necessary spatial dimension. The form and content of the *city* are all-important. This study of the flaneur should serve as a model for any type of knowledge production, including, of course, the more standard intellectual task in which Benjamin's work itself can be placed (a self-reflective dilemma of which Benjamin was acutely aware).

Benjamin's work here is therefore foundational in establishing the

introduction

importance of space for social analysis *and* intellectual self-reflection. A large range of recent studies have taken up aspects of the tensions of space (especially regarding the relation between the city and modernity) which Benjamin helped introduce to intellectual life. However, that relation between the intellectual and space — where space is both an object of investigation and also the site of such intellectual work — is an area which Benjamin problematises but which is not very often considered. As academics travelling from outside the area, our studies of western Sydney forced us to engage in these questions of the space of our intellectual work.

If Benjamin helped establish the ground for the recent works on modernity which give the space of the city such prominence,[47] he also lies behind the trend into research into the city and postmodernism. Instead of looking at the standard postmodern-city texts directly, we will consider here some feminist critiques of such work so that the problems of the position of the intellectual can be highlighted. These problems, as identified by Morris' critique of Horne, constituted a set of further difficulties which we needed to work through in our study of the space of the western suburbs.

The writings of Edward Soja and David Harvey have been subjected to a fairly thorough critique of this kind. In his book, *Postmodern Geographies: The Reassertion of Space in Critical Social Theory* (1989), Soja argues that the western intellectual tradition has in the past understood history as essential to a critical interpretation of social life and practice and for emancipating our thinking from the consequences of power relations. He suggests that now, however, we have to understand that space more than time may be hiding these 'consequences' from us. 'Human geographies become filled with politics and ideology.' The spatial dimensions in which we live our everyday lives are not natural or innocent; they are shaped by social forces and are, in turn, a 'shaping force' in social life.[48]

Focusing particularly on what he refers to as the spatial restructuring of Los Angeles since the mid-1970s, Soja seeks to understand the contingent but powerful forces that shape such a modern urban space as well as the way the space of that city — how it is organised spatially — plays a crucial role in what he refers to as the disciplining of labour.

'Totalising visions' will never do, he claims towards the conclusion of his book, as a way of trying to capture or pin down the spatial dimensions of a city such as Los Angeles, or to explain them. But at the same time he wants to insist on the importance of an economic order, 'an essentially exploitative spatial division of labour' as operating beneath the spatial dimensions of the city, the complexity of the modern experience of the urban — beneath what he refers to as a 'semiotic blanket'.[49]

Doreen Massey argues, however, that despite his disclaimers, Soja does set up a totalising vision of the modern city. The only axis of power that matters in his book, Massey argues, is 'that which stems fairly directly from the relations of production'. While Soja recognises the importance of referring to sexism and racism, he does not seriously address them as manifestations of relations of power and dominance. 'Modernity', Massey suggests, is defined in Soja's text, 'entirely in relation to capitalism, at times seemingly almost equivalent to it'.[50] Soja seeks to understand the space of the city as shaped fundamentally by the capitalist mode of production, even as he acknowledges the complexity and contingent nature of its history.

Massey also criticises David Harvey's book, *The Condition of Postmodernity* (1989), on the same grounds. Both this and Soja's text have had a major impact on scholarly debates in contemporary geography, she says, yet both represent a denial of feminism and the contribution it has made to the understanding of modernity. Harvey's analysis, Massey argues, provides an economistic exploration of the relation between the definition, production, and experience of space, on the one hand, and modes of production and class formation on the other. But it completely misses other ways, other power relations, in which space is also structured and experienced.[51]

Harvey sets out in his book to understand what he claims to be postmodernism — a shift in what he concludes to be surface appearances bound up with new experiences of space and time, rather than any fundamental change in the relations of production. Meaghan Morris accuses him of conflating a range of diverse phenomena as postmodernism and thus denying political differences, conflicts, and histories of struggle ('most spectacularly, feminism'). She expresses

introduction

dismay at what she sees as Harvey's attempt at a totalising, economistic explanation of the postmodern city: 'no Marxist, I thought, really claims that sort of mastery any more'.[52]

While seeking to understand, for instance, the preoccupation among Enlightenment thinkers with being able to visualise the world or a particular place from the standpoint of the 'seeing eye' of the individual, from the perspective of a human eye looking at the globe or specific location 'from outside', Harvey does not consider feminist critiques of this notion of detachment and the privileging of a particular point of view in the formation of the subject of modernity. Harvey is interested in the way these thinkers were involved in the social production of space as a means of dominating nature, in the interests of human emancipation and prosperity. By confining his analysis to these issues, Massey argues, Harvey fails to consider not only how this tradition of thinking actively influences the gender relations that contribute to the physical and social circumscribing of women's lives, but how this tradition has constituted the masculine as the universal subject form.[53] Harvey looks at how this Enlightenment tradition appeared to be revived by the moves to undertake massive programs of reconstruction and reorganisation of the urban fabric after the Second World War, but he is simply not interested in how these planning exercises sought to write gender onto the landscape through the design of new towns and outer-urban or suburban environments. He discusses how these planners declared themselves enemies of diversity as it was (and is) lived and played out in the space of the modern city, but does not contemplate that at the same time those planners were actively shaping particular social differences.[54]

Morris raises the question of whether postmodernism has now become a privileged space for Marxist self-reflection, a place from which Marxist intellectuals can articulate a sense of belonging to the nineteenth century European society of its 'origins' at the same time as they seek to avoid confronting the changes that have occurred since that time.[55] The sense of crisis with which Harvey seeks to engage may thus be as much a discourse about his own sense of crisis, than something which can be said to characterise contemporary culture as a whole. Similar issues have been raised by Massey and others. Massey, drawing on the arguments of people such as Zygmunt Bauman, canvasses issues

23

of whether the concept of postmodernism is as much 'a response by intellectuals to their own discomfiture, their sense of dislodgment from previous authority' and, in addition, a response among specific groups within the academy to a sense of crisis as positions of power and influence have shifted or disappeared. Massey suggests that such questions raise serious issues for all intellectuals and academics about 'the nature of their own writing, the power-structures of academe, and so on'. Indeed, she insists:

> these issues arise most acutely for those who are already established and, within these, for those who are members of the already dominant group of white males. For them, if ventures into post-modernism are not to represent simply an attempt at the restoration of their shaky authority as purveyors of truth..., and if it is to be more than another play for status within academe on the part of those who already hold, as a group, most of the positions of power, then there has to be a fundamental questioning of the way they go about their craft.[56]

Massey proposes that all intellectuals need to scrutinise their writing styles and the potential emptiness of some of the rhetorical moves they use, in addition to adopting a self-reflexiveness about the objects of analysis they constitute as the focus of their writings.

However, this feminist critique of these major works on the postmodern city does not require that such criticised theorising be simply dismissed. As our discussion of Adorno's 'constellation' epistemology suggests, Harvey and Soja's important perspectives should be preserved (in fact, some of our own research will rely directly on aspects of their theories). Criticism of their understanding adds to our ability to 'unseal the concept' and does not constitute a new truth progressing objectively beyond all previous answers.

readings of the landscape

As indicated earlier in this chapter, we are interested then in providing new readings of the landscape of 'western Sydney', at the same time as we explore questions of the social production of place, of home and belonging, and the spatialisation of social relations in the modern city.

introduction

In these terms some of the work of authors we have discussed in the previous section have influenced our studies, even though we have concentrated, in the context of this chapter, on the problems and debates about the locatedness of some of their preoccupations. So, for example, Soja's argument that ==spatiality is both a social product and one that shapes social relations== — echoing and extending the thesis of Henri Lefebvre's classic text, *The Production of Space* (1974) — is clearly crucial to our focus on the historical emergence and complex workings of the contemporary landscape of 'western Sydney'. Similarly, David Harvey's discussion of the preoccupation with the 'view from above' of Enlightenment thought and post-Second World War town planning provided a useful starting point for Lesley Johnson's analysis of the County of Cumberland Council Planning Scheme and its role in the emergence of the contemporary space of western Sydney.

Focusing on various aspects of the search for and attempts to create homely spaces in Australian urban and suburban life, we present speculations on the shaping of everyday identities and experiences of the population living in one outer-urban region — 'western Sydney' — since the Second World War. Lesley Johnson in chapter 2 focuses on the way our perceptions of the city have been shaped in the twentieth century. She looks at the role of town planners, government officials and the media in this process and, in particular, at the way they have set out to establish the dominance of a mode of visualising the urban landscape 'as if from above'. Using historical documents about the planning of Sydney produced after the Second World War, this chapter examines the function of the concept of 'urban sprawl' as well as other mechanisms in structuring perceptions of the city and its 'outer suburbs' so that it continues to be visualised in this manner. Lesley Johnson suggests that the population of Sydney was being asked in the 1940s and 1950s to take on the gaze of the planner and to visualise the supposedly problematic character of Sydney's development in apparently self-evident terms. She shows how architects and planners continue to presume this gaze to be a shared one between themselves and the general population, a gaze which enables them then to characterise the desires of the population of 'western Sydney' to live in suburbia as 'feral', out of control, irrational, while those who live in similar spaces on Sydney's North Shore are seen as respectable and rational citizens.

Michael Symonds, in chapter 3, reflects on the reasons why the western suburbs have been so denigrated by the Sydney centre. The nature of the European city and its relation to nature are argued to be necessary for understanding the west's position. Using an interpretation of Hegel, and incorporating Benjamin's study of Baudelaire, he argues that western Sydney has been cast out of the spaces which have been constructed by the European tradition for the journeys of the modern subject. The western suburbs are regarded as being part of a particular Australian tradition of relating to nature which the city of Sydney had to transcend in order to reach the cultural heights of modernity.

In chapter 4, Ghassan Hage takes ethnic food and the social relations constructed around it as the basis of an intervention in the debate on multiculturalism. He argues that there are two ethnic-food-related realities implicitly competing for the title of multiculturalism in Australia. The first is the reality of the private practices associated with ethnic food that migrants engage in and which lead to various modes of inter-ethnic interaction in the streets or the neighbourhoods where migrants live. The second is the reality of ethnic restaurants articulated to Sydney's cosmopolitan tourist scene. These two ethnic food scenes are each associated with a more general conception of multiculturalism. The first is a multiculturalism centred on migrant attempts to build themselves a home in Australia and the interaction with other ethnicities to which this gives rise. The second is a consumer-centred multiculturalism defined by the availability of ethnic commodities for cosmopolitan consumers. Hage argues that this divide is a spatial one given that the first reality is dominant in western Sydney while the second is largely an inner-city phenomenon. He engages in a critique of the dominance of the consumerist cosmopolitan perspective in inner Sydney's everyday life and deconstructs the relation between it and multiculturalism. Hage concludes by asserting the importance of re-centring the multicultural debate on the multiculturalism experienced in western Sydney.

Helen Grace in chapter 5 reads the space of the display-home village as utopian site, focusing in particular on HomeWorld II in the suburb of Prospect in Sydney's west. The chapter considers the evolution of the display home in Australia since the 1930s. It explores historical precedents to ideals of homely spaces through socialist housing

introduction

developments in the Soviet Union in the early twentieth century; model housing and industrial villages for the working classes in Europe in the late eighteenth century; and Ebenezer Howard's garden city in the late nineteenth century. From this general historical account the chapter moves on to examine the anxious emptiness and unoccupied intensity manifest in the details of the display home.

notes

1. Keith Willey, *When the Sky Fell Down: The Destruction of the Tribes of the Sydney Region, 1788–1850s*, Collins, Sydney, 1979, pp. 210–12.

2. ibid., pp.193ff.

3. There are a number of variations on the spelling of Dharuk, including Daruk, Dharug and Tharug.

4. *Sydney Morning Herald,* 21 January 1989, pp. 3, 78.

5. Peter Weir, *Whatever Happened to Green Valley?*, Film Australia, 1973.

6. Other examples include K. Mee, Living in the wild, wild west: frontier mythology and the depiction of place in western Sydney, conference paper, Institute of Australian Geographers Annual Conference, Townsville, 1994.

7. See chapter 2 in this book for further brief discussion of these moves.

8. This was most blatantly performed by the 'infotainment' program, 'Real Life', ATN Channel 7, 27 September 1993, where viewers were invited to exchange houses and see how 'the other half' lives.

9. *Sydney Morning Herald*, 30 May 1996, p. 5.

10. WESTIR is a community based organisation which provides an information service for the Greater Western Sydney region.

11. All the demographic information is provided by WESTIR unless otherwise indicated. The information compiled by WESTIR is primarily from the Australian Bureau of Statistics 1991 Census. Data from the ABS 1995 Census is now available.

12. There is no one 'official' definition of where western Sydney begins and ends. The region is defined differently by each organisation according to their purpose. The Greater Western Sydney Economic Development Board includes twelve LGAs in its definition, while the Western Sydney Regional Organisation of Councils (WSROC) includes only nine LGAs. Macarthur Regional Organisation of Councils (MACROC) is responsible for the remaining three LGAs. Yet again, the NSW Department of Education uses regional boundaries, not LGAs, to define western Sydney.

13 Greater Western Sydney Economic Development Board, *Australia Starts Here: Marketing Plan Executive Summary*, Sydney, 1996.

14 *Aboriginal Issues in Western Sydney*, WESTIR, Sydney, 1991.

15 M. T. Daly, *Sydney Boom Sydney Bust: The City and its Property Market 1850–1981*, Allen & Unwin, Sydney, 1982, p.111.

16 ibid.

17 See G. E. Fulop, How the west was won and lost: the politics of need in Western Sydney, PhD, University of New South Wales, 1992.

18 Department of Urban and Regional Development, *Community*, no. 4, October 1974, p. 9.

19 Diane Powell's book *Out West : Perceptions of Sydney's Western Suburbs*, Allen & Unwin, Sydney, 1993 deals extensively with media representations of western Sydney.

20 'A City Divided', *Sydney Morning Herald*, 5 October 1996, Spectrum, pp. 1s, 6s.

21 'Westie jibe slammed', *Sydney Morning Herald*, 30 May 1996.

22 In our original project proposal, we had outlined a major study on Aboriginal people in western Sydney that would have provided the material for a substantial chapter in this book. For a number of reasons it has not been possible to include such a chapter.
We are grateful to Maria Nugent for providing the material for this section of the introduction. The material comes from two research projects: one which investigated Aboriginal women's health in the western suburbs of Sydney which Maria carried out in collaboration with Dundi Mitchell and Veronica Arbon during 1992–94; the other is her doctoral research on La Perouse.

23 See J. Brook & L. L. Kohen,*The Parramatta Native Institution and the Black Town: A History*, UNSWP, Sydney, 1991.

24 ibid.

25 H. Goodall, *Invasion to Embassy: Land In Aboriginal Politics in New South Wales, 1770–1972*, Allen & Unwin in association with Blackbooks, Sydney, 1996, p. 291; see also NSW Legislative Council and Legislative Committee, 1967 *Minutes of Evidence Taken Before the Joint Committee of the Legislative Council and Legislative Assembly Upon Aborigines' Welfare*, Sydney, 1967.

26 *Dawn Magazine*, August 1993.

27 Goodall, p. 291.

introduction

28 ibid., p. 290.

29 NSW Legislative Council and Legislative Committee, para. 313. p. 41, 1967.

30 See Goodall, p. 334.

31 Mark Peel also notes this problem in his detailed history and analysis of the city of Elizabeth in South Australia, a city established as a 'new town' after the Second World War on the edge of Adelaide: *Good Times, Hard Times. The Past and the Future of Elizabeth*, Melbourne University Press, 1995.

32 Powell, p. 17.

33 P. Stallybrass & A. White, *The Politics and Poetics of Transgression*, Methuen, London, 1986, p. 191, quoted in Powell, p. 19.

34 Fulop, 1992.

35 See Stephen Hodge, 'Disadvantage and "otherness" in western Sydney', *Australian Geographical Studies*, vol. 34, no. 1, 1996, p. 41.

36 Pierre Bourdieu & Loic J. D. Wacquant, *An Invitation to Reflexive Sociology*, Polity Press, Cambridge, 1992, p. 69.

37 ibid., p. 72.

38 Theodor Adorno, *Negative Dialectics*, Routledge, London, 1973, p. 162.

39 ibid., p. 163.

40 Tim Rowse, 'Heaven and a Hills Hoist: Australian critics on suburbia', *Meanjin*, vol. 37, no. 1, April 1978, pp. 3–13. The history of Australian anti-suburbanism among Australian artists in particular has also been examined by a number of authors in the collection: Sarah Ferber et al. *Beasts of Suburbia: Reinterpreting Cultures in Australian Suburbs*, Melbourne University Press, 1994.

41 Sophie Watson, *Accommodating Inequality: Gender and Housing*, Allen & Unwin, Sydney, 1988, p. viii.

42 ibid., p. 19.

43 Powell, pp. 24–5; quotes taken from Robin Boyd, *The Australian Ugliness*, Penguin, Ringwood, 1968, p. 98.

44 Meaghan Morris, 'Cultural studies' in K.K. Ruthven (ed.), *Beyond the Disciplines: The New Humanities*, Papers from the Australian Academy of Humanities Symposium 1991, Occasional Paper No. 13, Australian Academy of Humanities, Canberra, 1992, p. 13.

45 ibid., pp. 20–1.

46 Walter Benjamin, *Charles Baudelaire: A Lyric Poet in the Era of High Capitalism*, Verso, London, pp. 36, 54.

47 See, for example, Marshall Berman, *All That is Solid Melts into Air*, Verso, London, 1983.

48 Edward Soja, *Postmodern Geographies: The Reassertion of Space in Critical Social Theory*, Verso, London, 1989, pp. 6–7.

49 ibid., pp. 246.

50 Doreen Massey, 'Flexible sexism', *Environment and Planning D: Society and Space*, vol. 9, 1991, p. 38.

51 ibid., p. 49.

52 M. Morris, 'The man in the mirror: David Harvey's "condition" of postmodernity', *Theory, Culture and Society*, vol. 9, 1992, p. 254.

53 Massey, pp. 45–6.

54 D. Harvey, *The Condition of Postmodernity: An Enquiry Into the Origins of Cultural Change*, Blackwell, Cambridge & Oxford, 1989, pp. 68–75.

55 Morris, pp. 275–6.

56 Massey, p. 34.

2. feral suburbia?

western Sydney and the 'problem of urban sprawl'

lesley johnson

> **feral:** 1. (of an animal or plant) wild, untamed, uncultivated. 2. a (of an animal) in a wild state after escape from captivity. b born in the wild of such an animal. 3. brutal [L ferus wild]
> *oxford english dictionary*

In 1994 the well-known Sydney architect, Philip Cox, was reported in the *Sydney Morning Herald* as saying that suburbia in western Sydney had 'gone feral'.[1] The newspaper article quoted Cox as attacking both politicians and architects for failing to address the problems of 'our outer area' where 'true dinkum Australian urbanism goes unchecked and unassisted'. As the text of his speech makes clear, his target was not necessarily suburbia itself. The suburban world of Sydney's North Shore and the harbour foreshores, he said, 'represents the best of the Australian way of life, the outdoors, landscape, identity, privacy and living opportunity'; suburbia, in this context, he declared, 'represents an Arcadia which is a true delight'.[2] The problem, Cox concluded, was that the suburban environment had 'degenerated' in the western areas of the city, where it 'cannot be called Arcadian or ideal'. Cox called on Sydney architects and planners to address the issues posed by these spaces, not to impose some design on the city 'as some cleansing agent', but to develop a coherent approach to the formulation of a notion of 'a true urban habitat' in which areas like Mt Druitt (in Sydney's 'outer' western suburbs) were as much the focus of their attention as Pyrmont (an older suburb in the 'heart' of the city).

Cox argued for the development of a uniquely Australian approach to urban design and pointed to the failure of Australian architects — and the forms of training they receive — in opening up such a possibility. The newspaper report of that speech, however, focused on his remarks about western Sydney and highlighted Cox's apparently negative attitude to this region.

In so doing, this newspaper article continued a practice of the metropolitan media that has now been well documented. A number of authors have drawn attention to the particularly negative media representations of the region known as 'western Sydney'. Diane Powell, in her book *Out West*, for example, has argued that, since the beginning of the 1980s, reports have been published in the metropolitan Sydney newspapers with great regularity, characterising this area of Sydney as a distinct region and focusing only on problems, social or economic. 'Western Sydney' in such contexts, she claims, plays the role of defining 'Sydney proper' — its imagined heartland — by being everything that it is not. That is, 'western Sydney' is portrayed as a place of excess — of crime, violence, poor health, unemployment and neglect; and a place of the lack of nearly everything — of facilities, services, culture and education.³

The pattern Powell and others have documented has four features. First, 'western Sydney' is frequently constituted as sociologically homogeneous by the media despite the enormous diversity in the cultural and socioeconomic backgrounds of its residents. Second, in representing the region as a unity, the media evokes a range of problems. Thus, although there are marked differences between suburbs and sub-regions in the area designated as 'western Sydney' on a range of indicators, the media largely ignore these differences and a unity of disadvantage and difficulties is portrayed. Third, the residents of western Sydney are depicted as victims of those problems. Rather than being seen, for example, as 'Aussie Battlers', Diane Powell points out, they are depicted as *being* disadvantaged, and as *having* problems; rarely as people struggling to do something about them.⁴ And finally, the media consistently find western Sydney convenient in their search to dramatise, give life to, their stories of urban issues. Information about crime, health, poverty, for example, are made into 'news' by providing what are represented as the 'telling examples' drawn from Sydney's west.

The *Sydney Morning Herald*'s report of Philip Cox's speech with its headline, 'Suburbia in the west has gone feral, says architect', reworked, then, what now appears to be a well-entrenched media theme. Cox's use of the word 'feral' provided material that the newspaper could readily take up in this way. It appeared to confirm once again that 'western Sydney' was a place that only had problems. The term invokes images of brutality, lack of cultivation or civilisation: 'western Sydney' as an unruly place — unkempt, unromantic, disorderly.

Various attempts have been made to counter these negative images of 'western Sydney' by groups in the region. The local media set out in the late 1980s, for example, to assert a positive sense of identity. The radio station, 2WS, for a short period, declared itself 'West and proud of it'. Similarly, the Greater Western Sydney Economic Development Board, established in 1992, nominated the region's problem of a negative identity as a major barrier to economic growth.[5] And Diane Powell's book itself was an attempt to challenge the ease with which the media have consistently conjured up negative images of the place in which she grew up. Yet, despite a range of moves to counter these ways of representing the region, the metropolitan media continue to appear to find them convenient.

My starting point, then is one context in which such caricatures of 'western Sydney' continue to play a powerful role for the metropolitan media in the process of making their stories news. In particular, I am interested in the way such representations of this region are regularly deployed to make newsworthy media stories about current federal and state government urban policies. Most frequently reported as focusing on 'the problem of urban sprawl', the issues addressed by various government agencies are brought to life by the media through images of the streetscapes and daily lives of the residents of Sydney's western suburbs. I am concerned with the statements made by the media, for example, in the ABC television report, 'Lost in Space', broadcast in September 1992, and in newspaper reports such as the one headed, 'Inquiry into Sydney sprawl' in the *Sydney Morning Herald*, where the streets of a suburb of western Sydney (Penrith) were chosen to demonstrate 'the problem'.

This is not to suggest that there are no problems of social disadvantage — unemployment, health, poor social services, pollution — in the region known as 'western Sydney'. Clearly there are; although, as already noted, the region is a highly diverse one. Nor am I suggesting that there is no such thing as urban sprawl. I want only to challenge the way in which 'western Sydney' is used to exemplify the problems of Sydney and, more generally, of urban development in Australia.[6] This trend continues the pattern which sets up this region as different, separate from, the rest of Sydney — set apart from the centre where we all live. It makes contemporary problems of urban planning into issues that arise as problems because of who *they* are and what *they* do.

Penrith streets in Sydney's west used to exemplify urban sprawl.
Sydney Morning Herald, 24 May, 1996, p. 1. Used with permission.

feral suburbia?

So, for instance, Philip Cox talks of 'feral' suburbans 'out west', as opposed to the respectable suburban populations living on the North Shore. This conceptualisation of the issue fails to recognise questions of class — social and economic disadvantage — and of political power: of the capacity of different groups to make their environment more like his 'Arcadia'. Similarly, it does not acknowledge the history and politics of infrastructure provision for different regions in cities like Sydney. Nor does it provide a context in which to consider the history of the aspirations of the people who have chosen to live in this region, except to characterise *them* as somehow unruly, irrational.

But, more particularly, I want to examine the *way of seeing* the urban landscape of Sydney assumed both by the very notion of 'urban sprawl' and by Phillip Cox's characterisation of suburban developments out west as 'feral'. I am concerned to denaturalise this way of seeing and hence the point of view it establishes as somehow objective or impartial. In this sense I am not suggesting that the metropolitan media are involved in some form of conspiracy against western Sydney. I am interested, rather, in its participation in and shaping of a particular way of visualising the urban landscape. I will explore the history of this structure of perception and how it has contributed to the difficulties of people living in the region known as 'western Sydney' in having their concerns heard or given adequate consideration in contemporary debates about urban planning and reform.

I will focus particularly on an important document of the post-Second World War period: the *Planning Scheme for the County of Cumberland*, first published in 1948. Although the term 'western Sydney' did not appear in this context, the conditions of its emergence *as a region* with a specific identity can be seen. And the term 'urban sprawl' was used. I explore the role of such documents in shaping the way in which the residents of Sydney imagine or visualise their city. The form of 'imagining the city' in which the residents of Sydney were invited to participate by the County of Cumberland Council continues, I suggest, to dominate contemporary media reports and policy debates about urban reform.

The mode of visualising the urban landscape promoted by the County Council had its historical roots in the emergence of the science of modern urban planning in the nineteenth century. I begin with a brief discussion of this tradition in Europe, Great Britain and the United States. Drawing on the recent work of a number of scholars from different fields, I will look at aspects of the history of the norms and structure of perception that I want to analyse and denaturalise in this chapter. I will then turn to an analysis of the document itself and how it was utilised by Sydney's urban planners in the 1940s and 1950s. Finally, I will seek to contextualise this document by looking at how the desires of the rapidly expanding population of Sydney were being shaped and articulated in this period.

imagining the city

James Donald, an English cultural studies scholar, argues that 'there is no such *thing* as the city'. Rather, it is a historically specific mode of seeing, a 'structure of visibility'.[7] He and a number of other authors have traced the emergence of our contemporary ways of discussing both 'the city' and 'the urban'. In pursuing this question, they suggest that an exploration of the historical nature of these concepts will facilitate new approaches to contemporary problems of 'the city'.

Donald documents the appearance of a new group of administrators and reformers in Britain in the mid-nineteenth century concerned with the rapid growth of urbanisation that had begun in the early decades of that century. Drawing on existing analogies and concepts from natural theology, physiology and political economy, figures like James Kay-Shuttleworth sought to find ways of understanding and managing the turbulent growth of the nineteenth-century European city.

Frequently using medical analogies, these early reformers developed new techniques of observation and calculation to render the city as 'a text' to be seen, laid open before them, and diagnosed. Cities like Manchester were divided into a series of districts that could be inspected, classified and regulated. These facilitated diagnostic maps of the 'social body' of the city and enabled identification of the sources of 'infection' and 'disease'. Just as the medical gaze sought to render visible the invisible — the internal landscape of the human body — through various techniques of measurement and intervention, so the new urban planners, through the collection of information and statistics about the population of the city and its districts, sought ways of making the invisible — the daily lives of this population — an object of scrutiny.

These reformers were finding ways, then, of representing spatially the social world they wished to regulate and ameliorate. They visualised 'the city' as a clearly defined space over which a grid, in the form of district lines, could be laid. And they conceived this environment as subject to rational calculation and control.

As these reformers developed more comprehensive means of representing the space of the city, Donald argues, they moved away from the medical analogies that had previously enabled them to think about or perceive the city as an entity or object, to a language of social engineering. They were now wanting not just to understand or *read* the city, but to redesign it and to shape the forms of life to be found in it. In the process of collecting statistics and information, they began to establish a set of norms of 'public health, decency, cleanliness and sanitation'[8] that would provide the principles according to which they could set out to transform this space.[9] The 'planned city', as Paul Rabinow comments in his history of the emergence of modern urban planning in France, was envisaged as 'a regulator of modern society'.[10]

Indeed the city was to become the laboratory of modernity.[11] Here, it was proposed, man would be able to subject his environment to rational control as well as freeing human existence from the bonds of tradition and superstition. Science would be harnessed to subdue the irrational and chaotic space of the nineteenth-century industrial city and create a new harmonious, radiant environment. Urban reformers proclaimed this science in the form of the newly emerging practices of social administration and town planning, objective and impartial. They believed the scientific techniques of these new disciplines provided all-encompassing analyses of the problems to be solved, as well as facilitating the design of a disinterested set of solutions. At the same time, these reformers were convinced that the other guiding principles of modernity would be addressed through the deployment of these human sciences. Democracy, social justice and a decent way of life for all would be accomplished through the new world order created by modern science.

Michel de Certeau, in his book *The Practice of Everyday Life*, talks about the 'concept-city' to suggest that both the practice and the theory of modern urban planning have, at least until recently, sought to reduce the complexity and contradictory character of *urban facts* to a transparent entity. Urban reformers of the nineteenth and early twentieth century hoped, as James Donald suggests, to render the invisible visible, through establishing a totalising perspective on the space of the city. This concept-city required a way of visualising the city 'as if from above' or 'from a distance' in the belief that objectivity and impartiality could be achieved in this way.[12]

The desire for such a perspective on the city can be identified in various contexts in the history of western thought. The new urban planners sought to assume this perspective, expecting that they could transform the lives of its population, erasing old forms of life and creating new ones. Adopting a satellite eye,[13] the planner set out to subject this space to 'his' rational will and to render the population that lived within it, rational, respectable and clean-living citizens.

De Certeau claims, however, that modern urban planning has never been successful in imposing its concept of the city on the space of the city itself. Using the metaphor of the pedestrian, he suggests that, in the practices of everyday life, people move about a city appropriating its spaces in a way not subject to the rational control of urban planners. There is no position from which these plural and complex tracks woven across a city landscape, de Certeau argues, can be *known* by the planner. The view 'from above' can only know or read the surface of the city. No amount of statistics or quantitative information can enable the urban planner to render the life of a city visible, a text to be read, known as a whole. Places are made up of fragmentary histories and stories, de Certeau suggests; memories that can only be revealed through fleeting glimmers but never be known or read in the mode desired by the urban planner. Instead, he says, these stories and memories are more likely, at any time, to undo the readable surfaces of the planned city.[14]

'urban … what's that word mean?'[15]

George Clarke, a graduate in architecture from the University of Sydney and a student at that time in its postgraduate Town and Country Planning course, became a planning officer for the County of Cumberland Council in 1954. In an interview with Paul Ashton, who has undertaken several important projects on the history of planning Sydney, Clarke describes how, after eighteen months in this position, he went overseas to gain a wealth of experience and knowledge of urban planning. He returned to Sydney in 1959 only to be met with the apparently crude question from a member of State Parliament to whom Clarke had been attempting to sell his new ideas on urban renewal and urban development: 'urban ... what's that word mean?'.

For Clarke, the idea of 'the urban' is quite transparent. He recounts, in the Ashton interview how, even as a child, he sat with his nose pressed against the windowpane of the living room of his parents' house in Randwick, absorbed in what he refers to as a 'synoptic view' of the suburban Coogee-Randwick area. His most dramatic experience of this view, however, was from the tower of the AWA building where his father worked, the highest building in Sydney during the 1930s. The 'synoptic view', he explains, 'implies an overall view, an all encompassing view which of course', he says, 'is what Gods and planners like, and indeed need, to take'.[16] *Seeing* 'the urban' is something that Clarke suggests came naturally to him. He affirms it as an unproblematic perspective, and one that anyone should be able to recognise as authoritative and necessary.

Clarke depicts members of his profession as trained 'utopian crusaders' in the 1940s and 1950s. Their theory and practice of town planning, he says, derived from 'the pioneering work of the English utopian and reform tradition', and he cites Jeremy Bentham as the key figure in this movement. The story of the history of the 'planning of Sydney', he tells in this interview, is of the slow recognition of the need to address the shape of the whole, rather than allowing the unregulated battles of competing interests to make de facto decisions about the form and shape of change in urban areas. 'The whole' is something he believes can be 'seen from above'. It was not, however, until the development of the City of Sydney Strategic Plan in 1971, in which he was centrally involved, that the will emerged, says Clarke, to be concerned with the whole — in other words, the will emerged to *see* 'the urban'.

Clarke's interview illustrates a number of the points already explored above in my brief account of some of the issues raised by contemporary scholars in their analyses of the modernist urban planning imperative.

home/world

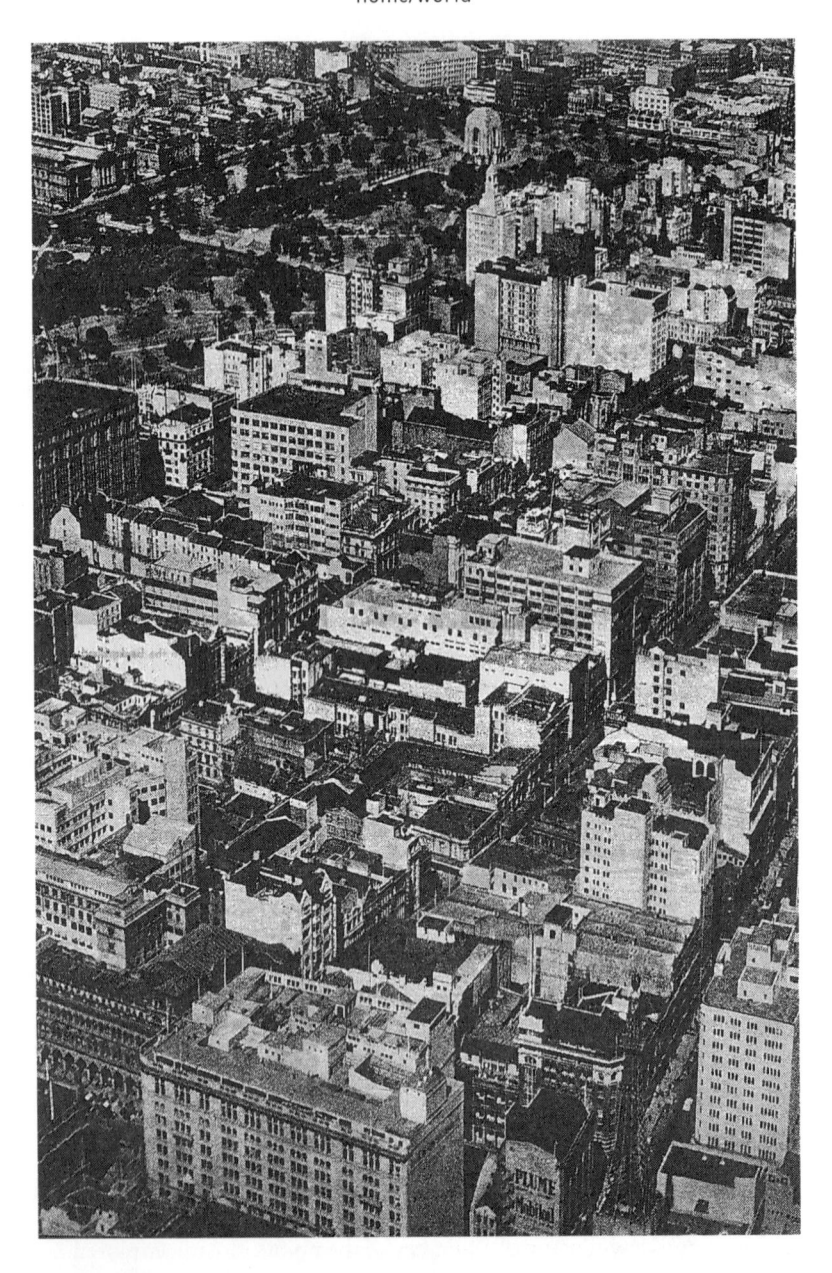

View from AWA tower taken in 1950.
The *Sunday-Herald*, 22 January 1950, p. 12. Used with permission.

Clarke indicates a firm belief both in his own capacity to adopt a god-like eye and view Sydney as a whole, and in the capacity of the professional planner to know and control the urban — the space he claims to be able to see clearly from this height. The modernist planning project he speaks for sought to utilise this view of the city to reveal its inner logic and to devise the totalising solutions of the master plan to solve its problems. The technical rationalism and superior knowledge of the planners, they believed, enabled them to divine what 'the public interest' was or ought to be and hence to shape the city in the interests of both progress and democracy.

Such beliefs were similarly articulated by the County of Cumberland Council, the body Clarke first worked for after receiving his initial training at the University of Sydney.

The County of Cumberland Council was founded in 1945. Attempts had been made in the early decades of the twentieth century to establish a similar means of planning for the 'Greater Sydney' region. A Royal Commission for Greater Sydney, for instance, was appointed in 1913. It recommended that an area from the Hawkesbury to the Georges River (and including Parramatta in the west) be brought under the control of a Greater Sydney Council. Yet a Bill brought to the State Parliament to establish such a body was allowed to lapse after its second reading. There appeared to be considerable opposition to the formation of a strong central planning authority that cut across existing local government boundaries.[17]

At least two developments during the Second World War, however, appear to have undermined this opposition. First, the establishment of a Ministry of Town and Country Planning in Great Britain in 1943 and its recommendations, which led to the New Town Act of 1946, created considerable interest in large-scale urban planning in Australia. Second, and more importantly, the formation of the Ministry for Post-War Reconstruction by the Commonwealth government in 1943 and a New South Wales Reconstruction Committee, established in 1941, both reflected and mobilised a general climate concerned with planning for major social change in the post-war period. Widespread commitment to significant social reforms emerged in the last years of the war and in the years immediately following. The experience of the Depression and the social dislocation caused by the war itself contributed significantly to the formation of this commitment, as did what was frequently referred to as 'the housing crisis' that had emerged during the war and which became more acute in the following years. Urban planning, then, was seen as an important means of achieving appropriate reforms of a large scale and significant nature.

Despite these developments, some objections to the formation of a central planning authority continued to be expressed. Such a move was depicted as authoritarian and dictatorial; the spectre of Hitler haunted parliamentary debates by the end of the war. In an attempt to deflect some of this criticism, the new County Council was made representative of local government councils rather than a totally new body: membership was drawn from ten councils around Sydney, elected by the sixty-five constituent municipal and shire councils. Formally established in 1945, the County of Cumberland Council published its *Planning Scheme* as a major report in 1948; after three years of delay, it was formally gazetted in 1951.

The *Planning Scheme* was indeed visionary. The 1948 report began with a quote from the poem by Erasmus Darwin called 'Visit of Hope to Sydney Cove', published in 1790:

> There shall broad streets their stately walls extend
> The circus widen, and the crescent bend;
> There, ray'd from cities o'er the cultur'd land,
> Shall bright canals, and solid roads expand.
> Yon glittering streams, and bound the chafing tide;
> Embellish'd villas crown the landscape-scene,
> Farms wave with gold, and orchards blush between.
> There shall tall spires, and dome-capt towers ascend,
> and piers and quays their massy structures blend;
> While with each breeze approaching vessils glide,
> and northern treasures dance on every tide![18]

With this poem the County of Cumberland Council declared their grand hopes for major changes to be effected through what they referred to as the 'science and art of town and country planning'. 'The Scheme', they announced in the opening pages of the report:

is much more than a collection of plans. It is a democratic instrument for the betterment of our daily lives, a medium through which the powers and abilities of our citizens may find constructive expression in their pursuit of happiness in a free society.[19]

The plan is perhaps best known for its proposal to establish a green belt as a strip of 'open country', utilising and linking existing scenic and bushland reservations around Sydney. The links were to be provided by retaining primary production areas; undeveloped, privately owned land; empty Crown land; and by reclaiming various waste lands — swamps and brickpits. The proposed green belt established a boundary between what was envisaged as 'Sydney' and areas planned as the site of satellite towns along the lines of England's 'New Towns'. St Marys, a suburb now clearly part of what is referred to as western Sydney, was discussed in particular as having all the characteristics necessary to take on precisely this new form of urban development.

The green belt was just one of the scheme's recommendations about increasing the amount of open space in the greater Sydney region. Such space, the council declared, would play a variety of roles. It was crucial to the leisure and recreation needs of the population, but it also provided a way of creating boundaries between areas. Housing could be separated from factories, and roads from buildings. And it would help establish the identity of districts.

The vision, however, was more utopian and romantic than these details indicate. The planned suburban development was imagined as a form of Arcadia. 'The aim is clear', the council announced:

> It is to recapture that affinity with Nature which gave contentment and stability to communities before the industrial revolution; to restore, on a scale befitting a great metropolis, the happiest features of the common and the village green.[20]

The importance of the image of a village community was even more evident in the description of the zoning of what the Scheme referred to as 'living areas'. Employment opportunities were to be dispersed throughout the city so that no-one would have to travel too far to work. But places of employment were to be segregated from where people lived. These latter areas were to include not only houses, but shops, schools, social services and community centres — all within a convenient walk. Satellite towns were to be created at St Marys, Penrith, Blacktown, Campbelltown, and on a smaller scale at Windsor, Richmond and Riverstone.[21] These developments would strengthen existing settlements rather than create new towns as was happening in England, but the principle would be the same: of establishing self-contained spaces, each with its own commercial centre, industrial employment and cultural and social facilities. Their location, according to the scheme, should be far enough from the city to discourage their use as mere dormitories for city workers.[22]

The County of Cumberland Council *Planning Scheme*, then, envisaged the future of what is now known as 'western Sydney' as forming, in part, the outskirts of Sydney at Parramatta for example, but mostly as forming a landscape made up of 'satellite towns', separated from the city by the green belt.

These proposals for open spaces and living areas were the solutions to the two major problems identified by the County of Cumberland Council: inner-city decay and urban sprawl. The 1948 report spoke of unplanned development over the years as having led to a pattern of land use in which the majority of the county's employees worked in the city's centre and either lived in unhealthy inner-city conditions or in mere dormitory areas that stretched along the network of transport systems. 'Generally', the report concluded, 'the development of urban areas has been a process of sprawl, a series of unplanned extensions, spreading from the centre'.

In explaining what they meant by 'urban sprawl', the councillors contrasted developments in areas like Bankstown and Blacktown with what they referred to as the neatness of Ashfield and Burwood and with the 'semi-rural' nature of Ku-ring-gai suburbs. Thus the contemporary landscape of the region of 'western Sydney' was represented in this context as 'urban sprawl' and suburbs like Philip Cox's Lindfield functioned as a contrast; at this stage, too, it appeared to represent the possibility of an Australian suburban paradise.

To persuade the residents of Sydney and the various factional interests

feral suburbia?

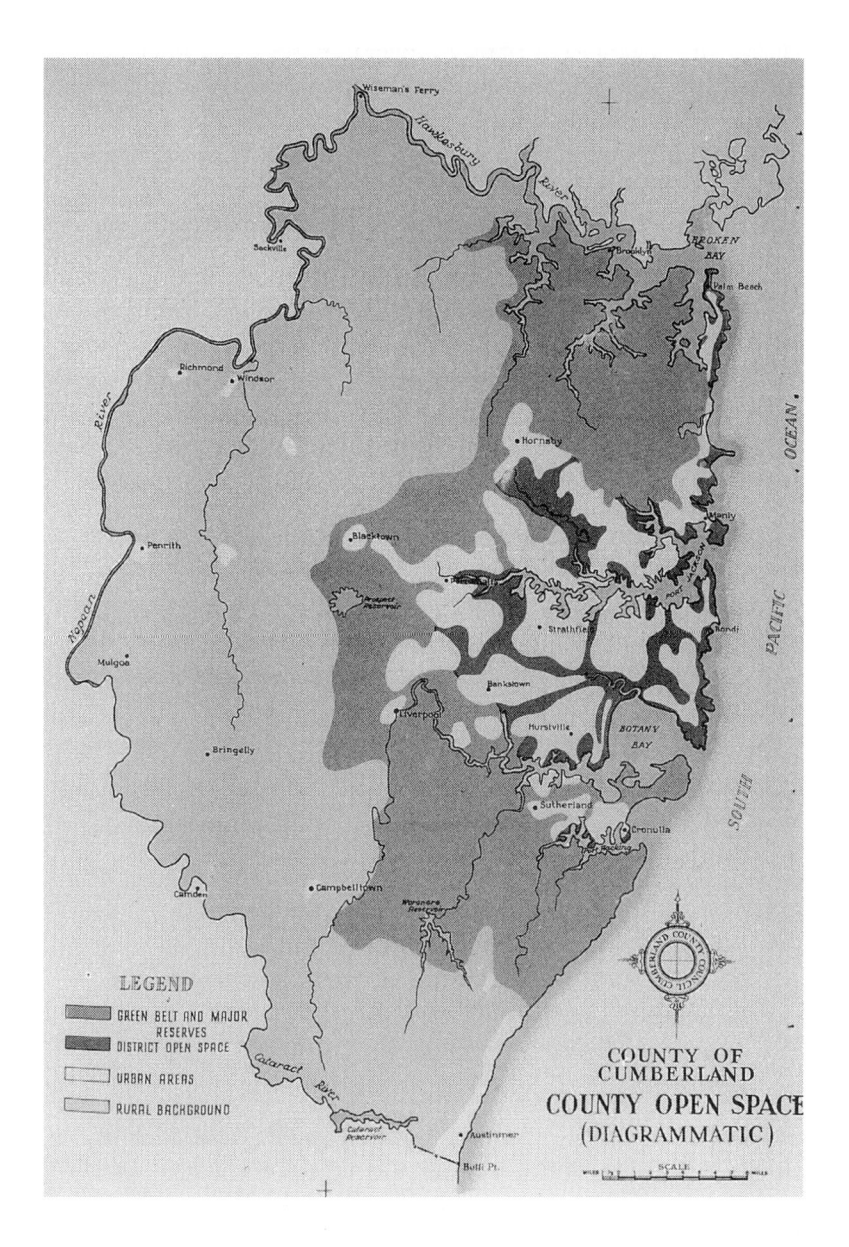

Map of County Council of Cumberland proposed green belt areas.
NSW Department of Urban Affairs and Planning

represented by local councils, community organisations and business agencies of the rationality of their proposals to solve this problem of 'sprawl', the County of Cumberland Council did not rely simply on the clarity of their analysis or the cogency of the arguments used in the 1948 report. They developed a number of strategies to ensure that all groups could *see* the problems which the *Planning Scheme* sought to solve. These included the use of extensive visual materials in the report itself; exhibitions explaining the scheme's proposals at the Sydney Town Hall and a number of local town halls; and a regular planning bulletin. Once the scheme was formally gazetted (in modified form) in 1951, other tactics were used too, such as taking groups of schoolchildren on trips around the city and to view an exhibition of the council's work and future plans.

'a people's plan'

The 1948 report is an impressive document. Filled with photographs and quotes from literary figures such as Somerset Maugham and T. S. Eliot, it invited the reader to join the councillors in their analysis of the city of Sydney — its problems and their solutions.

The report began by seeking to establish the rationality and objectivity of *seeing* the County of Cumberland as a whole. It provided an account of the county as the oldest defined region in Australia, named by Governor Phillip in a letter to Lord Nepean on 9 July 1788. The actual quote from Phillip shows the arbitrariness of this naming and the associated process of creating a defined space:

> As it is necessary in Public Acts to name the County, I named it Cumberland and fixed its boundaries by Carmanthian and Landsdowne Hills to the westward, by the southernmost parts of Broken Bay to the northward and by the southern most part of Botany Bay to the southward.[23]

As this quote suggests, the naming itself brought into being this place and the possibility of its future history.[24] It was not simply a question of any one individual naming this place and bringing it into existence. Phillip carried all the weight of the authority of the colonial government and its power both to treat the landscape as *terra nullius* and to mark it out for *feral suburbia?*

white settlers to perceive as a defined space. Through the formation of the County of Cumberland Council, then, the New South Wales state government was inventing this place anew one hundred and sixty years later, asking the residents of Sydney to see such a space as clearly identifiable and as an area that it would make sense to *see and plan as a whole.* Beginning with the statement from Governor Phillip, the 1948 report claimed the assistance of history and the stature of the figures invoked in this history to give such a naming authority. Similarly, this use of history gave authority — apparent objectivity — to the structure of perception that the council was seeking to encourage, to shape.

The report presented information about the region in written and tabular form as it set out to draw the reader further into this mode of visualising Sydney. 'Facts' about the region in the form of population data, geological information and land-use statistics were provided in impressive detail, creating a sense of an entity that could be mapped, defined and known. This is not to suggest that this feature of the report was in some way misleading or a ruse on the part of its authors. But the presentation of information about the region represents its existence as a fact, an entity to be known, rather than simply recording details about a place that pre-dates this process. As already suggested, this space or region was reinvented by the very formation of the council.

A wide range of maps of the region provided further apparently concrete evidence of its existence. But again, the maps did more than this. They asked readers to *see* the region *from above,* that is, with the god-like eye of the planner.

The use of maps and distance photographs in this document was particularly significant. The visual material appeared to be simply verification of the arguments; it operated to suggest that readers could see for themselves. Thus the report asked readers to bear witness to the squalor, the inner-city decay, just as they were asked to see 'urban sprawl' through the use of appropriate photographs. And the maps were showing the obvious good sense of both seeing and planning the area 'as a whole'. This material in the report of the *Planning Scheme* provided a form of training for its readers in its perspective. Residents were being asked to adopt a particular way of seeing, to join the urban reformers in the synoptic view.

home/world

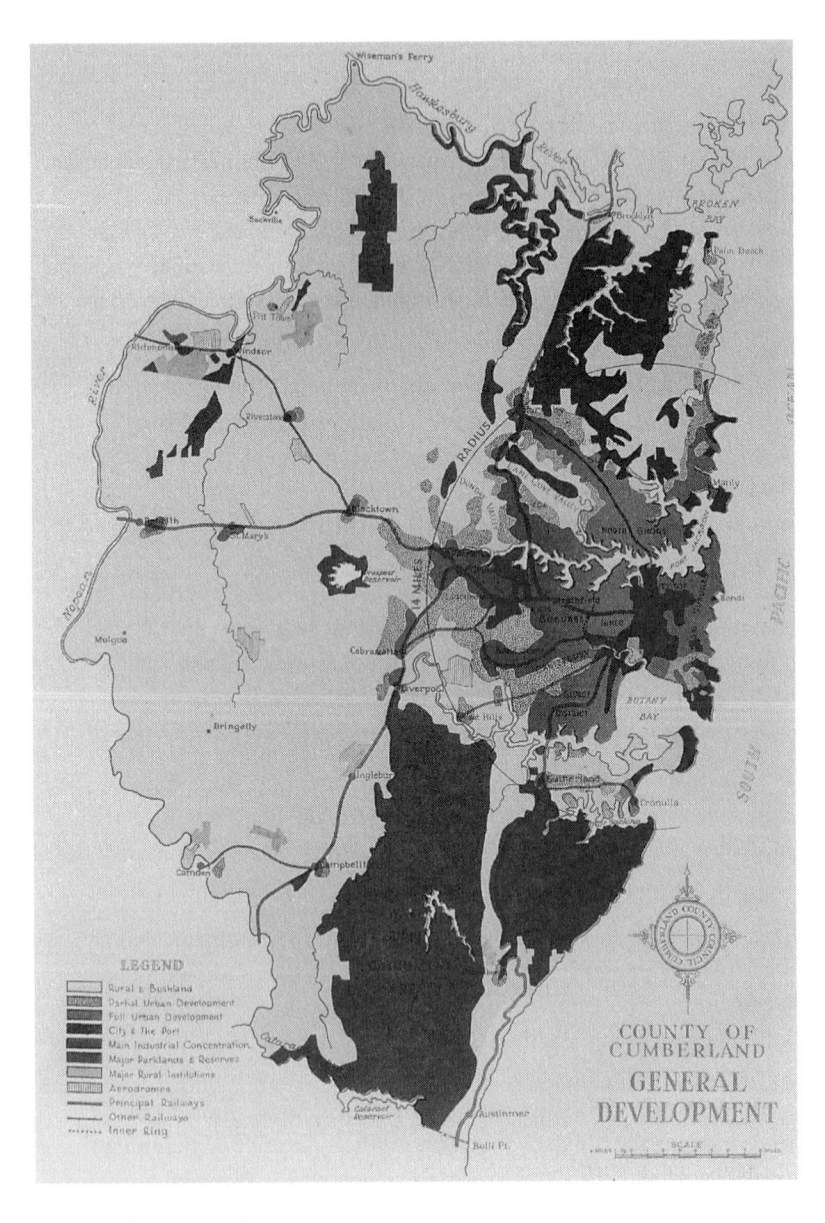

One example of the many maps used by the Cumberland County Council in its 1948 report.
NSW Department of Urban Affairs and Planning

feral suburbia?

County of Cumberland Council's views of urban squalor.
NSW Department of Urban Affairs and Planning. Used with permission.

home/world

23. Premature development means that land is neither town nor country. Trees and open spaces are slowly eaten up by scattered building on the metropolitan fringe.

County of Cumberland Council's views of urban sprawl.
NSW Department of Urban Affairs and Planning. Used with permission.

24. No-man's Land. Money spent without any return on roads and other services. Yards and yards of road per house, although there are many vacant lots within more developed areas.

feral suburbia?

KU-RING-GAI HOUSING
48. The individual house in harmony with natural surroundings, augmented by the imaginative garden treatment.

County of Cumberland Council's views of Arcadia.
NSW Department of Urban Affairs and Planning. Used with permission.

49. The reasonably high density of this street has not destroyed its natural beauty nor prevented the attractive garden treatment.

51

home/world

Very few of the residents of Sydney at this time would have had the opportunity to experience the 'synoptic view' that George Clarke claimed to have enjoyed as a young man growing up in Sydney. Unlike the Centrepoint tower or Australia Square building, the AWA tower was not available for local or international tourists to assume this perspective. And few had circled over the city in an aeroplane. In 1950 the Sunday supplement of the *Sydney Morning Herald* published a special feature, titled 'Sydney from the Air', which gave residents an opportunity to visualise their city in this way. Photographs were taken from many vantage points such as the Harbour Bridge, the AWA tower and from an aeroplane. But the report of the *Planning Scheme* of the County of Cumberland Council was seeking to introduce readers to more than simply this new way of looking at or visualising where they lived. They were being invited to adopt, from above, the totalising view. This viewpoint was claimed to enable both an objective diagnosis of the city's problems and the development of a set of democratic solutions.

The County of Cumberland Council, as already indicated, also held major exhibitions of its *Planning Scheme* in the Sydney Town Hall and in other localities, such as Bankstown. These exhibitions were to provide information about the scheme and an opportunity for the public to find out what was to happen in areas where they might be affected. Like the visual material in the 1948 report of the *Planning Scheme*, the exhibitions provided detailed presentations of the problems — photographs of inner-city decay and urban sprawl — and of the solutions in terms of 'looking at the whole'. These exhibitions were part of the training the council was seeking to provide so that Sydney would be *seen* — its landscape visualised and read — from a particular *point of view*.

The training involved is brought out most starkly by one of the activities that the County of Cumberland Council sponsored in the 1950s. Council officials took children on trips around the city of Sydney and to visit the council's exhibition about its current activities. They were being asked to take on the town planner's perspective and see their city from this angle. In 1955 the council ran a competition in which schools that had participated in the program were asked to submit essays by the children on the topic of 'Why Sydney should be planned'. In announcing the competition, the council suggested senior

feral suburbia?

Introducing Sydney residents to the 'view from above' of their city.
The *Sunday-Herald*, 22 January, 1950, p. 1. Used with permission.

53

students were 'junior citizens' and, as such, were a receptive and fruitful avenue for the dissemination of knowledge and information about the needs and benefits of planning.[25]

The children's essays diligently reproduced the messages they had clearly heard during their visit. The merits of the county's plans for zoning and living areas were dutifully recorded, as were the benefits of the proposed green belt. Similarly, the problems as defined by the council were reported back to them as issues of a history of a lack of planning, inner-city overcrowding and urban sprawl. A liberal use of red ticks in the margins of the essays told the students they were on the right track; comments were provided when they got it wrong.

One child sought to demonstrate that she could clearly visualise the city in the way required by providing a drawing of the rail and road patterns necessary, complete with a detailed key to interpret the various lines as seen from above. She also designed department store buildings with car parks on top and a polygon parking station, showing a ready willingness to imagine herself into a new modern city environment. The essays that received the most approval, however, were careful accounts of the council's problems, including those of inner-city decay and outer-suburbs sprawl, and its solutions. The council was seeking to train the children to *see the urban* and to see it as a space, a clearly defined entity as such, that could be subjected to the rational reforms of the town planner.

Only a very occasional glimpse can be caught in these essays of the lives of the children themselves and where these might fit within the spatial paradigm of the planner. Similarly, the 1948 *Planning Scheme for the County of Cumberland* provides very little opportunity to speculate about the lives of Sydney's residents at this time. Their social worlds were mapped out, documented, in the form of statistics and photographs of where they lived and worked. New social worlds were planned for them. But the perspective (which refused to acknowledge itself as a perspective) was of the master planner looking down on the whole. Though the chair of the council in its 1948 report announced it 'a people's plan',[26] in outlining the 'problem of sprawl', the possible motivations or desires of those who had chosen to move to Sydney's 'outer areas' were only scarcely contemplated. The County of

feral suburbia?

Photographs taken of the County of Cumberland Council Exhibition in the Sydney Town Hall.
NSW Department of Urban Affairs and Planning

home/world

Examples of children's essays submitted for the competition organised by the County of Cumberland Council on 'Why Sydney should be planned'. NSW Department of Urban Affairs and Planning. Used with permission.

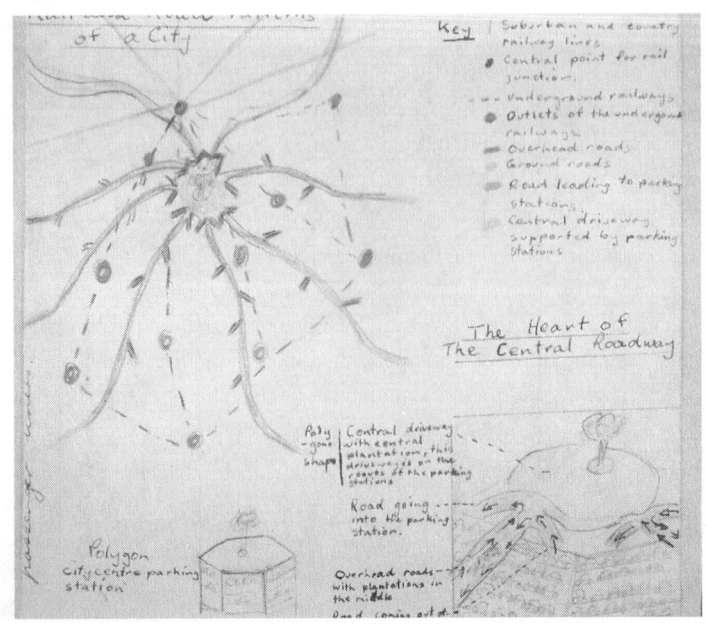

Cumberland Council plan speculated only briefly that the need for light and air may have driven people to move into such poorly serviced areas, with no amenities or community facilities.

This was predominantly, then, a document about shaping communities, everyday lives and identities to deal with the problems identified by the planner. The view from above, the view of the whole claimed by the authors of this report, purported to be able to know the city as an entity, a totality, and to read the surfaces of its landscape in order to both diagnose its problems and devise appropriate solutions.

private dreams and the 'public interest'

Once the 1948 report was published, the County Council called for submissions from the public about its plans. A wide range of individuals and organisations answered this call. Many of the objections were to the planned 'green belt'. Those from individuals, in particular, provide traces of the daily lives that otherwise scarcely registered in the *Planning Scheme*. They spoke of their blocks of land purchased to build a home in the future, a home they insisted they had a right to; a right that surely 'we fought for'. Letter-writers provided accounts of their hardships, of their years of saving, of the houses they frequently had built for themselves, of the dreams that had sustained them during the war, of their desires for a place for their family — for a safe space for children — and of their sense of their rights as citizens to fulfil their desires for such a place.[27]

The 1948 report of the County of Cumberland Council declared its *Planning Scheme* a democratic instrument for the betterment of everyone's daily lives. It asked citizens to take 'the synoptic view', the view from above and see that betterment as a matter of making collective plans into which individual lives would fit. As citizens, they were told, they were expected to adopt such a view. Similarly, the schoolchildren taken to the council's exhibitions were expected to embrace such a perspective as 'junior citizens'. But the objections of landholders affected by the zoning plans of the scheme invoked a different discourse of democracy and the 'public interest' about 'the rights of the individual' in which a democracy should enable its citizens to attain the collective achievement of their private dreams.

I am not suggesting that these dreams represent authentic or spontaneous desires of people opposed to the authoritarian imposition of the planner. These dreams were themselves, in large part at least, the product of various types of planning. They had been shaped, for example, by the rhetoric of the wartime period and the use of images of home, wife and family to forge a shared project of 'what we are fighting for'. They had been incited too by the popular media before, during and after the war, with their emphasis on images of domestic comfort as the sphere in which the individual could express not only his or her individuality but that they were the 'very best type of citizen'.[28] Politicians of various colours had also increasingly sought to speak to 'the people' in this form. Robert Menzies in his famous 1942 speech, 'The Forgotten People', began a powerful campaign to persuade men, in particular, that home ownership — 'one little piece of earth with a house and garden which is ours' — guaranteed both their manhood and their citizenship.[29]

And these dreams were to be sold, too, to potential migrants by the federal government after the Second World War.[30] While acknowledging the difficulty of providing adequate housing for its citizens in these early years, successive governments for the next two decades sought to attract migrants through films and written materials promoting employment prospects and the quality of life in Australia. In the 1950s, in particular, this propaganda used the new home on a quarter-acre block as symbolic of the quality of life Australia could offer. Photographs of happy migrants, either in public housing or homes they had built themselves, with accompanying stories, were sent overseas to be published in newspapers in the main source countries for Australian migrants to promote stories of successful settlement.[31] The reality in this period was as much about discrimination by public housing authorities, legal impediments to the ownership of land by 'aliens', shortage of building materials and problems with access to finance.[32] But by 1976 little difference could be seen in the rate of home ownership between overseas-born and Australian-born residents (68 per cent of householders either owned or were buying their own homes) and some groups of migrants, such as Greeks and Italians, had increased their home ownership by 1981 to between 84 per cent and 90 per cent respectively.[33]

feral suburbia?

An example of the images used to appeal to migrants' desire for home ownership. Department of Immigration and Multicultural Affairs

The ways in which the private dreams of a home of one's own were shaped by government and other agencies suggest that the sphere of everyday life is not quite as fundamentally unknowable as Michel de Certeau claims. The determination of the population of Sydney to own their own home, assisted by real estate developers pursuing their narrow economic interests and by local government agencies that refused to curtail their activities, appear to have been highly significant in undermining the ambitions of the master planners. But this determination, and the desires it appeared to articulate, were themselves, at least in part the product of planning, albeit of a different kind. An awareness of the history of the shaping of such desires suggests that the practices of everyday life that de Certeau claims to be opposed or resistant to the activities of the master planner, can themselves, even if never totally known or pinned down, be reshaped or given different forms of expression in the long term.

What I am questioning is the suggestion that the 'view from above' pursued by the urban reformers involved in the County of Cumberland Council in the 1940s and 1950s provided both an impartial and democratic instrument of planning. This 'view from above' relies on the notion of the master planner that reduces a knowledge of the city as a whole to a totalising perspective that reads only its surfaces. The complexity of the city and the needs and desires of the diverse urban populations — the lived experience of the urban — are reduced to this surface, to that which can be known and documented through population statistics and the mapping and monitoring techniques of social administration.

The County of Cumberland Council had not ignored the sphere of everyday life that objectors to the *Planning Scheme* were seeking to protect. On the contrary, its central preoccupation was with the rational organisation of that sphere through the zoning of the city and the creation of 'living areas' in which a sense of belonging and of community as well as a new type of worker could be produced. But, as a number of authors have noted, the pressure for housing blocks in the 1950s became so great that the New South Wales Labor government released 50 square miles (130 square kilometres) in 1959, extending the metropolitan boundaries and effectively unleashing the 'urban sprawl' with which the scheme had sought to grapple. Encroachment into the green belt had already occurred in the early 1950s because of the refusal of local governments to exercise the kinds of control required. By the early 1960s, both the green belt idea and the satellite town proposals had virtually died.

The commitment to a notion of the necessity of a planned society produced both by the experience of the Depression of the 1920s and 1930s and by the massive social dislocation of the Second World War had been important in creating the will to reform articulated by the *Planning Scheme for the County of Cumberland*. Democracy and social justice would be achieved, it was believed, through the use of the rational and objective tools of the town planner. But the participation of individuals and groups in this supposedly democratic endeavour was confined to the mode of formal and individualised objections to the plan. Complainants could only hope that their specific problems would be addressed, but the basis of their concerns, the fundamental issues underlying them, did not become part of the formal agenda of the County Council. They were being asked only to give their views on the solutions proposed by this agency, not to debate the way in which the problems themselves had been conceptualised.

'when one flies over the County ...'

In 1984, Nigel Ashton, chair of the State Planning Authority between 1964 and 1974, suggested that 'When one flies over the County' today, it is possible to see the metropolitan area of Sydney 'much as the County Scheme and the subsequent Sydney Region Outline Plan envisaged it...'.[34] Although the green belt and satellite towns did not eventuate, Nigel Ashton concluded, significant areas of open space planned by the County Council had.

And indeed, ironically, recent housing developments appear to be seeking to establish precisely the forms of 'living areas' proposed nearly fifty years ago by this scheme. Lendlease recently announced what they claimed to be 'a radical new development' for St Marys. They have commissioned an American architect, a proponent of what is referred to as 'new urbanism'. He designs 'communities that look like traditional old-style towns' with 'a traditional main street, with offices and houses above shops, and town squares, post offices, libraries and town halls occupying significant places'. 'Green corridors' are planned too and people are expected to walk everywhere rather than drive.[35]

Today we can all be expected to have flown over our city (if not in reality then with the assistance of a movie or television camera) and to have *seen* 'the problem of urban sprawl' from the point of view of the planner. But it is not simply the actual experience of this view from above that ensures that we see this landscape of Sydney as a problem. This way of looking is something we have been trained to do by government policy statements like the County of Cumberland Council *Planning Scheme* and subsequent state and federal government documents. And the media too have played their part in schooling us to 'see the sprawl'.

But are we still expected to discuss only the solutions, not the problem itself? And does that conceptualisation of the problem claim an objectivity for itself that relies on a belief in a god-like eye?

I am not suggesting that we should give up the impulse to plan this city, nor do I want to affirm some notion of democracy as simply the collective achievement of private and privatised dreams. Notions of 'the city' and 'the urban' can be important in enabling the integration of as many 'points of view' as possible and the various preoccupations and expertise of specialist planning groups: transport, energy, health, social, manpower, environmental.[36] It is of concern, however, that the concept of 'urban sprawl' springs from a notion of the authority of the planner that reduces an interest in the complexity of the city to an analysis of a surface claimed to be 'the whole'. Such a way of seeing sets up the desires of one section of the population as rational, and those of the 'others' — those who are said to be represented by 'western Sydney' — as feral, as out of control. Their points of view, their needs, understandings and sense of attachment to particular places, are thereby silenced, marginalised.

notes

1 *Sydney Morning Herald*, 13 September 1994, p. 7.

2 'A unique approach to urban design', Professor Philip Cox, speech delivered at the University of New South Wales, 12 September 1994, p. 8; this speech was subsequently published as 'Is there a uniquely Australian approach to urban design?' in *Urban Futures*, no. 17, 1995, pp. 20–5.

3 Diane Powell, *Out West.:Perceptions of Sydney's Western Suburbs*, Allen & Unwin, Sydney, 1993, p. xvii. In the 1990s some more positive stories have

feral suburbia?

appeared in the media, although these are still very much exceptions and often appear to be patronising. See, for example, 'Go west, yuppies', *Sydney Morning Herald*, Metro, 19–25 April, p. 13.

4 Powell, 1993.

5 Kathleen Mee, 'Dressing up the suburbs: representations of western Sydney', in K. Gibson & S. Watson (eds), *Metropolis Now: Planning and the Urban in Contemporary Australia*, Pluto Press, Sydney, 1994, p. 60.

6 Diane Powell draws attention to this issue, see Powell, p.33.

7 James Donald, 'The city, the cinema: modern spaces', in Chris Jencks (ed.), *Visual Culture*, Routledge, London, 1995, p. 92.

8 James Donald, 'Metropolis: the city as text', in R. Bocock & K. Thompson (eds), *Social and Cultural Forms of Modernity*, Polity Press, Cambridge, 1992, p. 428.

9 Donald, 'Metropolis', pp. 443–4.

10 Paul Rabinow, *French Modern: Norms and Forms of the Social Environment*, MIT Press, Cambridge, Mass., 1992, p. 12.

11 I am discussing here one particular concept of modernity — the governmental — in which the preoccupation was with rational control of 'man's' environment through the expertise and authority of particular social groups. The relationship between the city and modernity was conceptualised in quite a different manner in the nineteenth century by literary figures such as Charles Baudelaire.

12 Michel de Certeau, *The Practice of Everyday Life*, trans. Steven Rendall, University of California Press, Berkeley, 1988.

13 A term used by Paul Carter, *The Road to Botany Bay: An Essay in Spatial History*, Faber & Faber, London, 1987.

14 de Certeau, p. 110.

15 Paul Ashton, George Clarke interview, in *Planning Sydney: Nine Planners Remember*, Council of the City of Sydney, Sydney, 1992, p. 33.

16 ibid., p. 20.

17 Denis Winston, *Sydney's Great Experiment: The Progress of the Cumberland County Plan*, Angus and Robertson, Sydney, 1957, p. 28.

18 *The Planning Scheme for the County of Cumberland,* The Report of the Cumberland County Council to the Hon. J. J. Cahill, M.L.A., Minister for Local Government, Sydney, 27 July 1948, frontispiece.

19 *Planning Scheme*, p. xv.

20 ibid., p. 149.

21 All areas that are now included in various definitions of 'western Sydney' (see preface).

22 *Planning Scheme*, p. 79.

23 ibid., p. 1.

24 Carter, p. 46.

25 Department of Planning Library, EPA 26 108/66, Chairmans Minute No 127 — School Students — Essay Competition, 13 May 1955.

26 *Planning Scheme,* p. xvi.

27 Department of Planning Library, EPA 29, 125/15, Objections to the Master Plan — Individuals File.

28 Department of Planning Library, EPA 29, 125/15, Submission from residents in Willoughby.

29 Judith Brett, *Robert Menzies's Forgotten People,* Pan Macmillan, Sydney, 1992, p. 73.

30 *The Australian Magazine,* 4–5 November 1995, pp. 24ff.

31 For example, the Australian Department of Immigration and Ethnic Affairs collected a large number of such photographs between 1946 and the early 1970s. Similarly, *South West Pacific*, published by the Department of Information between 1946 and 1953, provided such stories for journalists working overseas, and films like *Australia and Your Future: Men Wanted*, also produced by this department, promoted a story of jobs, homes and sun.

32 See Ann-Mari Jordens, *On Accommodating Migrants*, Administration, Compliance and Governability Program, Working Paper No. 19, Research School of Social Sciences, Australian National University, Canberra, January 1994, pp. 27ff.

33 Jock Collins, *Migrant Hands in a Distant Land*, Pluto Press, Sydney, 1988, p. 169.

34 Nigel Ashton, 'Sydney: village to metropolis', a brief review of planning in the Sydney Region, Department of Environment and Planning, Background Paper, Sydney, 1984, p. 6.

35 *Sydney Morning Herald*, 1 November 1995, p. 4; see chapter 5 in this book for an analysis of this movement.

36 See Robert Beauregard, 'Between modernity and postmodernity: the ambiguous position of US planning', *Environment and Planning D: Society and Space*, vol. 7, 1989, p. 392.

acknowledgement

I wish to thank Julie Langsworth and Justine Lloyd for their assistance in collecting the material for this project, and more generally, for their support during the writing of the paper. I also wish to thank Pauline Johnson and Paula Hamilton for their comments on various drafts.

3. outside the spaces of modernity:

western Sydney and the logic of the european city[1]

michael symonds

In the eastern suburbs of Sydney where I spent my childhood in the 1960s, the term 'westie' was the ultimate insult. The tacit understanding was that 'westies' were essentially stupid, vulgar and so backward that they seemed to come from another time and place. Similarly, the western suburbs were imagined as ugly, featureless, dangerous and either too hot or too cold. It was commonly assumed that their distance from Sydney's east made a visit absolutely prohibitive (even though we travelled at various times during my childhood to the Blue Mountains for a day out, thereby traversing the whole of western Sydney in the process).[2]

And so years later, it was disconcerting to find myself working at the Nepean campus of the University of Western Sydney. For the first time in my life I had to seriously confront my long-held prejudices about Sydney's west. This self-reflexivity has been the impetus for the meditations that form the basis of this chapter and my consideration of the cultural object of the 'westie' and its supposed suburban habitat.

From my new location 'in the west' (and as someone trained in philosophy), I have come to think that we can look back towards Sydney's centre and the development of its suburbs in a way that highlights the interdependent and contradictory logics that lie at the heart of modernity. This perspective enables us to see Sydney emerging in the 1960s out of the long European tradition of the city. This was the logic it had to follow to become the cultural centre, the modern city, it now proclaims itself to be. But other contradictory logics were also at work. The ambivalence about questions of home, belonging and the freedom of the modern individual that has characterised modernity can be seen to be played out in the history of Sydney and the way in which Sydney's west has been conceived since the 1960s. At the same time, the view from Sydney's west suggests that these issues have taken a particular turn in the development of Australia's major cities.

This chapter explores these themes as a way of making sense of the specific ethics of space that enables the construction of Sydney's west as 'the bad suburbs'. From this perspective, a fundamental relationship between the emergence of Sydney as a world-class city in the 1960s and 1970s and the increasing condemnation of the western suburbs seems likely. It begins by tracing the tradition of the logic of the western city before moving on to questions of the modern individual — questions about the subject of the modern city or what sort of person is assumed to be appropriate to live in and be a citizen of this city. The chapter then goes on to explore questions about the search for the home in the suburbs, arguing that the logics of the city and home in western conceptions of modernity complement each other in the history of Sydney and serve to exclude its western suburbs. The chapter concludes by exploring the relationship of the city to nature in Australia, arguing that western Sydney is not simply denigrated because it is the centre's periphery, but because western Sydney is also understood as the centre's abandoned history.

While the emphasis in this chapter is on the logic of the modern city in the 'othering' of the western suburbs, there are clearly other factors involved. As indicated in the introduction to this book, Diane Powell emphasises a class view, arguing that the movement of the poor and the working class into these new suburbs lead to the stigmatisation of the west.[3] This is certainly part of the explanation. However, a predominantly or exclusively class analysis does not adequately explain the complexity of the image of the westie. This requires additional cultural explanation. Similarly, Powell identifies the suburban aspects of western Sydney as integral to its representation as a 'wasteland'. In the history of Australian representations of suburbia, this space is frequently depicted as boring and cultureless, especially when juxtaposed with the city.[4] While again I agree that this is a contributing factor, in itself it is not sufficient for explaining the view of Sydney's west as 'other'. The suburban ideal in Australia is also one where the lack of experiences of the city is balanced against the positive features of safety, tranquillity, cleanliness and even beauty — a good place to bring up the kids, as Hugh Stretton saw it in his praising of suburbia in his highly influential book published in the mid-1970s, *Ideas for Australian Cities*.[5] But these more affirming perspectives on suburbs are often lost in the constructions of the western suburbs that circulate in the Australian media. Again, further explanation is needed to explain the unrelieved negativity of perceptions of this particular suburban space.

But in suggesting that a process of othering needs to be considered in order to develop a more complex understanding of the 'westie' image, I want to avoid an uncritical adoption of a notion of otherness. For example, the framework developed by Edward Said in his seminal analysis of Orientalism cannot simply be applied to definitions of western Sydney. Said highlights the contradictory desires evoked in notions of the exotic which lie at the heart of definitions of the Oriental, at the same time as he reveals the clearly despised nature of this western construct. The westie does appear to have functioned as 'other' to the city inhabitants of Sydney in their self-proclamation as full cosmopolitan subjects. All that they desire not to be is displaced onto the formation of this other. But peculiarly, the westie appears to be understood as almost wholly lacking desirable qualities or attributes; there is nothing exotic about this image.

But this argument needs some qualification. The association of the space of western Sydney with the Aussie battler is one possible line of approbation. While the battler is a difficult image to pin down, it clearly does not only refer to the struggling poor. The image of the battler is of ordinary people imbued with a certain moral worthiness — a worthiness which is necessarily denied to the rich or high cultured. It is an image that conjures up an older, somehow better, traditional Australia. The power of its appeal can be seen at election time: politicians vie for battler appeal. But their interest is not simply the voting numbers involved. More importantly, the spaces identified with the Aussie battlers are considered some kind of moral heartland of the nation. In the 1993 federal election campaign, the contending party leaders, Paul Keating and John Hewson, both tried to exhibit this 'ordinary goodness' by invoking their respective western suburbs origins. In the 1996 campaign, Prime Minister Keating proudly and deliberately called himself a westie in a national television interview.[6] So, this slight positive attribute has to find a place in the overall picture.

The contention of this chapter is, then, that the logic of the western-European city provides an important key to understanding the power and politics of the damned image of western Sydney. Class and the history of Australian attitudes to suburbia are important to such an analysis, but they do not sufficiently explain the complexity of this issue.

outside the spaces of modernity

I the logic of the city

the city-as-cultural-centre

If the emergence of the identity of the western suburbs coincided with the cultural rise of Sydney as a city, the question arises as to what qualities constitute the city-as-cultural-centre. In other words, what was the pattern of development of Sydney which enabled it to be named as a place one no longer had to leave (go overseas) in order to fulfil oneself as a modern subject? At the same time, the logic of the city produced a space for the suburban home to function as the site for the losses involved in the life of the city. I argue that the western suburbs have fallen outside this twin logic of the city-as-centre and suburbia-as-home. They have been cast out of the spaces of modernity. This section of the chapter analyses these twin logics.

The identification of the city with modernity is a common and justified linkage.[7] But in trying to understand why the city is the site of the modern subject, it is a standard yet somewhat misleading tactic to begin with the late eighteenth and nineteenth centuries — with the historical time of modernity and the revolutionary process of urbanisation taking place in some European countries at this time. It is commonplace to focus on the cities of London, Paris and St Petersburg in this period in such analyses. Of course, much insight can be gained here but the origins of modernity and its sites lie in a much earlier time and space. It is by going back much further in time that the crucial relationships between the secular city, nature and death can be explored. And hence my contention is that through these formations the fate of the western suburbs can be more fully understood. Given the scope of the task, the historical possibilities seem overwhelming. A great deal of the complexity of the issues will have to be ignored in this chapter. However, I will briefly explore some key themes and salient points which will help to understand the relationship between Sydney-as-centre and its western suburbs.

early origins of the modern city

Hegel, in his classic text, *The Phenomenology of Spirit*, undertook a monumental endeavour to grasp the whole of the European–western tradition. Despite the clearly justified and considerable body of writing

69

that now exists criticising this work, Hegel continues to provide inspiration for understanding and tracing the origins of modernity. In particular, through a discussion of the ethical life of Ancient Greece in the fifth century BC, he shows how the basic conflicts of the European tradition can be identified as existing very clearly at this time. He argues that they were given their most forceful representation in the play *Antigone*, by Sophocles.

To recount the story of Antigone: Antigone is the daughter of Oedipus and Jocasta. Her two brothers, Polyneices and Eteocles, kill each other on a battlefield outside the polis of Thebes. Creon, the king of Thebes, decrees that the body of Polyneices cannot be buried or honoured since he had been fighting against the Thebans. Creon ordained that anyone performing the burial rites was under penalty of death. Antigone defies the city law in the name of the Gods, nature and family. As a result, she is walled-up in a cave where she kills herself. The blind soothsayer, Tiresias, predicts doom and condemns Creon. Creon eventually changes his mind, bowing to the signs of an older divinity. But it is too late. Creon's son, Antigone's fiance, finds her body and kills himself. Creon's wife, Eurydice, also commits suicide. Creon admits his guilt and ultimately Antigone's cause is proclaimed as right.

Hegel discusses *Antigone* in the beginning of his move to develop a theory of *Geist* (Spirit) in *The Phenomenology of Spirit*. And while it is notoriously difficult to give an account of Geist a few remarks are needed: Geist is the great Hegelian shift to history beyond Reason (where Reason can be seen particularly in abstract philosophical solutions, for example at its highest level in Kant). History has an essential telos, with philosophy needed as the ultimate self-consciousness of this dialectical progress of history as Spirit. Spirit is the progress of 'the living ethical world'.[8] It is 'the ethical essence that has an actual existence'.[9] Its understanding gives the meaning of history.

Antigone, as the beginning point of Spirit, illustrates the most basic dialectical contradiction. Hegel describes it as the conflict between the human and divine laws. The human law is of course represented by Creon and the polis; and Antigone represents the divine order, family and nature. These two laws are seen to be in balance by Hegel.

The whole is a stable equilibrium of all the parts, and each part is a Spirit at home in the whole, a Spirit which does not seek its satisfaction outside of itself but finds it within itself, because it is itself in this equilibrium with the whole.[10]

And each knows the other. On the one side is the state as the realm of the universal, and for Hegel, of course, the future. It is the site of the gathering subject — of freedom and self-consciousness. This is the place of the human law. On the other side is the sphere of Antigone's law, the divine, which has its legitimation in the 'nether' world, that is, with the gods, but especially with death.

> For the commands of government have a universal, public meaning open to the light of day; the will of the other law, however, is locked up in the darkness of the nether regions…[11]

The divine law points to existence beyond the human achievements of the city. It is also said to be natural. This can be interpreted as indicating the non-polis terrain of nature, where the gods and tradition must still rule. Polyneices' body lies outside the polis walls, and Antigone has to bring it into its place in enchanted nature by means of the burial rites. Antigone represents the enchanted cosmos which gives death a meaningful place. Thus, by perfoming the rites, 'she weds the blood relation to the bosom of the earth'.[12] Since death and suffering have this meaning, Antigone deliberately seeks them, and embraces them as her destiny. It is her end and her fulfilment. Antigone says: 'I will bury my brother; and if I die for it, what happiness! … There is no punishment can rob me of honourable death'.[13]

Antigone's sphere is also one of the particular, according to Hegel. Here Hegel explores how the universal law of Creon (which will be developed by western reason) applies to all the people of Thebes impersonally, including Antigone. It is this law which is denied by Antigone in the name of her own dead brother, since he is a member of her family and the object of her personal particular love. 'Convicted of reverence — I shall be content to lie beside the brother whom I love. We have only a little time to please the living, but all eternity to love the dead'.[14]

But note how the particular of Antigone has a universality itself within the divine order. It is a universal based on the family and which can include the particularity of personal love as opposed to the necessary impersonality of polis reason. (It should be stressed that it is this realm of Antigone that Hegel wants to deny but, in the end, regain for himself.)

The balance between these known, interdependent but contradictory laws will necessarily be upset because of what Hegel terms the deed.

> What appears as order and harmony of its two essences, each of which authenticates and completes the other, becomes through the deed a transition of opposites in which each proves itself to be the nonreality, rather than the authentication, of itself and the other.[15]

That is, with Polyneices' death, the balanced, complementing spheres cannot be maintained. They are doomed to crack. Knowingly flouting the human law, Antigone performs the funeral rites and welcomes death. At this stage of Spirit — the very beginning, with the state so young — Creon must finally accept the law of the enchanted cosmos. The state is overwhelmed by the ethical space of the divine order.

Creon is the nascent subject of the West. He acts and reasons within the mundane polis and is not trying to avoid any preordained fate (as, for example, Oedipus tried to do) or escape ancient magical beings (as did Ulysses). His deeds and reasons are his alone, possible only within the polis limits, with no divine intervention or advice. He alone bears responsibility for the terrible outcome when he admits his error and goes back to the divine law. But in this he reveals his subjectivity in being able to change, even if it is in denying the realm of the possible subject. Antigone, by contrast, is all constancy and filled by outside forces. She is at one with a natural order which is made meaningful by including the realm beyond human life.[16]

For Hegel, the state as the sphere of free subjectivity will triumph and the household gods will be brought into its determination.

> Human law in its universal existence... is, moves and maintains itself by consuming and absorbing into itself the separatism of the Penates, or the separation into independent families presided over by womankind.[17]

There will be a final resolution, not in Antigone's favour, but in the end of Spirit's development, with Creon. The state itself will come to be considered as god-given. It is the telos of history that Antigone's sphere will come to the free subject, as part of the state. At least this is the movement which Hegel sets up as the absolute end of history.

However, Hegel has to admit that the family, and its particularity, 'presided over by womankind',[18] is always a concern even at the end of the state's historical triumph.

> Womankind — the everlasting irony (in the life) of the community — changes by intrigue the universal end of the government into a private end, transforms its universal activity into a work of some particular individual, and perverts the universal property of the state into a possession and ornament for the Family.[19]

That is, although the human law of the state has increased enormously since the time of Creon's failed beginnings, it cannot, even at the end of its development, completely absorb the Antigonean sphere of particular love. A remnant of all Antigone triumphantly and tragically represented remains and is necessarily beyond the reach of the power of the human law. So even on his own philosophical terrain Hegel cannot make the final absolutist achievement work.

Given this serious admission by Hegel himself, and the necessary rejection of any idea of some great final, idealist totality, it is arguable that the dialectic of Antigone is still with us. The state (the site of reason) is very much more developed, of course, as Hegel articulates; and its leaders will certainly not bow to some itinerant soothsayer today and return to the magical tradition. Also, the other side is no longer the divine law of the family — the enchanted realm has been lost in the state's–reason's vast development. Importantly, nature has been disenchanted by reason and for the state. The rise of natural science and Protestantism in the sixteenth and seventeenth centuries is the most obvious cause of the de-magicalising of nature and the overthrowing of a divinely meaningful cosmos like Antigone's. But all that Antigone espoused is not therefore lost. There is still a sphere of family love, duty and self-sacrifice; and death and suffering maintain a trace of meaning here. It is the space of the particular still, but without the universal provided by the gods of the underworld. The gains of the subject, of the state and freedom are at the cost of the ancient whole as a place for meaningful death; but a place for the maintenance of the Antigonean ethical lineage can still be discerned.

This small space, the remnant of Antigone's enchanted sphere, is what we often call home. The idealised vision of home contains a peace and familial love which points back to Antigone, but the full ideal cannot today be realised because the wider realm of enchantment and meaningful death is missing. The crucial point, which arises from Hegel's beginning with Sophocles' play, is how the city, as the site of the human law, was formed in relation to a specifically enchanted nature, as the place of the divine law of Antigone. Nature should play a fundamental part in any adequate understanding of the city; and the desires of home will be entwined with the city's development once this Hegelian starting point is adopted.

The problem facing Creon, at the very beginning of the city's development, was to try to gain a self-sufficiency for the space of the polis in the face of the enchanted cosmos. (This is meant as a legitimating, cultural self-sufficiency, not an economic separatedness.) Vitally, the polis, at least in this representation, would be trying to establish this cultural position in purely secular terms, that is, against the divine law of Antigone and Tiresias. Creon would attempt a reasoned defence of his human law which had reference only to the internal nature of the city–state.[20] Here, and only here, could the highest human achievements be accomplished. Outside the city walls one had to accept the older law of the gods.

This starting point of Hegel's Spirit can be used to understand the logic of the European–western city which Sydney in the late twentieth century will also be fated to follow. Despite the vast changes since Sophocles' time the city is still seen as the necessary space for the pursuit of the secular heights of human cultural achievement. It has to try to offer a certain self-sufficiency in terms of the current historical determination of what such secular achievement might be. In other words, for contemporary understanding, a city will have attained this level of cultural self-sufficiency if individuals do not have to leave it in order to fulfil themselves as modern subjects. The city can be considered a centre if this completion of secular opportunities is established, as will be seen when we consider a tradition of understanding the city which stretches from Plato to contemporary Sydney.[21]

the city-as-secular-centre

Within two decades of the first performances of Antigone, Plato was born. In the most widely read of any Greek classic, the *Republic*, Plato wants to argue for a polis which can sustain itself against the forces of tradition and enchanted nature — a conclusion opposed to Sophocles' claim in *Antigone*. Here, very clearly, the polis is the demarcated site for the highest, secular, human achievement. For Plato this is the development of human reason as embodied by the minutely trained philosopher–kings.

The standard criticisms of the *Republic* stem from the shock felt by latter-day liberals to the measures Plato advocated to try to gain a self-sufficiency for the polis against the Antigonean forces. Infanticide, eugenics, the expulsion of the artists, the denial of familial (particularly maternal) attachments — all these seemingly terrible policies are aimed at maintaining the cohesive unity of the city–state. For it is only through such cohesion that the secular centre can be secured against the strength of the divine law, and only in this space can reason be fully achieved by the elite few. Plato goes about describing the structures and institutions which constitute this human space. And it is clear that the unity and preservation of the polis is absolutely paramount. Socrates, Plato's champion, will finally give his definition of justice (the key problem of this dialogue) as everyone just doing their own job.[22] The strangeness of such a definition is allayed if Plato's task is understood as following the logic of the city, particularly when the fate of Creon is remembered. That is, if everyone does their own job, as Plato has determined, then the city will be impervious to the outside realm and human reason will flourish.

This ideal of the city as providing all that is needed for human cultivation (a centre) is emphasised in Plato's *Phaedrus* in the following scene:

> *Phaedrus:* What an incomprehensible being you are,
> Socrates: when you are in the country, as you say, you are

like some stranger who is led about by a guide. Do you ever cross the border? I rather think that you never venture even outside the gates.

Socrates: Very true, my good friend; and I hope that you will excuse me when you hear the reason, which is, that I am a lover of knowledge, and the men who dwell in the city are my teachers, and not the trees or the country.[23]

The ancient Greeks reveal to us the basic forms which we are still trying to perfect. And the most cursory sketch of the western tradition indicates how the city is the necessary site for the usually acknowledged highspots of cultural development. Hence, the Renaissance existed within the city limits of such centres as Florence, Rome and Venice. Later, Habermas emphasises how the cosmopolitan opportunities of London's coffee-houses of the late eighteenth century contributed to the growth of the public sphere.[24] And a great deal of recent work has focused on the experiences which the modern city has to offer — from Baudelaire's Paris to Woody Allen's New York. Indeed, this logic of the modern city continues to be one pursued by Sydney and Sydneysiders.

The modern subject demands to experience all the possibilities which great cities offer. This consumption of urban life has become one of the conditions for achieving the secular, cultural heights of subjectivity.[25] The type of subject, whose successful cultivation became the standard against which the city of modernity was measured, was the artist. The artist could not only experience the city, they could also give expression to life in the city. Hence for Baudelaire, the great nineteenth-century definer of city modernism, the ideal city-dweller is 'an "I" with an insatiable appetite for the "non-I", at every instant rendering and explaining it in pictures more living than life itself'.[26] And again:

Few men are gifted with the capacity of seeing; there are fewer still who possess the power of expression. So now, at a time when others are asleep, Monsieur G. is bending over his table, darting onto a sheet of paper the same glance that a moment ago he was directing towards external things.[27]

Maintaining the artist as the ideal of the experiencing and expressive individual is the goal of the logic of the modern city (as much as the philosopher of Reason was for Plato's polis). Sydney seems to have pursued this logic of the city successfully since the 1960s — becoming a centre when 'the artist' did not travel to other cities in the world to fulfil himself or herself.[28] A rough turning point can perhaps be identified at the moment at which overseas travel for aspiring modern subjects became non-essential. A cultural trail of Australian ex-patriots can be traced up until the 1960s (for example, culminating with Clive James and Germaine Greer). The period immediately following this, from the late 1960s and early 1970s, can be identified as a period in which Sydney vastly increased its cultural offerings.

Not only did the city need to provide rich experiences, it also needed to develop the venues of artistic expression. For a city to be able to proclaim itself as world-class it had to possess companies, venues and schools for high culture (the ballet, opera, theatre and orchestra). If one event epitomised this, it was the building of the Sydney Opera House. Despite the compromises, its completion as a site for artistic experience and expression, as well as being a work of art itself, in such a dominant location, is highly indicative of the logic of the modern city.[29]

II home and modernity

city and nature

This brief historical overview has traced the logic of the city-as-centre from the time of the ancient Greeks. But while the logic can be understood as constant, there are clearly historical shifts between the 'polis ideal' and the contemporary city. The complexities of these shifts are beyond the scope of this chapter. However, one of the major shifts in the western tradition has to be mentioned. Whereas Plato's Socrates thought he could learn nothing from the trees and countryside, nature today is usually regarded as a fundamental source of experience and inspiration. For Plato, outside the polis walls lay the traditional divinities of an enchanted nature which in fact threatened the secular, cultural achievements of the city itself (and to which Creon tragically succumbed). But, as already mentioned, with seventeenth-century natural science (among a range of other factors), nature was disenchanted. It was made safe to be included in the range of the city-dwellers' experiences. The romantic movement of the late eighteenth and nineteenth centuries would provide us with one such vision of nature as experience. For example, a romantic poet like Wordsworth would advocate a solitary walk in nature as providing a great enlargement of human subjectivity. This would have been considered an extraordinary proposal before nature and the urban subject could be brought together in the name of experience.[30]

Nature was aestheticised and could be regarded as an extension of the city subject. One could lap up all the city had to offer and then go to the country (or travel generally) to be part of this disenchanted, romanticised nature. And nature could be felt as not only beautiful, but its magical past could also be invoked as part of the possible life of the modern 'I'. (An example is contemporary white Australian city-dwellers going out into the bush to experience the Aboriginal Dreamtime.) But such limited memories of enchantment are fodder for the sensibilities of modernity, and not the recovery of Antigone's underworld.

Disenchantment meant that the threat of the Antigonean world was completely gone. But the triumphant human law of the city, in all its manifestations, could not recover what had been lost in this victory. For us now to list some well-known dilemmas of modernity, as exemplified by the city, will necessarily point us back to the idea of home as the inescapable remnant of the shattered Antigonean cosmos. Max Weber provides one of the best accounts of this loss.

modernity and loss

Weber wrote his most influential works in the first two decades of the twentieth century. Although he was a supporter of the developing structures of the modern world, such as capitalism, science and democracy, he still found them highly flawed. The points of critique here are fairly familiar, but Weber's particular understanding can significantly help us to sort out the city's logic of success and loss.

A first point is associated with the standard criticism of modernist culture as being isolating, alienating or lonely. Weber's gloss on this aspect is to stress the impersonality of, for example, the modern bureaucracy and the law. For Weber the progressiveness of a democratically attuned bureaucracy (as with the provision of state welfare), or the benefits of an impartial legal system (blind justice), are necessarily accompanied by the treatment of welfare clients and the legally accused with a somewhat cold, detached impersonality. General laws and rules must apply to all equally, without irrational associations and sentimental attachment.[31] Recall how this was Creon's defence for his punishment of Antigone.

This Weberian form of understanding as both gain and loss can be applied to the city and the crowd. The modern city provides the freedom which the anonymity of sheer numbers allows (away from the gaze of suburban neighbours and family), but can also result in the extremes of impersonality and loneliness.[32] It is the loss of the particular, especially as it is known in family love, as we saw with Antigone and her brother.

A second, closely related point is generally put in terms of the modern ethic of individualism riding roughshod over ethics of care and love. Weber expresses this notion as the impossibility of success in the spheres of modernity (the economy, politics, art, the erotic and science) without forgoing the ethic of 'brotherliness'. Such an ethic has its clearest expression in some types of Christianity. Again, for Weber, the loss of such an important ethic is the necessary accompaniment to the pursuit of money or power or beauty or truth. And trying to achieve such values enables the triumphs of the modern to unfold.[33]

These Weberian spheres of modernity are, on the whole, to be found in their greatest glory in the city. Here is the site for these purely human values. Again, the contrast is with Antigone's family love of her brother.

Lastly, the decline of religion and the consequent loss of the meaning of life and death are large themes in Weber's work. Because of its sheer secularity modernist culture is meaningless and senseless. There is no place for meaningful death. The disenchantment of the world, with which modernist culture begins, guarantees such loss. Weber captures this dilemma in the following way:

> The peasant, like Abraham, 'could die satiated with life'. The landlord and the warrior could do likewise. For both fulfilled a cycle of existence beyond which they did not reach. Each in his way could attain an innerworldly perfection as a result of the naive unambiguity of the

substance of his life. But the 'cultivated' man who 'strives for self-perfection', in the sense of acquiring or creating 'cultural values', cannot do this. He can become 'weary of life' but he cannot become 'satiated with life' in the sense of completing a cycle. For the perfectability of the man of culture in principle progresses indefinitely, as do the cultural values.[34]

Like Antigone, Abraham and the peasant could fulfil their cycle of existence because they lived and died in an enchanted cosmos where their life and death had meaning. But with modern culture, or the culture of the western city, there is no such completion. Rather, it is endless: there is constantly more to experience and more to achieve. But such quantity of culture is senseless because the place for death is absent.

In this Weberian sense, the losses of particularity, love and meaning symbolise the failure of modern culture. While the logic of the city will result in the triumph of western culture, such achievements will necessarily be accompanied by experiences of these lacks. In order to try to regain what has been lost, the idea of home is needed as a counterveiling weight to the logic of the centre. For the urbanised western world, suburbia becomes the prime site for this ideal of home. In this way, the ideal of the suburban home is imagined to consist of a personal and particular love, and a peacefulness befitting a 'satiated' end of the journey from the endless culture of life in the city.[35] City and suburbia work together to bring back the unity of the very beginnings of Spirit (to use Hegel's notion). But this twin compensatory logic of city and home cannot succeed.

As already stated, 'home' can be regarded as a vastly reduced reminder of the cosmos of Antigone. It cannot provide the desired completion of the 'indefinitely progressing' culture of the city. As the logic of the city can only end in weariness, the logic of the home is not the place of satiation. It is not the final resting place because it no longer contains the door to the underworld. Instead of the cycle of existence being fulfilled here, there are only frustrated *repetitions* of attempted compensation for the loss of the Antigonean whole. To understand the logic of 'home', which is the necessary accompaniment to the logic of the city, we must try to grasp the workings of such repetition. But what are they?

the logic of home

First, these repetitions might be understood as a continual return to dreams of the goodness of home in which the Antigonean drama is reworked (with Antigone's law triumphant). An obvious example of this can be seen in popular narratives of mainstream cinema which appeal to notions of the family, home and love. Two films illustrate the point. In *Regarding Henry*, Harrison Ford plays an unscrupulous, successful lawyer who is returned to the ethic of the family when his rational capacity is severely reduced due to a gunshot wound to the head. In the film, the immorality of the city is both exposed and rejected, while the particular love of home is extolled without qualification. The ending is harmonious unity (and guaranteed audience tears). Similarly, the title character in *Forrest Gump* can be understood as exhibiting Antigone's ethic. He easily inhabits the spaces of its expression through his lack of guile — successful in the human sphere only because of chance and his naivety. But, in the end, he returns to his family home as his rightful moral space. He can do so because he never follows the human law.

However, with the success of western logic, the ending of these films is not the return of King Creon and the capitulation of the state, but rather it is only the individual stripped of full membership of the sphere of universal reason and denied his or her full subjectivity, who can fully regain this place of love and absolute meaning. On this individual level, the human is once more subordinated to the memory of the divine. There can be the recovery of the old unity when the western subject is cut out of the hero and he can really return home. In this type of cinema the desire for the old resolution is repeatedly pursued, and even briefly achieved. The standard happy ending provides a fleeting glimpse of a home which is part of some greater ordering where the final answers are certain and good (as Antigone knew them). While its specific content is vague, it can be understood in terms of the ideas of an Antigonean space. The idealised home at the conclusion of the film has recaptured a past of unified ethical sense; the final scenes allow us entry into the sensibility of an ancient realm. But when the film ends, that teary feeling of unqualified goodness is inevitably dispersed. With the sunlight comes the return of our knowledge of the dominant law. But we will be back. Again and again. (And Hollywood knows it.)[36]

Second, the expression 'going home' hints at repetitious, yet unsatiated, desires for meaning in the modern world. In this phrase, 'home' can be understood as representing the end of the subject's journey from the city or state (that is, going home to the suburbs). Following Adorno and Horkheimer's discussion of the Odyssey, 'home' becomes the compensation for the loss of unity with an enchanted nature which the subject must lose in order to create itself. As Odysseus' reason overcomes the enchanted forces of the old nature in his journey home to Ithaca and the constant Penelope, he begins to emerge as a western subject. In defeating the Cyclops and avoiding the Sirens he enlarges himself in terms of will, rationality and experience. But such disenchanting of nature means that the old unities are forever lost and Odysseus is alone. The deep desire for the ancient attachments finds an object in 'going home' and the subject continues its journey of self-realisation. On the development of the western subject, Adorno and Horkheimer say: 'It is a promise of the way home. It is homesickness that gives rise to the adventures through which subjectivity (whose fundamental history is presented in the Odyssey) escapes the prehistoric world.'[37]

But this journey's end cannot regain the past unity, and hence it will ultimately be dissatisfying. In fact it will mark the denial of the subject itself ('I am nothing', says Creon when his realm of existence as subject has been renounced).

In the home, the dominant ethic is one of sacrifice of the self, and this can be experienced as simply boring because it deprives the subject of the varied experience integral to the growth of the modern self. Under such conditions, the subject will have to leave home to realise itself. In order to seek its subjectivity, the modern Ulysses journeys back to the city from the suburbs. But again the subject will be seeking to regain the lost unity in the very production of itself and once again will seek home. In this, a compulsive repetition can be seen as acting as compensation for modernity's denial of a possible resolution for the basic dialectical dilemma.[38]

Third, these repetitions can further be seen in modern-day preoccupations with 'homemaking'. As argued throughout the chapter, the home is the site of attempts to recreate the enchanted whole of

Antigone — the place of particularity, love and meaning for suffering and death. But this can only partially succeed. This pursuit becomes one of making the home an interior self-sufficiency. This can be seen in the allure of the detached home with its own garden, a sort of mini-cosmos. The ordering and cleaning of this small space of interiorised meaning can for some become paramount. Hence the repetitious routine of home duties tries to maintain this Antigonean space. Of course, there are other forces at work here beyond this interiorisation of meaning. For example, there is the necessity of eating and the pleasure which may ensue from home decorating. But the necessities and pleasures of being at home might more fully be explained by incorporating this understanding of loss and the repetitions of reconciliation.

But if there cannot be this internal completion, in these small isolated spaces, then completion is attempted from outside, that is, from the 'human' world. Within capitalism, 'home' also means a 'nice' home furnished with consumer goods, endlessly updated. 'Home' as meaning the ethical space of love is supplemented by 'home' as the 'dreamhome' of advertisements. Again, such human elements will not regain the lost meaning — in fact, they stand in contradiction to lost unity. But with Creon's success in the West there is nothing else to be sought. Resolution is desired. But to seek it here, as is our fate, is to make certain that the repetitions of loss continue indefinitely.[39]

The continuous shuffle between the spaces of home and city and the constant making and re-making of the home mark the fate of modernity. Of course, our self-consciousness is one of freedom and agency, so that this fate is commonly not acknowledged. In the end, our fate is forgotten or denied in order to fulfil it (with the space of home as a prime site for such repetition). Indeed, this very repetition will come to be regarded as freedom itself. Furthermore, there is still the hope of resolution where the two spheres, knowing each other's laws (interdependent yet contradictory), will be reconciled. Much contemporary discussion of balancing career and home assumes such a resolution. But, just as in Hegel's understanding of the perfectly balanced realms of Greek ethical life, the deed will intervene to upset this goal: actual children, jobs and desires of the subject will pit one law against the other. As such, the goals of the city and of the home would seem unable to be harmoniously and equally pursued.[40] In this way, as already shown, the logics of the city and of the home develop together,[41] feeding off each other's inadequacies. The endless novelty of modernist cultural experience is tied to the repetitions of the familiar in suburbia.

III understanding the western suburbs

the western suburbs' relationship to nature

From the perspective of western Sydney we can look back on the development of Sydney and its suburbs in terms of these interdependent logics. We can see Sydney, from the 1960s on, as emerging out of the long European tradition of the city. This was the logic it had to follow to become the cultural centre it now proclaims itself to be. Vitally, gaining the desired level of modernity in the city has to be accompanied by the *losses* incurred by reaching this level. The history of the fall of Antigonean nature, and the consequent need for the reconciling repetitions of 'home', are the necessary additions to the formation of the city as a centre. Especially, death and its loss of meaning have to be given their place beyond the city walls.

City and home are the spaces of the modern subject. But the western suburbs, in their full derisory configuration as the habitat of the westie, constitute a space where modern subjectivity is denied. To come from the west of Sydney is to be perceived as lacking the basic requirements for subjectivity. In its standard form you are just a 'yobbo'. How then might the fate of the western suburbs be explained by using this account of the spaces of modernity?

In the first instance, the western suburbs of Sydney are represented as lacking the experiences of the city-as-centre. This can help to explain why the modern subject, in search of itself, must leave such places. In contrast, the centre of Sydney built up an array of cultural institutions to match international cities. But it is insufficient to explain the west as simply being in need of the life of the city. Many other spaces also metaphorically lie outside the city 'walls' but are not so stigmatised. But what the tracing of the origins of modernity illustrates is that the most important way of understanding the denial of the city–home logics is to grasp the differences between the relations to nature in these western suburbs of an Australian city and the European model. While Hegel's reading of *Antigone* provides a starting point for these speculations, the specificities of the local Australian context for the success or failure of the dialectics of Spirit need to be uncovered.

The tale of Antigone reveals how the city as the secular site for human achievement formed itself against a divinely ordered nature. The subject would develop itself in the city, and eventually nature itself would be disenchanted and be an important part of modernist experience. But the enchanted history of nature would never be lost. It would be remembered in some romantic artistic experience (which many modern subjects still desire) and in the creation of the longing for home (which the space of suburbia is often imagined as approximating). This relationship to nature had to be gained in the Australian context (specifically for the inhabitants of Sydney) in order for the logics of the European tradition to be realised.

But popular images of Sydney's west as an ugly, barren wasteland seem to indicate that this tradition of European experience of nature is perceived as being absent there. The natural setting of Sydney's west is understood to lack both beauty and a history of enchantment. It lacks the tranquil prettiness of the leafy suburban home, and cannot provide the rich experiences of the romantic visions of the natural. The Antigonean beginning point seems to be missing. How can this be explained?

The west's real and imagined relationship to nature can be understood as being located at the end point of a specific Australian tradition — a highly influential tradition of Australian experience of nature which disallowed the possibilty of the European modern subject from the outset. Australia was, from some of the earliest colonial descriptions, considered a barren, ugly and virtually uninhabited landscape. The convenient legalism of *terra nullius* partly flowed from this understanding.[42] *Terra nullius* provided the legal foundation for the possession of the land by British imperialists without the need of a treaty with Aboriginal landowners. But the term and concept also indicate an experience of the landscape as non-enchanted: as a blank space which was antipathetic to the endeavours of the human species. As the explorer John Eyre wrote in 1845:

> I have myself observed, that no part of the country is so utterly worthless, as not to have atttractions sufficient

occasionally to tempt the wandering savage into its recesses. In the arid, barren naked plains of the north, with not a stick to burn for his fire... the native is found, and where, as far as I could ascertain, the whole country is equally devoid of either animal or vegetable life.[43]

Earlier, in 1770, Joseph Banks described 'New Holland' as 'in every respect the most barren countrey [sic] I have seen' and as 'thinly inhabited even to the point of admiration'.[44] From this perspective, the land was so hostile that a few 'savages' could only just survive. In this *terra nullius* — this empty land — the rich European mythologies of the magical cosmos seemed as improbable as Aboriginal ownership.

Within this tradition the possibility of the subject (in the western Hegelian sense) was disallowed not only because the environment seemed unable to be tamed by European methods, but also because there was nothing to disenchant (as opposed to the European tradition beginning with Antigone and Odysseus). If ideals of 'home' and romantic sensibility have their origins in this enchanted past and, furthermore, if the creation of the subject developed through the very acts of disenchantment of this natural realm, then these elements of the European model were missing from this time and space of the colonial experience.[45]

This is clearly stating the case too baldly. There are of course many examples of successful 'taming' of the land (in an economic sense at least). There too existed a romantic appreciation of the beauty of the Australian bush (for example, the Heidelberg School of painting).[46] However, at the same time, it can be argued that perhaps the most vigorous form of national identification in Australia's history stridently diminished the possibility of enlarging the modern subject because of the inescapable brutality of nature. Here I am referring to the so-called radical tradition covering the period from the 1890s beginning with Henry Lawson and others and culminating with Russel Ward's 1950s account in *The Australian Legend*.[47] The early European experiences of the Australian landscape, as evoked by Eyre and Banks, continued with this radical tradition. For example, the following extract from a piece called 'Some Popular Australian Mistakes', which Henry Lawson wrote in 1892, illustrates this:

outside the spaces of modernity

1. An Australian mirage does not look like water; it looks too dry and dusty.

2. A plain is not necessarily a wide, open space covered with waving grass or a green sward, like a prairie...; it is either a desert or a stretch of level country covered with a wretched scrub.

3. A river is not a broad, shining stream with green banks and tall, dense eucalypti walls; it is more often a string of muddy water-holes — 'a chain of dry water-holes', someone said.

4. There are no 'mountains' out West; only ridges on the floor of hell.

5. There are no forests; only mongrel scrubs.[48]

This experience and representation of the space of the Australian bush bred the anti-individualism of the tall-poppy syndrome and the contempt of high cultural aspirations as 'bullshit' (to adopt the expression from Donald Horne in *A Lucky Country*[49]). In this sense, the European ideal subject was stifled in favour of the loose array of ethics centred around 'mateship'. Instead of a relationship with nature based on its enchanted quality (as in a traditional relation of cosmic unity or in the subject developing through the losses and gains of disenchantment), a strange secular mimetic relationship developed. Nature could not be overcome, or entered into through religion or art, so it was imitated. But it was imitated in such a way that the human subject is humbled. One of the best examples of this is seen in Russel Drysdale's paintings, where the long, frail human figures imitate the lines and the colours of a harsh bush setting.

Further, this tradition means that the suburban mythical haven of 'home' cannot exist because the necessary history of nature is absent. That is, if nature is regarded as an unenchanted, intimidating force then the Antigonean lineage is lost. Lawson's much-scrutinised story 'The Drover's Wife', where the threat to the family from the snake under the house can be interpreted as a constant, overwhelming threat of a hostile, inhuman landscape, is a good example of this. 'Home' as constituted by the repetitions of loss of the ancient place for meaningful death, and which acts as a necessary extra-urban dimension of the secular city, is not able to be constructed here. The landscape forbids it — there is not the history of (dis)enchantment, only a dangerous, Godless, ugliness which allows just minimal human survival and not the patterns of European culture. Death, and its meaninglessness, will be coped with differently; and the cultural consequences of the European tradition of existential senselessness will not be followed. Thus, the losses of modernist culture, which have formed the city-as-centre as well as the 'home', cannot be given their rightful place.

It is this specific Australian relation to nature which must be escaped for the European–western subject to emerge. But it is this form of nature which is imposed on Sydney's west. A significant part of the 'otherness' of the west to the Sydney centre is a remnant of this old Australian nature. In other words, the west gains its poor reputation by being associated with a specific, Australian colonial relation to nature which prohibits the Hegelian construction of the subject from the beginning. The image of the western suburbs as a cultural wasteland is the very past Sydney had to expel in order to establish its modern reputation as a city centre. In this sense, the western suburbs becomes Sydney's historical waste.

The identification of the west with this anti-subject tradition of Australian nature arises in a number of ways. The western suburbs grew after the Second World War, away fom the coast and without a city in the sense of a centre. It was developed in a bush setting before (or contemporaneous with) the formation of an essentially Australian, city space. During this time it was considered to be 'out in the sticks'.[50] Consequently, the secular, mimetic relation to nature could, to a certain extent, be maintained in this space. These new suburbs tended to consist of a series of flat, single-storied houses with red-tiled roofs, a bare backyard with a solitary Hills Hoist.[51] They too imitated an intimidating vision of Australian nature which they could not rise up to confront. In this way, the 'home' itself could not be secured against these forces (as in the example of 'The Drover's Wife'). The place was imagined as ugly and dangerous and hence not properly suburban. Undoubtedly, an additional factor that contributed to the association made by the city elites between the west and this so-called radical tradition was that it was the poor and working class who first populated the area. In other words, the Australian lower classes represented by the radical tradition and the actual new inhabitants of these fledgling suburbs shared a similar perceived culturelessness. This link becomes even clearer when one considers that the prime, derisory image of the west and the archetypal old Australian mate is the same — the yobbo, 'Anglo' male.

In other words, the western suburbs tended to grow up within a tradition of a specific Australian relation to nature which would enable it to be the site of the city's full-blown, myth-making need for an 'otherness' to escape this very *terra nullius* heritage. The 'westie' is the city-dweller's other in the sense of developing out of, and being located within, a natural realm which cannot fulfil the requirements of modernist culture. This is not to argue for the truth of the uniform image of the west, but to note that there were sufficient connections to the Joseph Banks-Henry Lawson understanding of Australian nature to enable the undifferentiated 'westie' mythology to arise.

The development of the relationship between Sydney and its west was based on the imagined need to escape from a past, colonial Australian tradition of the bush. This historical linkage put the west into, not just a different cultural space, but also into a different cultural time. It was the colonial 'barbaric' past as the other. Such an odd, space–time configuration perhaps starts to make sense of how impossibly far the west seemed to be away, much further than just its geographical distance from the city centre. It also begins to show that, when combined with the imagined lack of the appropriate conditions for the European subject, the diversity of the western suburbs largely fails to be recognised; the multifarious migrant population and the largest Aboriginal population in New South Wales become lost in the space–time of the west. It is still *terra nullius*, where only a few 'savages' and the anti-subject of the mimetic male colonial can survive.

At the same time, it must be noted that the creation of this 'other' in the west is complemented by a number of additional factors which establish Australia, and particularly Sydney, as free from this limiting relation to nature and which provide the conditions for the emergence of the modern subject. For the modern subject, Australian nature is brought firmly into the realm of experience. It is aestheticised by being represented and imagined as essentially beautiful. During the 1970s, rainforests and coral reefs became the pivots of Australian identity as opposed to the hostility of the desert.[52] Brett Whiteley's lush forms and colours were favoured over Drysdale's dry and barren image of Australia.

Furthermore, suburban gardens from the 1970s went 'native', demonstrating the appreciation of local Australian flora as beautiful and the right type of nature to create a 'home'. The previous garden standards, which had been resolutely English, were usurped. In fact, in 1960 Robin Boyd gave a description of Australian suburbia which within ten years was almost totally overthrown:

> The bush is so far removed from the European image that one cannot contemplate attempting to come to terms with it in suburban society, to meet it at least half-way down the garden path. A principal article of suburban faith is that these primitive landscape elements must be eradicated from the home environment in the same way as one would deal with a digusting-looking tramp seen weaving his way in through the front-gate.[53]

And crucially, with the fuller recognition of Aboriginal cultures, Australian nature is given an enchantment, with all the rich contradictory outcomes which flow from such a recognition for the development of the European-western subject. For Australian nature to gain its own magical cosmos allows a local history of the losses this implies, as well as providing a source of romantic experience for the modern subject. The logics of Spirit, as we saw with Hegel, can now be fully followed here. Put simply, instead of Eyre's description of the bush as a nullity, tourists now travel out to the desert to enter into the Aboriginal Dreamtime. It enriches the modern subject and gives an appreciation of what has been lost.

The local Australian experience is shaped into the correct forms for the possibility of modernity. The intricate pattern of city, home and nature, which an examination of Hegel has helped reveal, is followed in Australia, with Sydney as its centre. But the west is left out of this design, except that it does function as a much-mocked reminder of what has been left behind. But what of the other suburbs of Sydney?

outside the spaces of modernity

Why did they not share the west's fate? There are perhaps a number of explanations: the northern and eastern suburbs were much wealthier; the houses were often more than one storey;[54] they had a leafy or English garden 'feel' up until the 1960s; and they were closer to the coast. Generally, they did not exhibit, especially in the wealthiest parts, a mimetic relation to the Australian bush. In this sense, it is arguable that they were more like distant suburbs of London than of Sydney. The way in which the coastal houses of these suburbs seem to gain height when looking out to sea (and back to Europe), compared with the flat and low dwellings a little further inland, perhaps is also symbolic of this different relation to nature. In other words, the identity of the northern and eastern suburbs was formed on the basis of European models, and as such, they could effectively turn their backs on the harsh, anti-subject landscape of the Australian interior (or, closer to home, the western suburbs).

It was only as Sydney gained status as a modern centre that these suburbs (as signified by the emergence of the cult of the native garden) turned their gaze for the pursuit of the logics of the European subject increasingly to Sydney itself. This meant that to live in the older suburbs of the east and north was to be able to adopt the great European–western logics of city and home within Australia because Sydney had at last succeeded culturally.[55]

the end of the 'westie'?

The mythology of the 'westie' is alive and well today. However, the phenomenon may one day become a thing of the past. The western suburbs will probably never achieve the status of the now most wealthy addresses in Sydney, but they will probably be able to reach the standard suburban ideal of 'home'. They will be tied into the logics of city and home and not be left outside as they are now. Some small reflections of the centre's glory will be exhibited in the growth and recognition of restaurants, theatres and businesses. Today, multi-storied townhouses and blocks of units are the standard architectural forms, not the old low-level style of dwelling. The phenomenon of Sydney notables 'coming out' and admitting their western suburbs origins is indicative of a certain change in perception. The most significant factor, however, will be the development of the cultural elites of Sydney into a form where there is not the strong functional need for this other of the 'westie'. Perhaps only then can we say that the old cultural cringe has gone.

The demise of the 'westie' caricature would seem to be an unmitigated good. However, there was that small side of the imagery which valorised the ordinary, and seemed to allow a place for an outlook which recalled some value in the old colonial battler position. A memory of the virtues of the radical mateship tradition is recalled. The westie was not just a yobbo, but the ordinary person who had some justified scepticism about the achievements of the city. To stand outside the logics of the European history of the subject, as was forced on the western suburbs, perhaps enables a perspective back to the city which will find the pursuit of modernity highly desirable, but also lacking in some fundamental respects.

This chapter, written from the University of Western Sydney, Nepean, has been caught in this very dilemma. In other words, although mythological, the 'westie' depiction had such force that it did link up to the critical, radical tradition and created the cultural space for a sceptical gaze back to the origin of the mythmaking (as well as promoting the desire simply to deny the charges as false). But the overwhelming logics of the European–western tradition of space will probably just sweep all this aside. The western Sydney of the future will almost certainly fit into the Hegelian dialectical pattern of city and home as surely as is now the case for the rest of Sydney.

notes

1 Earlier versions of some of the ideas expressed in this paper appeared in 'Imagined colonies: on the social construction of Sydney's western suburbs', *Communal/Plural*, no. 1, 1993.

2 As indicated in both the introduction to this book and in chapter 2, this view of Sydney's west continues to gain public expression in various contexts, but it is also a view now contested very vigorously.

3 Diane Powell, *Out West: Perceptions of Sydney's Western Suburbs*, Allen & Unwin, Sydney, 1993.

4 See chapter 1 for a discussion of this history.

5 Hugh Stretton, *Ideas for Australian Cities*, Georgian House, Melbourne, 1975.

outside the spaces of modernity

6   Interview with Andrew Denton on Channel 7, 'Keating Unplugged', 1 November, 1995.

7   See Marshall Berman, *All that is Solid Melts Into Air*, Verso, London, 1983 and, as probably the seminal work for this view, Walter Benjamin, *Charles Baudelaire: A Lyric Poet in the Era of High Capitalism*, Verso, London, 1983.

8   G.W.F Hegel, *The Phenomenology of Spirit*, Oxford University Press, Oxford, 1977, p. 265.

9   ibid., p. 265.

10 ibid., p. 277.

11 ibid., p. 280.

12 ibid., p. 271.

13 Sophocles, *The Theban Plays*, Penguin, Ringwood, 1947, pp. 128–9.

14 ibid., p. 128.

15 Hegel, p. 279.

16 Steiner stresses a contrasting interpretation where it is a conflict between two divine orders (G. Steiner, *Antigones*, Clarendon Press, Oxford, 1984). But this hardly makes sense of Hegel's stress on the *human* law and the whole thrust of the *Phenomenology*. Note also how the common interpretation of Antigone's action as an example of individualism versus the state, and even as exhibiting some strong sense of subjectivity, works against Hegel's unfolding of the history of the West as the development of such freedom. Interpretations such as these illegitimately import the end point back to the beginning, from a Hegelian perspective. Other important, contrasting interpretations of Hegel on Antigone have been expounded by Jacques Derrida in *Glas* (University of Nebraska Press, Lincoln, 1986) and by Hyppolite in *Genesis and Structure of Hegel's Phenomenology of Spirit* (Northwestern University Press, Evanston, 1974).

17 Hegel, pp. 287–8.

18 There have been a number of specific feminist critiques of this section of Hegel's work. See most recently K. Oliver, 'Antigone's ghost: Undoing Hegel's Phenomenology of Spirit', *Hypatia,* vol 11, no. 1, Winter, 1996. Unfortunately, Oliver disregards the divine aspect of Antigone's law and the fact that this section comes at the beginning of Spirit. Other feminist criticisms can be found in: L. Irigaray, 'Love of same, love of other' in *An ethics of sexual difference*, Cornell University Press, Ithaca, NY, 1993; L. Irigaray, 'The eternal irony of the community' in *Speculum of the Other Women,* Cornell University Press, Ithaca, NY, 1985; C. Willett, 'Hegel,

Antigone and the possibility of a women's dialectic' in *Modern Engendering: Critical Feminist Readings in Modern Western Philosophy* (Bar On, Bat-Ami, ed.), SUNY, Albany, 1994.

19 Hegel, p. 288. This point is also made in W. G. F Hegel, *The Philosophy of Right*, Oxford University Press, Oxford, 1967, pp. 114ff.

20 Sophocles, pp. 143ff.

21 Here we have to leave Hegel, since he tends to lose the spatial aspect of the European tradition, which can be found in the beginning of Spirit with Antigone, as he goes in pursuit of the universal absolute in the last phases of *The Phenomenology of Spirit*.

22 'we affirmed that justice was doing one's own business' (Plato, 'Republic' in *The Dialogues of Plato*, trans. Jowett, University of Chicago, Chicago, 1952, p. 349).

23 'Phaedrus', in Plato, p. 117.

24 J. Habermas, *The Structural Transformation of the Public Sphere*, Polity Press, Cambridge, 1989.

25 See Berman, for some examples; and C. Taylor, *Sources of the Self*, Cambridge University Press, Cambridge, 1989, for an overview of some of the forces which have shaped this type of subject in modernity.

26 C. Baudelaire, *The Painter of Modern Life and Other Essays*, Da Capo, New York, 1964, p. 9.

27 ibid., p. 12.

28 This is not to say that the artist is the only type of modern subjectivity possible; nor to deny that many still go overseas to get to the 'real' centres like New York.

29 A history of this cultural transformation of Sydney, in terms of the actual sites and the accompanying debates, has yet to be written. However, Julie Langsworth and I are engaged in writing this story of Sydney's cultural trajectory.

30 It should be noted that although many of the romantics, such as Rousseau, were great critics of the city, there was a strong sense, particularly in later romanticism, that there was still a need for urban training and experience for such judgment or art to be allowed a place in the modernist discourse. Without such city legitimation any cultural offerings are usually judged as at best primitive or, at worst, as coming from a country bumpkin.

31 M. Weber, *Economy and Society*, University of California Press, Berkeley, 1978, pp. 956ff.

outside the spaces of modernity

32 See Simmel's famous essay on this in G. Simmel, 'The metropolis and mental life', in *The Sociology of George Simmel* (K. Wolff, ed.), Free Press, New York, 1950.

33 M. Weber, 'Religious rejections of the world and their directions', in *From Max Weber* (H. H. Gerth & C. Wright Mills, eds), Routledge Kegan Paul, London, 1948.

34 ibid., p. 356.

35 Fishman gives an appropriate definition: 'Suburbia, I came to believe, must be understood as a utopia in its own right. Its power derived ultimately from the capacity of suburban design to express a complex and compelling vision of the modern family freed from the corruption of the city, restored to harmony with nature, endowed with wealth and independence yet protected by a close-knit community.' (R. Fishman, *Bourgeois Utopias*, Basic, New York, 1987, p. x).

36 The examples from film employed here refer to a specific form of male hero. The female roles I find more difficult to fit with the argument. The mother-ideal maintaining the place of particular love is common and easily incorporated into the theory being offered here, for example, the mother (Sally Fields) in *Forrest Gump*, or the wife (Annette Bening) in *Regarding Henry*. However, the female leads in *Thelma and Louise*, for example, need more complex argument. An interpretation of this film can be given from the perspective of the above argument (which, it should be noted, flies in the face of the celebratory reviews the movie enjoyed on release). Thelma and Louise enter into the classic male Odyssean journey of the subject discovering itself in the human world. The interesting point for the current argument is how their deaths (driving off the edge of the Grand Canyon after being surrounded by police) are completely severed from the Antigonean lineage and, although shocking, prove senseless. Their suicides do represent escape and confrontation like Antigone's, but all they gain is oblivion, not meaning. And there is no possibility of the human world being ethically challenged. On the contrary, their deaths are the affirmation of their pure subjectivity, and so cut off from the site of Antigone's ethic. It is death without home (and nor do their deaths gain sense through defence of the state, like Eteocles'). The triumph of Creon's sphere is apparent and the contradictions remain unresolved. The audiences' pleasure in the mythic unity of the happy ending is denied, for Creon, not Antigone, is upheld in the end despite the obvious criticism of male authority. The repetitions of home are fled from in this example, but they are not clearly understood.

37 T. Adorno & M. Horkheimer, *The Dialectic of Enlightenment*, Verso, London, 1979, p. 78. Note that Adorno and Horkheimer will go on to discuss the fascist homeland and not the suburban ideal referred to here.

38 It takes but a small extension of Horkheimer and Adorno's ideas (in fact to include, more explicitly, the idea of meaningful death) in order to see this homeward journey of the Western subject as an exhibition of the two laws Hegel describes at the beginning of Spirit. The unity with enchanted nature which Ulysses must sacrifice as he pursues his subjectivity is the same meaningful order which Antigone can call her own. Ulysses' reason propels him away from a world of magical beings but this is also the cosmos where the underworld can have a place in the overall scheme of things. Ulysses can be placed with Creon in representing the human law in an early, contradictory opposition to the divine, at least in terms of Horkheimer and Adorno's interpretation. And through this interpretation the lines between Antigone and home can be better understood. The journey's end of the subject, home, will also be an impoverished version of what had been initially vanquished. An Antigonean place in the underworld had to be forsaken in the name of reason and state but our journeys home vouchsafe this primary loss as our final, unrealisable desire.

39 Other outside forces, like reason itself, in the form of expert advice, will also be used as supplement. The state will also be needed, especially when poverty prohibits a family from being able to achieve the current historical standard of home in this double sense of ethics and consumerist ideal. Again, resolution is sought from areas which will provide comfort but which will also maintain the contradiction.

40 However, just such a reconciliation is one of Richard Sennett's major, recent aims; but in my view, although it cannot be argued here, his attempt is not successful. See R. Sennett, *Flesh and Stone: the Body and the City in Western Civilization*, Faber & Faber, London, 1994, pp. 26, 27 for example.

41 As a qualification, the lack of direct engagement with the *sexual* aspect of home and Antigone should be given a brief explanation. By emphasising the *ethical spaces* of modernity, for example, city and home, it might be possible to sever the natural sexual division which Hegel and most others always assume, while retaining the dialectical insights of Spirit. This is why I have not used the familiar terms 'public' and 'private'. These expressions are almost completely defined in gender terms and private loses the wider Antigonean perspective. This is usually the case because most analyses, in confronting the male political philosophy tradition, begin with a dominant public sphere and tend to overlook the immediate prehistory and the vital relation to death within the enchanted cosmos. Hence most feminist critiques of the western tradition will start with Plato or Aristotle, and not, as Hegel does, with Sophocles.
Perhaps the argument here could have some impact on the maternal ethic debate, as exemplified in the work of Carol Gilligan, by casting the problems in terms of ethical spaces rather than sex. This could incorporate many of the critics of Gilligan who show that different ethics are not just female,

especially in other cultures. Ethical space is here created through the force of things like reason, nature, subject and death. It could also allow a possible recognition of colonial differences in that the alignment of such forces helps to explain certain ethics, like mateship in Australia, which although sexist do imitate some of the elements of the Antigonean view. (A non-European relation to nature, the subject and reason, coupled with a critical distance to the city–state could build the space for this anti-Creon ethic.) The question of how the sexual character of this ethical space contingently developed in the West might then be attempted.

42 See H. Reynolds, *Aboriginal Sovereignty*, Allen & Unwin, Sydney, 1996, chapter 2 especially, for a discussion of this point. *Terra nullius* might be translated as the land of nothingness or of no account, but it clearly indicated a place in which there was an absence of human culture.

43 Quoted in Reynolds, p. 20.

44 Quoted in Reynolds, p. 17. Further bleak portrayals of the Australian landscape can be found in R. Gibson, *The Diminishing Paradise: Changing Literary Perceptions of Australia*, Sirius, Sydney, 1984, chapter 4 especially.

45 This point is reinforced by Patrick O'Farrell's summation of the Irish migrant experience: 'witness the conversation…in the 1930s between two Irish Presbyterian ministers, Reverend Samuel Angus from Antrim and Reverend Jock Steele of County Down. "Dr Angus, you do believe in theophanies [the manifestations of God to man]?" He smiled, "Well, now, in Ireland yes, but not in Australia". Reverend Steele adds: "This was my own belief… Somehow the Australian landscape, inland, is dry, brown and empty. You see the hills but there is no one or spirit in the emptiness".' O'Farrell goes on: 'Home, "my own people", had been left behind; the need for home, for belonging, for a secure connection with history, was couched in the language, not of hope or search, but in that irrevocable loss; they spoke laments'. For O'Farrell the land in Australia was 'beyond love or management' since 'God was not here' (P. O'Farrell, 'Landscapes of the Irish migrant mind', in *Stories of Australian Migration* (J. Hardy, ed.), University of New South Wales Press, Kensington, 1988, pp. 39, 40).

46 Or, for example, see the mid-nineteenth century, highly romantic descriptions of the beauty of the Australian bush, and nobility of the Australian Aborigines, by the German migrant Hermann Beckler, discussed in J. Voigt, 'The Australian experience of a German doctor: Hermann Beckler's letters and writings on the fifth continent', in Hardy.

47 R. Ward, *The Australian Legend*, Melbourne University Press, 1966 (1958).

48 B. Kiernan (ed.), *The Portable Henry Lawson*, University of Queensland Press, St. Lucia, 1976, p. 128.

49 D. Horne, *The Lucky Country*, Penguin, Ringwood, 1964.

50 Powell, p. 51.

51 Even the most common building material of the western suburbs — fibro — is an indication of this relation to nature. It is certainly cheap, a necessity for the working-class owner–builders, but it also gave poor protection against the extremes of temperature (see Powell pp. 72ff, for details). Nature is relatively untamed and intrudes on the human without beauty or enchantment. In fact fibro was so closely identified with the west that rugby league supporters of western suburbs teams referred to themselves as 'fibros'.

52 This basic cultural shift is accompanied, and determined by, the spread of the environmental movement and the tourist industry.

53 R. Boyd, *The Australian Ugliness*, Penguin, Ringwood, 1980 (1960), p. 95.

54 Bachelard stresses the importance of the vertical, with cellar and attic, in his idealised memory of a child's experience of the house, especially as he relates this to the ability to imagine and be fully human. Bachelard universalises this European home, which should be placed in contrast to the Australian mimetic flatness (G. Bachelard, *The Poetics of Space*, Beacon, Boston, 1969, p. 17).

55 The southern suburbs of Sydney had many of the characteristics of the west, but because of their proximity to the coast were not associated with the old hostile bush ethos and, hence were saved from the same stigma.

4. at home in the entrails of the west:

multiculturalism, ethnic food and migrant home-building

ghassan hage

> Everything which is eaten is the food of power.
> elias cannetti, *crowds and power*

This chapter extends the preoccupation of previous chapters with the question of home in western Sydney. Part I is concerned with the 'home-building' practices centred around the production and consumption of food and the kind of intercultural interaction it gives rise to. At the most immediate level, this examination of migrant home-building practices draws attention to the importance and the vitality of migrants' attempts at making themselves feel at home in Australia. This practical reality stands against the (mis)conception of migrants as constantly yearning for 'back home' at the expense of living their lives in Australia. My considerations in part I are based on research with Lebanese migrants in the Parramatta area.

In part II, I argue that 'multiculturalism' increasingly refers to an experience of cosmopolitan consumption grounded in a reality largely created by international tourism. As such it has much less to do with the migrant home-building explored in part I. Nowhere is this more apparent than in the ethnic eating scene where multiculturalism is defined according to the availability of ethnic restaurants for cosmopolitan consumers rather than on the basis of the ethnic food-centred migrant home-building. This touristic based multiculturalism I call cosmo-multiculturalism, and I argue that the cosmo-multicultural subject conceives of ethnicity largely as an object of consumption.

In Part III, Cabramatta is used as a site for the further exploration of cosmo-multiculturalism. I stress the importance of re-centring multiculturalism and the multicultural debate around the everyday reality of migrant home-building and intercultural interaction in western Sydney. Otherwise, it is argued, we are in danger of debating a vacuous conception of multiculturalism, a 'multiculturalism without migrants'.

The chapter critically evaluates the cosmo-multicultural claims of multicultural superiority by showing the class and ethnic power relations which constitute their conditions of possibility. It is shown that cosmo-multiculturalism is primarily a class discourse aimed at establishing a cultural distinction between its cosmopolitan subjects and western Sydney dwellers, who are constructed as lesser multiculturalists or even racists on the basis of their assumed inability to appreciate cultural diversity. It is argued that such claims are only possible from the vantage point of a reality which involves minimal intercultural interaction between cultural subjects. Further, it is shown that the cosmopolitan relation of consumption is itself grounded in an inter-ethnic power relation which allows for the availability of ethnicity as an object of appreciation by the cosmopolitan subject.

As a reading of migrant home-building in part I and cosmo-multiculturalism in parts II and III will show, there is a tension between the representation of these two realities within the same concept of multiculturalism. To the extent that 'cosmo-multiculturalism' is predominant in the centre while the other multiculturalism predominates in the western suburbs, the tension between them is also a spatial struggle over the significance of the concept. It is a struggle between which of the two realities is to hegemonise multiculturalism: the lived reality of the centre or that of the periphery? If this struggle is largely implicit it nevertheless finds its most apparent manifestations in the centre's discourse that aims at claiming multicultural superiority and at devaluing the multicultural experience of western Sydney.

I migrant home building

In this first part of the chapter based primarily on interviews conducted with Lebanese migrants mostly living in suburbs around Parramatta on their attempts to make themselves feel at home in Australia, I begin by analysing the general process of migrant home-building.[1] I then examine more specifically the practices of home-building associated with food. Finally, I move to an examination of the nature of the food-centred intercultural transactions made between the dominant culture and migrants.

multiculturalism, food and migrant home-building

The relation between home and food is an essential one. Its ideological power is constantly exhibited in various items of everyday life such as the status of the home-made on the food market. That a quiche, for example, is labelled 'home-made' at one's local delicatessen distinguishes it from the mass-produced. This makes it exude that specifically homely goodness: intimations of sound nutrition, careful choice of ingredients and careful labour (of love). That is, it becomes a bit of 'mother's cooking' which at an important level, is of course a continuation of breast-feeding, the most homely of the homely yearnings or fantasies. In much the same vein, the myth of being handed a 'mother's mouthful', *lu'mit 'umm*,[2] is among the most powerful gendered structuring themes of the yearning for *lib-blehd* or *blehdna*, the national home, 'our national home', or 'back home' among the Lebanese in general, and certainly among Lebanese migrants in Sydney. The yearning for a 'mother's mouthful' is one and the same as the yearning for 'back home'.

In some of the early academic writings on Australian multiculturalism there is often a critique of those multicultural perspectives that trivialise ethnic cultures by reducing them to matters of food, dance and other 'superficial' cultural elements.[3] Though pertinent at one level, this critique leads indirectly to devaluing the importance of the production and consumption of ethnic food as the locus of practices with which migrants try to make themselves feel at home in Australia.

In what way does the multiculturalism of food delineate the possibility of a homely living for migrants? There obviously is no single answer to this question. The answer differs according to variables such as the nature of the ethnic presence in a specific area, the different ways in which ethnic food is produced and consumed, and increasingly, as we shall see in part II, the degree to which those practices are incorporated in the circuit of touristic capital. It is because of these differences that the answer to this question necessarily brings to the fore both the objective and the subjective aspects that differentiate Sydney's inner city and its western suburbs.

on the nature of homes and home-building

Emile Benveniste, in his seminal work, *Indo-European Language and Society*, gives a documented historical substantiation of the common saying 'a house is not a home'. He differentiates between the linguistic roots of the conceptions of 'home as family', that is, as an affective social unit, and 'home-as-construction', or what we refer to as house.[4] In this sense, home-building is not necessarily, but can be, the equivalent of house-building or domestic space building. House building does not necessarily include the attempt to build a familial, comforting and 'homely' space, and home-building does not necessarily involve house construction. It is on such a basis that I would like to suggest a definition of home-building as *the building of the feeling of being 'at home'*. It is in this sense that I am considering the home as an affective construct: an affective edifice constructed out of affective building blocks (blocks of homely feeling). For it to come into being, to be successfully erected, this homely affective structure has to be built with affective blocks that provide either in themselves or in combination with others four key feelings: security, familiarity, community and a sense of possibility.[5] They are the feelings that it is the aim of home-building to foster and maximise, to put together into a liveable structure.

Security

The feeling of security is of course one of the most basic feelings we aim to foster in our homely space. This feeling derives from the availability of what we consider as necessary to the satisfaction of basic needs and from the absence of harmful threatening otherness. But this is not enough. For we can be in such a space without being in our own homely space. A deeper sense of security and homeliness emanates from the space where we not only have but where we feel empowered to seek the satisfaction of our needs and to remove or exclude threatening otherness. That is, home is a place governed by what we consider to be 'our law'. We can feel secure where the law of the other rules but we cannot feel 'at home'. To be at home a person has to feel to a certain degree a wilful subject in the home. This is, for example, the difference between a servant's and a housewife's belonging to a home.

Familiarity

The feeling of familiarity is generated by a space where the deployment of our bodily dispositions can be maximised. It is where we feel in possession of what Bourdieu would call a well-fitted *habitus*. Clearly not every *habitus* operates in the spaces in which it has historically evolved and where it is most at home. It is because each *habitus* is endowed with what Bourdieu calls after Spinoza a *conatus*, a tendency to persevere in its own being, that a *habitus* will aim at home-building: the creation of the space in which its strategic dispositions can be maximised. This involves the creation of a space where one possesses a maximal practical know-how: knowing what everything is for and when it ought to be used. It also involves the creation of a space where one possesses a maximal spatial knowledge: knowing almost unthinkingly where one is, and where one needs to go for specific purposes and how to get there.[6] This sense of familiar knowledge implies spatial and practical control which in turn creates a sense of security.[7]

Community

The feeling of community is also crucial for feeling at home. Above all, it involves living in a space where one recognises people as 'one's own' and where one feels recognised by them as such. It is crucially a feeling of shared symbolic forms, shared morality, shared values and most importantly perhaps, shared language. A home is imagined as a space where one possesses maximal communicative power in Bourdieu's sense — that is, the capacity to speak appropriately in a variety of recognisable specific situations. It is a space where one knows that at least some people can be morally relied on for help (family or friends).[8]

Sense of possibility

Finally, and this is something often forgotten in theorisations of the home, a home has to be a space open for opportunities. Most theorisations of the home emphasise it as a shelter but, like a mother's lap it is only a shelter that we use to rest and then spring into action, and then return to spring into action again. A space which is only a shelter becomes, like the lap of the possessive mother, a claustrophobic space and loses its homely character.[9] Consequently, a homely space has to be open enough so that one can perceive opportunities of 'a better life': the opportunity to develop certain capacities and skills, the opportunity of personal growth and more generally, the availability of opportunities for 'advancement' whether as social mobility, emotional growth, or in the form of accumulation of symbolic or monetary capital.

This notion of possibility is crucial in understanding these homely feelings. This is because homely structures are more an aspiration, an ideal goal guiding practices of home-building, than an existing reality and what propels people into home-building is precisely the recognition of a future possibility of more security, familiarity, and so on. People always live in an approximation of the ideal home. Their homes are never secure, familiar or communal enough and they never allow for as many opportunities as one yearns for. Homes are homely because they provide *intimations*, hints of those feelings, and the possibility for more.

migrant home-building: the fostering of positive intimations

From the moment of arrival migrants encounter intimations of new possibilities. But contrary to what is often believed, the intimations of lost homelands as well as more obviously those of 'new homelands', should be seen as 'affective building blocks' used by migrants to make themselves feel at home where they actually are. They are part of the migrant's *settlement* strategies rather than an attempt to escape the realities of the host country. And if homely feelings are based on such intimations, home-building can then be seen as the practice of fostering these intimations and seeking more of them. My intention here is not to theorise migrant home-building by opposing it to nostalgia or by displacing the importance of the latter in migrant daily life. Rather, I argue, nostalgic feelings are sought as a mode of feeling at home where one is in the present. That is, nostalgic feelings are affective building blocks in the sense defined already. They are used by migrants to engage in home-building in the here and now.

In cultural studies the analysis of migrant nostalgia has been largely concerned with its manifestations or otherwise in literature.[10] This has led to an exclusively intellectualist conception of the phenomenon.[11] No work in cultural studies has aimed at examining the everyday life discourse of nostalgia accompanying the settlement of 'non-intellectual' migrants in Australia or elsewhere, let alone perceiving its implication in an active–positive (in the sense of optimistic) form of home-building. Writings on migrant homes appear as if there are no migrants living in them.[12] And commentators more often associate migrants with a concept of nostalgia equated with homesickness.[13] In this sense nostalgia is assumed to be the exact opposite of home-building: a refusal to engage with the present, and a seeking of an imaginary homely past as a hiding place from the present time and space.

But nostalgia is nothing more than a memory of a past experience imagined from the standpoint of the present to be homely. Clearly, nostalgic feelings do not only abound in migrant life but in everybody's life. They guide home-building in the present because people seek to foster the kind of homely feeling they know. And nostalgic feelings are invariably those homely feelings they remember having experienced in the past. Thus when people yearn for a communal life, their understanding of such a life is guided by the kind of communal feelings they remember having had in specific situations in the past. This is why this yearning for homely communality translates into an attempt to build the past conditions of its production.

Such nostalgic homely feelings can be sought or triggered accidentally, but, far from being an escape, they are more often deployments actively fostered to confront a new place and a new time, and to try and secure oneself a homely life within them. Consequently, the fostering of nostalgic feelings is one of the main aspects of home-building. It is only when faced with the impossibility of home-building that nostalgia can degenerate into a debilitating homesickness. This is why such a homesickness decreases the longer migrants have been residents of a new country. The length of stay translates into a more developed ability to engage in home-building, that is, among other things, to recognise and exploit new possibilities and opportunities for the fostering of nostalgic feelings.

Nostalgic feelings are experientially triggered. They can be triggered by an experiential absence, a negative intimation, or a presence, a positive intimation. Here is an example of a negative intimation that emerged during an interview with a Lebanese man telling of his early days in Australia:

> I had been here for around six month and I was driving back home to Punchbowl from Liverpool where I had gone to see the owner of a petrol station who had advertised for a job. I can't remember exactly where now, but it was pretty deserted. And I got this flat tyre and I had no spare. I couldn't speak English...not that there were many people driving by. I

started walking. Then it got dark and, as I was walking, I started to think of myself heading to the village. Sometimes when I returned late to the village from Tripoli, I used to have to take a bus that stopped a fair distance out of the way. So I had to walk the rest of the way home. But invariably I meet someone I know driving up and they give me a ride. And that's how I began to think of home. I started thinking that soon someone I know was going to turn up. I started remembering all the people with whom I took rides. I could even remember the details of their car, the sound of the horn, what they said to me. I got so engrossed by my thoughts that I really thought I was home. And when I heard a car coming I turned around hoping it will be…for some reason I just though it was my brother. But it wasn't…[He has a tear in his eye. The story he was telling happened ten years ago.] I had to walk all the way home. I arrived home around three o'clock. I couldn't speak to anyone the next morning.

[He sighs] …*Su'bi elhijra* [migration is a difficult thing].

Nostalgia here is triggered by a direct experience of lack of homely feeling of familiarity (lack of practical and spatial knowledge) and lack of communality (lack of recognition and the non-availability of help). As such the nostalgic experience and the remembering triggered by it is an essentially depressive one. It is the accumulation of this kind of nostalgia that produces states of homesickness.

Unlike this example, positive nostalgia is not necessarily induced by a direct experience of lack. It is triggered by a positive presence which comes to fill a passively and only potentially existing lack. That is, the person does not necessarily go around feeling they lack something. It is the encounter with an object which creates both the yearning for the past homely experience associated with it, and in that very process the feeling that the object was lacking. Thus, it is the positive encounter with a person, a sound, a smell or a situation which offers an intimation of an imagined homely experience in the past: an experience of 'back home'. These intimations operate like 'imagined metonymies' in that they are fragments which are imagined to be traces of an equally imagined homely whole, the imagined past 'home' of another time and another space.[14]

at home in the entrails of the west

Below is a classical nostalgic passage published in the Lebanese Australian newspaper *El-Telegraph*. It is a populist poem written to invoke the experience of listening to the Lebanese singer Wadih El-Safi. No other male singer has ever reached the national superstar status of El-Safi. His songs and his voice have become part of Lebanese folklore. Because of their constant broadcasting, their usage in schools and on virtually any private or public occasion, Wadih El-Safi has become rightly known as the 'Voice of Lebanon'. This makes listening to El-Safi a particularly suitable trigger of nostalgic feelings among Lebanese migrants in Sydney, and indeed across the world. What better reminder of the nation than the voice of the nation itself.

> Sing O Voice of Lebanon and takes us back through your voice to our homes. Pull us out of here and deliver us from the tortured life of exile.
>
> Sing to us of Lebanon, sing to us your hymns that make us adoringly kneel in the shadows of the cedar tree. Sing to us our traditions, (and) our forefathers...sweating under the olive tree, and take us back to where we've known peace just as today we know war.
>
> Sing oh Wadih, return with us and let your music weave the web of memories and hope, so that we remember the smell of early morning coffee as it brews, and the sight of blessed grapes as they hang heavily from the vines on our homes' roof-tops...[15]

Like listening to the taped message of the relatives sent with the recent arrival to Sydney, the voice operates as a conduit to the imaginary world of the homeland (as 'back home'). Song and music, in particular, with their sub-symbolic meaningful qualities (see Kristeva),[16] are often most appropriate in facilitating the voyage to this imaginary space of feelings. It is in this sense that they operate as *intimations* of the imagined homely nation left behind. The voice operates as an imagined metonymy, in the sense that it is metonymic of a totality that does not and has never existed, but which is imagined as a homely totality from the standpoint of the present.

It is important to stress that despite the rhetorical form 'Pull us out of here and deliver us from the tortured life of exile', this voyage is not a desire to be there. This might appear as a difficult point to sustain but this mode of delivery is a ritualistic 'moaning' in exilic cultures. Like the person interviewed earlier, if someone is *really* experiencing a tortured life of exile, they would not be able to 'speak to anyone the next morning' let alone sing about the need to be delivered from the life of exile. Positively experienced nostalgia does not necessarily involve a desire to 'go back'; more often than not, the 'pull us out of here and deliver us from the tortured life of exile' is a desire to promote the feeling of being there *here*. People try to foster intimations of homely feelings, of situations such as they are imagined to have been experienced. For Lebanese migrants this might include: upholding familial law as one's own law; surrounding oneself with socially and culturally recognisable and pleasing objects, smells and sounds to promote specifically 'Lebanese' feelings of security; owning one's home; ensuring that one is surrounded by Arabic-speaking people; having family around; having familiar house decoration to promote Lebanese feelings of familiarity; creating Lebanese 'neighbourhoods' and Lebanese shopping centres; and holding Lebanese parties to promote feelings of Lebanese communality.

But, it should be stressed again, the aim is not to go back. It is to foster these homely intimations so as to provide a better base for confronting life in Australia: to build a shelter from 'social and cultural crisis', but also to have a base from which to perceive and grasp Australian opportunities. It is in this sense that nostalgic feelings are used in the process of home-building in Australia. This will be clearly shown in relation to the practices of home-building centred on the nostalgic feelings triggered in the production and consumption of food.

migrant home-building and food

Part of the history of early Lebanese migration to Australia, like many early migration histories, is one of deprivation of familiar fruits, vegetables and other ingredients. One of the interesting elements of this deprivation is the emergence of creative practices of substitution. This shows that even negative nostalgia does not necessarily lead to passive depression. One Lebanese who lived in Bathurst in the 1940s told this story:

at home in the entrails of the west

> Although some tahini arrived by boat every now and then, we used to go through long periods without it. Sometimes we used to really crave for tahini dishes. Finally, we improvised: either Mum or Dad, I can't remember, probably inspired by the similarity between the texture of peanut butter and that of tahini, decided to grind some of it with garlic and oil and we used it as a substitute for tahini sauce with a grilled fish. Long after, when tahini became always available I used to sometimes crave for the peanut sauce!

In this climate, the very encounter with yearned-for fruits and vegetables triggered strong intimations of 'home'. Home food not only provides intimations of security in that it represents a culturally determined basic need for nutrition, it also provides a clear intimation of familiarity in that people know what to do with it, how to cook it, how to present it and how to eat it, thus promoting a multitude of homely practices (unlike facing the unknowable: for example, Salman Rushdie's description of the Indian migrant facing the English kipper in *The Satanic Verses*). Furthermore, food also provides a clear focus for practices of communality, especially in collective eating either in private or in public spaces. In the following interview, a Lebanese woman tells an exceptionally graphic story of the homely intimations triggered by an encounter with Lebanese cucumbers, which Australian Lebanese, except for some who managed to grow them in their garden, were deprived of until the late 1970s:

> *Nayla*: It was incredible. I was visiting my sister who lived on the other side of the station. On the way back, I stopped to get some beans for dinner and here they were…I touched them…I held them in my hands. They were firm. It was like touching my mother [her mother lived in Lebanon]. Shawki, the shopkeeper, saw me, smiled and nodded: 'yes…there's Lebanese farmers growing them down near Liverpool. No more mushy stuff'. That's how we refer to the Australian cucumbers. I bought two kilos, although we were poor then, and they were very expensive. I ate one on the spot in the shop. Adel [her husband] used to say, almost every day, how much he missed the taste of Lebanese cucumbers. When Adel came back from work that day, I made a tomato

and cucumber salad with garlic and lemon because that's what I really felt like, and brought it to the table and said to him 'close your eyes', and I put the plate in front of him. When he opened his eyes, he looked at the plate and it took him a little while to realise what I was making such a fuss about. And then [laughter]

[Adel, her husband interrupts laughing: No don't tell him…it's very embarrassing.]

Nayla: Yes.

[Interviewer: Come on, you must tell me, what did he do?]

Nayla [laughing]: He got up, he kissed me and he started dancing and singing something like *Ya 'ayni 'al khya*r [Oh I love you cucumbers]!!

[Everyone laughing]

It all sounds so silly now. But the cucumbers really made us happy. It was like reuniting with a close relative.

In this homely scene generated by the cucumbers, we see both the nostalgic elements triggered by the cucumbers but we also see how the practices of fostering intimations of being in Lebanon (represented in the making of the salad which makes the cucumbers yield their potential homeliness) are at the same time practices of home-building 'in the here and now'. Like with all practices of fostering intimations, these migrant practices of home-building are about providing the agents of the practices with a stable homely structure from which they can have access to a better life in Australia. This can be mildly seen in this short extract from an interview where the usage of Lebanese coffee after a period of deprivation made the interviewee not only more at home but also better able to face his day:

I started making coffee in the morning like we used to have it in Lebanon. You know, *subhiyyeh* [early morning]. Whenever I have time to just sit down and drink it, I am immediately transported to our apartment in Beirut…Initially, when I started having the coffee in the morning I was noticeably different and happier at work so much so that one of my workmates asked me: 'how come you're so enthusiastic these days John?'. I said to him: 'I've been drinking Lebanese coffee in the morning'. He looked at me, shook his head and said: 'Bloody wogs...I don't know...'

Just as much as food provided the basis for homely practices within the private sphere, it also provided the basis of practices of home-building in the public sphere, in particular in fostering intimations of homely communality. This is how an article in the *Sydney Morning Herald*, whose coverage of the food scene in Sydney dates to the immediate post-war era, describes the process:[17]

> As each wave of immigrants to Australia settled in, little knots of eateries, evocative of the old world, served as meeting places where lonely groups of migrants chatted in their native tongue and recreated the tastes of home.[18]

An article in the same newspaper some twenty years earlier describes a more specific process involving the 'Ceylonese Tea Centre' in the early 1970s:

> It isn't surrounded by the neat green slopes of tea bushes — only the roar of Castlereagh Street traffic — but it's the nearest thing to home for the 5 000 or so Ceylonese who live in Sydney...
>
> At night, if there is a special occasion, the Ceylonese gather to eat food characteristic of their spice-rich island...The Tea Centre invites Ceylonese wives to cook their favourite dishes for the celebration held at the restaurant.[19]

Although the tradition of public eateries has never been dominant among Lebanese migrants, village clubs have always provided, and continue to provide, an alternative where on weekends and on specific occasions someone's house or a hall is transformed into a village party. Men and women sit around large barbecues of grilled meats, chicken and garlic. Often the party ends with a *dabkeh* danced to the sound of traditional mountain shepherds' music.[20]

migrant home-building, food and the dominant culture

Despite all the homeliness fostered by private and public culinary practices of home-building, there was one sense of homely communality which, according to many older Lebanese migrants, remained minimal until the mid-1970s. This had to do with the culinary recognition and appreciation of the dominant culture. The dominant culture's appreciation of the value of the migrants' food and other cultural forms was a source of pride for migrants in a social setting where there was very little recognition by 'Australians' of 'ethnic value'.

Before the multicultural era, many culinary practices of home-building happened away from the 'Anglo gaze' — the gaze of those positioned in the space of the dominant 'Anglo' culture. There is an abundance of stories, told by the older interviewees, of secretive eating to avoid being seen by members of the dominant culture. This story happened to a Lebanese family holding a party in their backyard for their son's first communion in 1962:

> Our neighbour, who had been quite friendly, looked from above the fence and was talking to my husband. Nagibeh was taking out a plate of *kebbeh nayyeh* (raw meat with crushed wheat pounded into a paste) and when she saw him, turned around straight back to the kitchen. She said she didn't want the neighbour to think we were cannibals! My young sister, who's always been a bit of a troublemaker (mal'uneh), took the plate from her hand and said: 'let him think what he wants'. She went out straight to him and said would you like to try our raw meat! Nagibeh hid her face with her apron! The neighbour looked at my sister and said: 'Raw meat! I am going to call the police!'. And he left. Nagibeh ran to my sister and said: 'See, I told you! All you ever do is put us in trouble!'. We all started talking at once, each proposing what we were going to tell the police when suddenly the neighbour reappeared on the fence with a plate and said: 'Well are you going to give me some of this meat or what?'!

Despite the specificity of this neighbour's reaction, it is clear that the whole story is structured by an implicit fear of the Anglo gaze and its imagined rejection of the migrants' food. It is this imagined gaze which was to be increasingly transformed by the advent of multiculturalism.

Of course, multiculturalism did not constitute a magical clean break with such a reality, and the official multicultural discourse of a move from monocultural assimilation to multicultural plurality exaggerates the before and after of this historical transition. Clearly, it is not the case that there were no cross-cultural culinary interactions that predated multiculturalism. At the same time, the negative Anglo gaze has not totally disappeared; even today, as a number of interviewees indicated, children in some schools are still taunted about their 'ethnic lunches'. Nevertheless, one only needs to examine any historical document concerning migration and food in the pre-multicultural era to see that the multicultural story has a solid basis in reality. For instance, an article in the Sun-Herald in the early 1950s asked:

> Are you satisfied with chops and eggs...? Or are you one of the growing number of Australians who stop at a city or King's Cross delicatessen on their way home to buy salami sausage? If you include yourself in the second group, you are under the good influence of our new compatriots...whom Mr. Caldwell called 'New Australians'.[21]

The 'real New Australians', the article goes on explaining, have not had a chance to open restaurants and shops yet, but 'their influence takes the more subtle form of "peaceful invasion" by example'. Although the writer of the article is clearly sympathetic to the transformation himself, boldly stating: 'I've had a salami myself', he nevertheless thinks it wise to assure any worried reader that in their attempt at a peaceful invasion the New Australians 'are not encouraged by their Federal sponsors':

> An official of the Department of Immigration became quite officially indignant at the suggestion that New Australians might be introducing their food habits into Australia: 'That's not the idea at all', he said. 'What we want is for these migrants to become absorbed into the Australian community, not to bring their own habits with them.'[22]

As the article itself indicates, stories of migrants changing the eating habits of Anglo-Australians clearly predate multiculturalism. It emerged within a number of interviews conducted with elderly Australians, for example, that there is a whole history of working-class Australians 'eating Chinese' during the Depression. Despite the mythologies which made it disease-ridden food, it was considered 'the best nutrition you can get for very little money'. Nevertheless, it is clear that multiculturalism did enhance the climate for culinary intercultural interaction.

Lebanese interviewees were asked whether they knew, and whether they had had any meals with, their 'Australian' neighbours in the street. This question was more often than not routinely answered in the affirmative, and on many occasions researchers were introduced to 'the neighbours'. In one case, a Lebanese family from Westmead introduced the researcher to their neighbour, who had adopted the standard Lebanese mixture of minced meat, onions and pine nuts (*lahmeh w'snoobar*) in the making of her meat pies. The neighbour informed her that:

> When we first had some at Wafa's, my husband and I thought it was the best minced meat we've ever tasted...She taught me how to do it and I decided to try and make a meat pie with it...Everyone, including the children, thought it was a nice way to make a meat pie if we felt like something different.

Clearly, similar multicultural encounters remain today part of the everyday life of many people, and as the interviews indicate, most certainly in the western suburbs. Along with the practices of home-building, it is such encounters that constitute a homely and an *interactive* culinary multiculturalism, based on interaction between different cultural subjects.

However as a prelude to my critical assessment of cosmo-multiculturalism, it is important to keep in mind the complexity of multicultural encounters such as those described earlier: their mix of racism and tolerance, of friendliness grounded in relations of power and hints of the capacity for domination. While many of the stories in these interviews have happy endings, there are many others involving abuse and even mild violence by Australians offended by the smell or the sight of a particular dish. One Lebanese described how he used to find his lunch box tipped in the rubbish bin until he decided to do what others did and order a sandwich.

It was clear from the research that it would be ludicrous to classify these interactions with a simple 'racist' or 'not-racist' binary, as the intercultural interactions varied not just according to how long people knew each other, their levels of education, whether they had children, degrees of assimilation, and so on. But the relation itself and the conception of the other within it was also always ambivalent and constantly fluctuating. While interviewing a taxi driver who for all practical purposes was a racist raving about 'wogs taking over', the door of his apartment opened and an Indian person walked in to be introduced by the taxi driver as 'my flatmate'. Such an example is far from being an odd case. These forms of contradictions were commonly encountered features of 'racism' as it circulates in the general population. They were the rule rather than the exception. For example, many Lebanese we interviewed had stories about how their neighbours *were* prejudiced when they first moved in but how they became 'nicer' later on. Other Lebanese had stories of different reactions by different members of the same Anglo family. In one case, a man was described as very prejudiced in the presence of his daughter who was going out with their son. They all discussed the 'old man' as if it was a family problem rather than by classifying it with an outraged 'racism'. Clearly, the longer people knew each other the more openly they interacted. This did not mean that prejudice disappeared but rather that it was 'managed' more openly within the relation and was no longer pathologised:

> They were auctioning the house next door to us and there were two bidders left. Both Asians. Jack said to me: Those bloody Asians are buying the whole country! I said to him: You're a bloody racist! I am Asian too you know! He said: Nah! you're Lebanese, you're all right. But they're a problem, there's too many of them. I said: you probably said the same thing about me when I first moved in here. He got pissed off and he said: You know what, I did, and maybe I shouldn't have changed my mind!

A similar kind of ambivalence is found in intercultural culinary encounters where eaters and feeders interact 'nicely' across cultures while, at the same time, the power relations underlying this interaction can be sensed. In the following interview with an elderly Lebanese woman, one comes face to face with embryonic elements of the multicultural and cross-cultural culinary scene as they developed out of early encounters, but also one senses the relations of power in which they were grounded:

> I still remember him very well. His name was Pat. He died before we left Redfern; Raymond went to his funeral and there was no-one at the church except his two sons. I remember the time he came into the fruit shop and we got to know him. Tony [her son] had just come back from school and I was carrying a plate of *kebbeh bil sayniyyeh* [kebbeh cooked in the oven] for him to eat. I don't usually carry our food into the shop just in case customers are offended, but I unthinkingly had the plate in my hand when Pat came in. He looked at me and he said: 'I know what that is. That's *kebbeh* isn't it?' I was very surprised that an Australian recognised our food. This was the first time ever. I said to him: 'Are you married to a Lebanese?' and he said with a smile — he had a real cheeky smile: 'No, but I wish I was'. Then he told me that he had been to Lebanon during the war, and that he loved Lebanese food. So I went straight to the kitchen and got him some. Then he became a regular customer and I always had some food for him. He lived alone the poor thing. Raymond used to joke whenever he showed up and say to me: 'Here comes our restaurant customer, prepare the table'. Anyway, from a joke it became a real thing. You know, it is funny. I always felt he gave us the idea to open a restaurant and I always feel sad, even now, when I think that he died without visiting it. But, you know, Australians are funny, they help you when you're needy but they don't like it when migrants are doing well. I feel as if he resented us becoming restaurant owners.

Again, at the end of this very homely reminiscence there is nevertheless a trace of the power relation between the majority and the minority. In the Anglo working-class, the often mentioned 'Australian funny behaviour' is clearly grounded in both a historical sense of cultural dominance and the fear of losing such dominance; on the part of migrants there is also a certain 'over-sensitivity' based on their own sense of being on 'someone else's land'. This relation of power, however, does not stop the encounter from being experienced as a homely one.

It should be stressed that there are no contradictions in a culinary interaction grounded in an unequal relation of power yet being equally experienced as homely by both sides of the interaction. After all, this is the basis of the dominant mode of patriarchal homely interaction. Home cooking and 'mother's cooking' always interpellates two subjects who are differently implicated in this homely structure but who are nevertheless supposed to feel equally at home: the feeder (subject) and the fed (object), the 'feeding function — source of nutrition' (object) and the eater (subject) — Mum and whoever is moaning for the food — the rest of the family. Each can be an active subject or a passive object of the home depending on whether the discourse emphasises eating or feeding. Despite the primacy of the eater within it, a patriarchal but communal home, which promotes the belonging of all will have a combination of both these discourses, allowing both feeders and eaters to experience themselves as subjects of the home despite the structurally unequal relation of power between them.

As argued earlier, the feeling of being a subject is crucial for the homely experience of security. Subjectness here is meant to emphasise the experience of wilfulness and the capacity to exercise it. This is in opposition to being an object of someone else's will.[23] The more a discourse reduces the mother to an object or source of nutrition, the more she acquires the status of the servant or cook which does not 'fully' belong to the home, and the less homely the whole system of relations becomes for both eaters and feeders. A mothering subject is at home as a feeding subject and the children are at home as eating subjects, all under the watchful eye of the 'appreciative' fathering subject who has to be fed, but whose presence communicates the imperative of the Law that secures the mothering subject as a source of nutrition, while ensuring she or he experiences her or himself as an active feeder. This is roughly what might be called the subjective structure of the 'culinary-nurturing home'.[24]

It is as a continuation and generalisation of this subjective structure that the multicultural discourse is supposed to make of multicultural Australia a culinary-nurturing home. It is a place where many 'sons and daughters of the nation' feel at home 'eating ethnic' and where many ethnic 'mothers' enjoy feeding and being appreciated. In it everyone feels a bit of a subject. All of this happens under the watchful eye of a well-fed paternal government whose presence communicates the imperative of the multicultural Law which regulates the availability of the eaten and the access of the eater. Like all such discursive structures, the dominant multicultural discourses of food are eater-centred, and they vary in the degree to which they emphasise ethnic feeders as active central subjects.

In recognising the dimension of racism and domination I want to make it clear that my aim in criticising cosmo-multiculturalism in Part II is not to idealise such interactive culinary practices and set up a nostalgic dualism between the 'good old' cosy ethnic family restaurant where genuine multiculturalism takes place and a 'cold' cosmopolitan eatery which is non-multicultural. Rather, my critique aims at questioning the increased association of multiculturalism with cosmopolitan practices without aiming at devaluing cosmopolitan eating as an experience.

II cosmo-multiculturalism

In this second part of the chapter, I argue that cosmo-multiculturalism is a discourse which positions 'ethnic feeders' simply as passive feeding functions in a field where migrant subjects have been erased and where the central subject is a classy and more often than not an 'Anglo'-cosmopolitan eating subject. Cosmo-multiculturalism is part of a more general practical field of a 'multiculturalism without migrants': a multicultural reality made of institutions that seems to exist without any migrant subjects to sustain it. My critique shows how the media-instigated debates about multiculturalism often take this 'multiculturalism without migrants' as their object. In the process, it is somehow 'forgotten' that multiculturalism in Australia is, or at least *ought to be*, above all about migrant lives and intercultural interaction. This part of the chapter is based primarily on research about restaurants in the ethnic eating scenes of the Glebe–Newtown area of inner Sydney, the Parramatta area and the Penrith area.[25]

the field of culinary cosmo-multiculturalism

The tendency towards measuring differential degrees of multiculturalism in terms of the quantity and quality of available 'ethnic' food, and primarily 'ethnic' restaurants, in a street or neighbourhood, is the prevalent form in which multiculturalism is conceived and expressed in everyday life in Sydney. Residents of Sydney's inner-city suburbs such as Glebe and Newtown interviewed about their 'ethnic eating' clearly perceive their restaurant experience as a multicultural one.[26] Often, they engage in a competitive discourse each trying to mark the superiority of their suburb by outlining the number of ethnic restaurants and the number of national cuisines available to them. Claims such as 'We have five Thai restaurants' or 'We have an African and a Burmese restaurant' made by residents of Newtown are challenges that have to be met by the residents of Glebe who have a whole array of strategic deployments available to them to dismiss the Newtownian claims of multicultural culinary superiority — from emphasis on higher quality to a highlighting of greater diversity. Because it is primarily grounded in an inner-city experience of cosmopolitan consumption, I refer to this 'multiculturalism' as culinary cosmo-multiculturalism.

As far as ethnic restaurants are concerned, cosmo-multiculturalism emphasises the availability of an experience of ethnic food where ingredients are 'fresh' and where dishes are 'authentic' in the sense of not being 'watered down' to cater for a 'western palate'. But cosmo-multiculturalism is also marked by an emphasis not just on the availability of diversity but on an internationally sanctioned quality of diversity and the capacity of cooks to manipulate it and be creative in deploying it. The high-culture end of cosmo-multiculturalism aims precisely to boast an Australian culinary scene capable of competing with the best in the world, providing Australia with the means of international culinary distinction. This is exemplified by recent cosmopolitan deployments aimed at the presentation of a unique 'Australian cuisine'.

Clearly, the migrant-created culinary diversity facilitated the presence of certain elements, experiences and practices, the raw material, as it were, used by inventive chefs in bringing about the phenomenon. Because of this, culinary cosmo-multiculturalism does represent a phenomenon related to migration. At the same time, however, it is the product of forces which are far more linked to tourism and the international circulation of commodities than to the circulation of migrants. These two processes are often uncritically perceived as adding up to a common experience without an analysis of the differences between them.

In a recent article analysing a similar phenomenon in London, Cook and Crang analyse the following piece from *Time Out* magazine:

> The world on a plate. From Afghani ashak to Zimbabwean zaza, London offers an unrivalled selection of foreign

flavours and cuisines. Give your tongue a holiday and treat yourself to the best meals in the world — all without setting foot outside our fair capital.[27]

In explaining this discursive deployment, Cook and Crang point out that it conforms to a long-established conceptualisation of cultural geographies through the figure of the 'cultural mosaic'. But, as they explain with the help of Appadurai and Chambers:[28]

> the mosaic is not the only spatial figure that this globalized plate draws on. It also depends upon, and refers to, a variety of 'cultural flows and networks'…in particular of migrations and of tourisms. We can give our tongues a holiday because a world of 'foreigners' and 'foreign flavours' has come to cosmopolitan London.[29]

Despite the usefulness of their analysis, Cook and Crang succumb to the fetishistic logic of their object of analysis by not differentiating between the effect of foreigners establishing themselves to live in London, and foreign flavours arriving either with those foreigners or appearing independently on the market. Cosmo-multiculturalism, like cosmopolitan eating elsewhere in the world, has more to do with the market of foreign flavours than with the market of 'foreigners'.

Historically, the trend towards the formation of an international eating scene predates the intensification of international migration and multiculturalism. One the most successful cookbooks published in Australia in 1952, and running over eighteen editions, was titled: *Oh for a French Wife!*. Yet it is not possible to explain the valuing of French cuisine in Sydney, or anywhere else in the world, as a migration-related development.

Michael Symons, in his popular history of Australian eating, shows that, not only was Kings Cross already a cosmopolitan enclave in the 1950s but that even in the mid-1930s there were publishing companies with names such as 'The Cosmopolitan Publishing Company' publishing books of international cuisine, with what proclaimed itself to be 'the First Australian Continental Cookery Book' published in 1937.[30] Furthermore, international mobility and travel, starting with the returned soldiers who were mentioned to us in a number of interviews as the earliest 'appreciators' of ethnic food, played an important role in fostering intercultural culinary interaction. Symons mentions the case of Frank Margan, who:

> didn't agree with the 'official fictions' about the influx of migrants bringing their wine-drinking habits and teaching us about food and wine...It all happened because 25 000 of us were coming back every year, after tasting the Medocs and the Graves and the vin ordinaire. It wasn't the migrants, he concluded, it wasn't them it was us.[31]

Consequently, the importance of post-war migration in producing culinary changes in Australia has been shown to be somewhat exaggerated. But there are a number of reasons why the two processes of cosmopolitanism and multiculturalism have merged in public discourse. Among these, most important has been the increased deployment within middle-class Australia of multicultural diversity as a means of cosmopolitan distinction on the world scene. This was clearly exemplified in Sydney's Olympic 2000 bid, where Sydney's cultural diversity was exhibited as proof of the city's cosmopolitan and international nature.[32]

The conceptual merger was officially sanctioned in the 1988 Fitzgerald Inquiry into immigration and multiculturalism.[33] In the inquiry's report the concept of cosmopolitanism enters the orbit of multiculturalism, sometimes as a synonym, and sometimes even as a substitute. The inquiry's usage of cosmopolitanism showed a new preoccupation with the relation between cultural diversity and Australia's identity on the international scene. Emphasising diversity was seen partly as a strategy of encouraging touristic activity and the investments of touristic capital, and partly as a way of providing 'Australians' with a new 'high-culture' definition of themselves.

What further facilitated this partial fusion was that the cosmopolitan competitiveness of the 'we have more and better restaurant'-type of viewpoint shared with official multiculturalism a peculiar evolutionary conception of cultural change. This evolutionary multiculturalism sees cultural history as a movement from an inferior assimilationist monocultural state to an increasingly superior state marked by increased diversity and plurality. Multicultural culinary histories within this mould often tell a story marked by a before, where food was largely Anglo-Celtic, monotonous and boring, and an after, where thanks to the influence of immigration, food becomes diverse and interesting. According to this view: 'the influx of migrants has been the biggest single influence in changes in Australian eating habits'.[34] And this change keeps leading to even 'higher' realms of culinary diversity from mythological, but not necessarily incorrect, stories about Sydney offering 'more diverse eating experiences than Paris'[35] to stories about friends having 'a 5-year-old who insists on extra chilli with her Thai noodles…'.[36] Some venture that we have reached the ultimate stage of this culinary revolution:

> I knew the revolution was complete when I was at the newsagency the other day and noticed a booklet called *Step-by-Step English Cooking*. Part of a Family Circle series that includes such titles as *Step-by-step Cajun Cooking* and *Step-by-Step Lebanese Cooking*, it contains recipes that generations of Australians learned at mother's knee: shepherd's pie, roast beef with Yorkshire pudding, apple crumble, trifle, even scones and pikelets. Once the staples of the nation, they're now just another variety of ethnic food.[37]

Because it is in keeping with this evolutionary account, the competitive Glebe–Newtown mode of deployment of cosmo-multicultural culinary superiority appears in continuity with such a multicultural discourse. What marks it from the latter, however, is its fusion of notions of diversity with notions of classiness, sophistication and international distinction. For cosmo-multiculturalism, not only was 'before' monocultural, it was also totally unsophisticated.

> Not so long ago two things were certain at wedding receptions; the couple would probably be divorced within ten years and a prawn cocktail would be part of the meal. The former hasn't changed much, but the beloved prawn cocktail isn't the sensation it was in the past.
>
> At Oatland House in Dundas, prawn cocktails were once the order of the day, but alas no more. 'People are a little more educated', Carmel Smithers says, 'Adventurous even'. Prawns are popular though, but prepared in different ways. Cooked in fresh ginger and honey, for instance.[38]

It is within this process, where the emphasis is on 'education', 'sophistication' and 'adventurousness' that culinary multiculturalism — symbolised here by the use of ginger — fuses with cosmopolitanism — symbolised by the adventurous addition of honey — to define not only a culture of abundance of otherness, but one of inventive and daring cooks creatively making use of such otherness. Necessarily, this also requires the emergence of a palate capable of going all the way with such daring cooks. That same palate has to also be able to go all the way with whatever an ethnic eating experience requires. An article in the *Sydney Morning Herald* maintained that: 'Given the Australian palates' rapid acceptance, Sushi addiction is clearly a phenomenon that could revolutionise the local restaurant scene'.[39]

What makes a cuisine such as sushi highly valued within cosmo-multiculturalism is that it is perceived to embody a whole cultural experience, and culinary cosmo-multiculturalism ultimately aims to provide the eater with something like an international touristic adventure. This was clearly exemplified in the London advertisement reproduced earlier. A patron of a Nepalese restaurant, asked why he liked the restaurant said: 'I like the clothes that the people who work there wear. It is interesting to observe the culture through the food experience.' This is a crucial aspect of cosmo-multicultural eating in both cosmopolitan ethnic restaurants and the 'adventurous and creative' international ones. As one restaurant manager explained, the eater is offered a 'dining experience' rather than 'a meal'.[40]

Cosmo-multiculturalism involves the production and consumption of food with a consciousness that these practices are occurring in an international field where the standards of excellence and daring and of what is 'real creativity' or 'real authenticity' are set internationally. Opening up the market for the migration of those who can enhance the nation's competitive cosmopolitan capacity is crucial. In July 1986 it was reported that 'chefs head the list of Australia's requirements for skilled immigrants in 1986–87'. But given that the presentation of the food and the way it is offered were just as much a part of the cosmopolitan dining experience as the preparation of food, also high on the list were skilled waiters.[41] The whole set of internationally sanctioned and largely implicit rules of production and consumption begin to operate as a form of symbolic violence, setting the parameters of acceptable creativity.[42] Consequently, in Australia as elsewhere, the emergence and spread of the provision of such a dining experience has involved the setting in motion of an increased 'policing' of the production and consumption of cosmo-multicultural food. Bodies such as the National Tourism Industry Training Committee have become interested in surveying the professionalism of cooks and the degree to which they have received formal training.[43]

Accompanying this process is the emergence of an aristocracy of cosmo-multicultural producers and consumers who set themselves up simply and subtly as 'those who know how to do it best' and a hierarchy of those who possess 'more' or 'less' cosmo-multicultural capital. Officially and popularly recognised cosmo-multicultural high priests emerge, acquiring the recognised power to classify, judge and rank, and therefore the capacity to allow or disallow eating experiences, which also involves making and unmaking restaurants, for those who have the capacity to appreciate them.[44]

All of this happens within a clear awareness of Australia's presence in an international culinary field and a search for distinction within this field. In March 1984 Australia held the First Symposium of Australian Gastronomy where someone declared: 'I think there is an Australian cuisine, but it is difficult to categorise because there is so much going on'.[45] Two years later, while explaining the making of a dish with goat meat, the famous Australian cook Josephine Pignolet casually throws in: 'the goat has to be Australian'.[46] The very capacity of deploying such strategies of international culinary distinction, the very possibility of thinking 'that', as Foucault would say,[47] indicates not only the presence of this international market but also the degree to which the history of this market has been internalised by those involved in it to such a degree that they can professionally manoeuvre within it.

cosmo-multiculturalism and class

Culinary cosmo-multiculturalism constitutes therefore a field of possible strategies of class distinction. It is made up of people with different capacities for appreciation and different tastes all linked to the extent to which they have accumulated 'cosmo-multicultural capital'. As such, just as much as there is a division between cosmo-multiculturalists and non-cosmo-multiculturalists, there are various classes of cosmo-multiculturalists relative to degrees of attainment and capacities for distinction. The field is dominated by the culinary high priests who expect 'the goat to be Australian' and who aim for a more or less pure cosmopolitan experience rather than a multicultural one. But the forbidding cost of such a culinary experience makes it the reserve of those who are rich in economic capital. However, economic capital is not enough. A cook who owns two restaurants, one in Balmain and one in Lane Cove, explained to me that he finds it very hard to 'sell' the adventurous dishes he offers in Balmain to his Lane Cove clients. Although, the Lane Cove clientele are as rich, if not richer, in economic capital, they are, as he put it, 'generally speaking too traditional' and 'very Anglo' in their tastes. They lacked the cultured sense of adventure of the Balmain clientele, who were 'more aware of international trends'. Consequently, there is a specific kind of 'cosmopolitan capital' that people can accumulate through exposing themselves to international trends and experiences. And this is not solely related to the possession of economic capital, although the possession of economic capital for travel, for example, can be of help.

Generally, the cosmo-multicultural field offers a wide range of strategies for those who are less endowed with the economic capital necessary to savour 'up-market' culinary experiences. Thus, it is in the culturally and educationally-endowed but relatively economically poor settings of Newtown and its surroundings that the strategies of savouring 'the vegetarian authenticity' of Asian food among what some call the 'tofu set' flourish. This 'Asian vegetarianism', while not necessarily a 'classy' eating experience for more economic capital-endowed eaters, still provides its followers with a means of distinguishing themselves from the real or imagined monoculturalism of a mainstream lacking both class and the capacity to appreciate culinary diversity. Many of the Anglo-background people interviewed in this category clearly saw it as a way of distinguishing themselves from what they perceived as the culturally undistinguished Anglo-Saxonness from which they originated. One defined his ethnicity as 'boring white middle-class trash'. Another declared that 'Anglo food sucks and, you know, the western beef-centric diet is a boo-boo'. For another the migrants' ethnic food is seen as 'better than my (Anglo) ethnic food — tastier and easier to digest'.

These cosmo-vegetarians also distinguish themselves from the economically-rich cosmo-multiculturalists by constructing themselves to be in possession of more cosmo-multicultural 'knowledge-capital', either on the basis of travel, which allows them to make knowledge claims about what 'authentic Asian food' is really like, or on the basis of reading and education which allows them to make nutritional knowledge claims about 'what is good and healthy for you', such as: 'I tend to like Asian food, because, and this is a medical thing, it's more easily digestible'. When talking about Chinese food one interviewee wished that 'more people understood it'. In this 'communist' wish for an equally distributed capacity to understand among all people lies the underlying claim that not everyone understands. These eaters can distinguish themselves through the implicit claim of a superior capacity to understand.

In processes such as these, the various deployments of cosmo-multicultural tastes operate as indicators of class position, and especially as indicators of the degree of accumulation of economic and cosmopolitan capital. As Bourdieu has put it in a classical passage:

> Taste classifies and it classifies the classifier. Social subjects, classified by their classifications, distinguish themselves by the distinctions they make, between the beautiful and the ugly, the distinguished and the vulgar, in which their position in the objective classifications is expressed or betrayed.[48]

It is in laying the foundations for this class-differentiated social map of taste that cosmo-multiculturalism differentiates itself most from multiculturalism. For not only does it distinguish between an unsophisticated before and sophisticated after, it also creates various splits in Australian culture between a sophisticated us and an unsophisticated them. What is more, and this is what makes it of particular interest to us, in Sydney, this difference is spatialised into another difference between the sophisticated 'here' and the unsophisticated 'there', where the there is the homogenised construction 'western Sydney'.

cosmo-multiculturalism, class and western sydney

The availability of genuine ethnic food and of cosmopolitan ethnic eateries connected to the circuit of global tourism is seen by many as one of the crucial differences between the city on the one hand, and its western suburbs on the other. If cosmo-multiculturalism is perceived to have taken Sydney into the sophisticated after, according to its main spokespeople, it has failed to take western Sydney with it. There, people are still in the before: generally speaking, an unsophisticated and backward steak-and-chips-eating and beer-drinking population. Western Sydney is yet again seen to be lacking. Here it is lacking cosmopolitanism and cosmopolitans. For example, one interviewee mockingly claimed in relation precisely to the demonised 'prawn cocktail': 'You can still have one in Parramatta'. In a similar mode of differentiation, a chef working at a 'top' city restaurant after having worked at a Parramatta restaurant solemnly claimed that both the customers and the chefs in Parramatta were historically 'behind'. He said that in 1975–76, restaurants in central Sydney were serving Steak Diane. That was fashionable then, but now no-one would dream of serving it. But you still find it on menus in Italian restaurants in Parramatta. He said that the further you go out of Sydney, the worse it gets. 'Customers out there', he maintained, 'were at least ten years behind'.[49]

Clearly (and despite the special case of Cabramatta which will be examined later) to the extent that generalisations can be made about an area called 'western Sydney', it *is*, and visibly so, less integrated in the circuit of international touristic capital. And the statistical figures of the Australian census clearly show that a higher proportion of the population that inhabit it does lack economic, cultural or educational capital or all of them.[50] So the area does lack cosmopolitanism and cosmopolitan consumers, even if to a far lesser extent than the stereotype implies. This can be clearly seen in the difference between the total network of restaurants available in the inner-city suburbs and in places like Parramatta and Penrith. Thus, using as an 'objective' criteria the cosmo-multicultural centres' *subjective* criteria of taste — which is made objective through its operation as a mode of symbolic violence — the spatial differences in the kind of food and the kind of eating experience provided by supposedly equivalent restaurants can readily be seen.[51] Many elements operate to create an effect of differentiation here: the food quality and mode of presentation; the mode of deploying 'authenticity'; the work culture itself — such as the 'sophistication' of the cooks, the waiters and the waitresses, and the way all of those relate to the clientele; the clientele's mode of eating and dressing; the quality of the paper on which the menus are printed; the quality of the printed material; the restaurant's furniture and its layout; the service; the wine list, and many more. All of these work to establish a reasonably stable spatial hierarchy of taste and sophistication in which the further west one goes, the more lacking the restaurant scene generally is.

This 'objective' spatial hierarchy is often implicitly recognised subjectively by the agents themselves, particularly the cooks and the restaurant owners.[52] It is not that it is easy to find a restaurant owner or a cook willing to say 'we are not as good or as sophisticated as an equivalent restaurant in the city'. The hierarchy is acknowledged in the taking of the city as the standard. Statements such as 'we are as good as any of the best restaurants in inner-Sydney' made by many restaurant owners in Penrith or Parramatta already reveal the relations of hierarchy in which the statements are being made. Such is the logic of cultural distinction, analysed so well by Bourdieu,[53] that those who aspire to be as good as those who are perceived to be the best become involved in an impossible struggle: even if they do well according to the standards of the dominant, they can only reveal themselves to be 'lacking' by the very fact that they are 'parvenus', 'forever-trying-to-become', as opposed to merely 'being' who they are.

These modes of class differentiation are most apparent in the strategies established around cosmo-multiculturalism as a mode of consuming *diversity*. 'Diversity' of ethnic cuisines is a key concept deployed on an everyday life basis by cosmo-multicultural subjects. 'I enjoy the diversity', 'I like the diversity', 'The diversity available here is amazing, if it wasn't for the diversity…' were commonly used to express people's culinary experience.

How can diversity be consumed? The question is more difficult than it seems, for the people who utter this sentence are not referring to a plate on which they had a bit of Lebanese food or a bit of Thai. They are talking about the fact that they like being able to eat Thai in Newtown one night, Italian in Glebe on another night. Furthermore, it

at home in the entrails of the west

is not merely a matter of the consumption of different ethnic cuisines, but the consumption of the very difference between them. Cosmo-multicultural eaters have to be capable of expressing their eating experience by condensing it in space and time. Cosmo-multicultural advertisements often exemplify this condensation — as in the concept of 'the world on a plate' in the London advertisement. A Melbourne advertisement does the same using the metaphor of the smorgasbord: 'You'll be greeted by a world of exotic experiences on the streets of Melbourne. And each street has its own cultural character. To find out more about Melbourne's smorgasbord of ethnic experiences, see your travel agent'.[54]

But how can anyone experientially imagine themselves to have 'the world on a plate' or 'to consume a smorgasbord of ethnic experiences'? This can only be done by maintaining a certain distance from the materiality of the food consumed so that the experience is not just that of eating a hot curry that causes a sweat, but to 'eat' that very difference between the curry and the pesto. That is, the culinary experiences have first to be hoarded: 'I had this pesto last night and that Laksa two nights ago', for instance. Second, there has to be a recognition of the potential culinary experiences open in the future: 'We have to go to this new Tuscan'. Third, and at the same time, what has been accumulated and projected have to be kept present as part of each eating experience. As one interviewee put it: 'I like Asian food in general, I like a bit of Indonesian and Thai and Indian and Nepalese and Japanese too. I think it is a privilege to be able to have the variety'. This is how people manage to consume diversity.

Such a mode of consumption does not presuppose the possession of economic capital, although the latter, as is often the case, can help. More important is the possession of a cosmopolitan capital that allows a sublimated approach to otherness where people can *and know how to* rise above a too-materialist functionality. It is an experience specific to those who are cultured enough to know how to eat more than 'just' to satisfy their hunger and their taste buds. It is a form of detachment of the palate similar to the detachment of the gaze analysed by Bourdieu:

129

> The detachment of the pure gaze cannot be dissociated from a general disposition towards the world which is the paradoxical product of conditioning by negative economic necessities — a life of ease — that tends to induce an active distance from necessity.[55]

In opposition to this experience stands the experience based on need and on a straightforward conception of taste. Below are excerpts from an interview with a working-class Maltese–Australian who works as a guard in a shopping centre and who eats at a Vietnamese restaurant there. One can see an excellent example of the materiality of the experience governed by notions of size and taste, rather than that of difference and diversity:

> *I*: ...the mussels, you weren't too keen on them?
>
> *S*: Oh, I've never tried them but it's not my cup of tea, I just don't see what they see in them. They're like a big snot to me. They're like oysters.
>
> *I*: Have you ever had the tofu stuff or the beancurd stuff [used in some Lao–Thai dishes offered at this restaurant].
>
> *S*: No, I won't eat any of that.
>
> *I*: No vegetarian stuff.
>
> *S*: Nup. See I like meat, so.
>
> *I*: What about the soups?
>
> *S*: Yeah, I eat their beef soup, that's all right. Actually I was sick last week, she give me beef soup, it was all right.
>
> *I*: So you can't remember anything specifically that you turned your nose up at?
>
> *S*: No. Normally if I don't like it — if she says 'Oh try this' and I say 'I don't like it' I won't eat it. It's like these desserts (an Asian sweet stall directly behind us). That makes my stomach turn, you know. It's just things that I don't like I stay clear from.
>
> *I*: Have you tried them?

S: Nah, I won't try them. It just turns me off. It's not like you go to Maccas and say 'There's a hamburger. I like that, I'll eat that'. It's just not the same.

I: You know what you're getting there [at McDonald's].

S: It's just I don't know what I'm getting and I don't like it, don't like the look of it, all runny and sloppy and shitty.

The point is not, of course, that cosmo-multiculturalists do not have such a direct materialist experience of food. Rather, it is that such experiences are driven into the cosmo-multicultural unconscious where the non-cosmopolitan and the non-classy, 'runny, sloppy and shitty' as it were, lurks. This is why they are then pathologically transferred geographically and articulated to the geographical unconscious of the centre and made to look as if it is a specificity of the inhabitant of Western Sydney.

As analysed by Dianne Powell, it on the basis of strategies of differentiation which manage to create their own reality that discourses seeing Western Sydney as lacking emerge. They are continuations of the structuring of the stereotypical representations made of the area, by the self-proclaimed centre, around axes such as lack–excess, brutality–finesse and crude–refined.[56] But, there is more to this construction of Western Sydney as lacking cosmo-multiculturalism and cosmo-multiculturalists than the typical regional stigmatisation of what is considered as a less classy area. For, probably as a natural by-product of the fusion of cosmopolitanism and multiculturalism, the discourse that sees western Sydney as lacking culinary cosmo-multiculturalism constantly slips into portraying it as lacking multiculturalism.

It is in this domain, where the cosmopolitan and the multicultural part of the discourse contradict with each other, that the problematic nature of the meaning of 'multiculturalism' in the cosmo-multicultural discourse emerges. For here was a multicultural discourse (based on the consumption of otherness) declaring one of the most multicultural regions of Australia (in terms of inhabitance) 'ten years behind', as it was put by one interviewee. This is extended further to the point where the inability to appreciate the culinary diversity available in cosmo-multicultural ethnic restaurants is perceived as 'racist' according to the 'classy' multiculturalists of the centre!

home/world

An Italian–Australian patron of a Vietnamese restaurant in Cabramatta explained to me: 'It is already getting very crowded in all the restaurants here. Lucky the locals are idiots who don't know what they've got. All they think about is "Asian invasion" '. An inner-Sydney restaurateur, asked if he would open a restaurant in the western suburbs said jokingly: 'No bloody way. They're all rednecks out there. They'd blow my restaurant up if I ever offer anything more ethnic than spaghetti bolognaise'. Even if said as a joke, this discourse implicitly equates the inability to appreciate ethnic food with being a 'redneck'. A Lebanese restaurant owner from the eastern suburbs sees Penrith as full of racists who wouldn't know what hummus means, let alone other more sophisticated dishes. It is partly on the basis of such stereotypes that western Sydney is perceived to lack multiculturalism.

What is at stake in the cosmopolitan critique of western Sydney is a struggle over what multiculturalism is, rather than just a struggle over who is multicultural and who is not. Western Sydney does not offer within its practical everyday life a different definition of what 'cosmopolitan consumption' ought to be like. Therefore, restaurants there are bound either to remain outside the competitive cosmopolitan game — remain unaware or unconcerned by the yearning for cosmopolitan status — or, as we have seen, mimic the cosmopolitan inner-city restaurants and be forever constructed as lacking. But this is not the case with multiculturalism. In this domain, western Sydney does have a very viable lived multicultural reality to offer as an alternative. It is precisely this multicultural reality of migrant home-building and intercultural interaction that has been emphasised in the first part of this chapter. In the cosmo-multicultural version of things, if an area is more multicultural than another, this appears to have less to do with who *inhabits* it, who makes a home in it, and the degree of interaction between different cultural subjects within it, and more to do with what multicultural commodities are *available* on its markets and who has the capacity to appreciate them. The latter is a multiculturalism of availability, the former is a multiculturalism of inhabitance and cross-cultural interaction. Because each of these multiculturalisms is grounded in a different part of Sydney, where it is dominant, the concept of multiculturalism is also spatially torn between the pull of the inner city and that of the western suburbs.

But this pull is not equally strong on both sides. It is cosmo-multiculturalism that is becoming the dominant popular mode of conceiving of multiculturalism as such. A very common process through which the dominant centre's ways of seeing come to dominate and superimpose themselves on different realities is taking place. This is, as always, facilitated by the centre's monopoly over the means of representing social experiences, especially in the media. Inner-city journalists immersed in the cosmo-multiculturalist experience have unconsciously contributed to a generalised equation of the love of ethnic food with non-racism and vice versa! A typical newspaper article, for example, combines a celebration of the evolutionary conception of Australia's culinary diversity with an attack on the figure of Geoffrey Blainey. Somehow it is supposed to make natural sense that the appreciation of culinary diversity should be anathema to someone constructed as a backward 'racist' monoculture-lover:

> You don't have to be as ancient as I am to remember when Australian cuisine was a remote province of the British Empire, with Mrs. Beeton as Governess General. If you wanted a bottle of olive oil, you had to go to the chemist for it, feeling a bit foolish, as it was expected that you wanted it for constipation...
>
> It really is marvellous that a nation's eating habits should have been so transformed in a mere 40 or so years...Eat your heart out Geoffrey Blainey.[57]

A good indicator of the scale of their dominance is the extent to which cosmo-multicultural conceptions of multiculturalism are naturalised so that their specificity goes largely unnoticed. It takes a serious effort when talking about ethnic food to think of anything other than 'ethnic restaurants', for example. Asked which areas of western Sydney were 'multicultural' as far as 'ethnic food' was concerned, using specifically the words in inverted commas, thirty-two out of forty-one inner-city interviewees from different socioeconomic backgrounds only mentioned Cabramatta and Bankstown. A person who mentioned these also added what was clearly implicit in many of the responses: 'there is nowhere else to go otherwise'. This is, of course, a reasonable perception of things from an inner-city perspective. However, it reveals the depth of the association of the multiculturalism of ethnic food with ethnic restaurants as opposed to, for example, migrant home-cooking: where there are no ethnic restaurants there is no culinary multiculturalism.

III multiculturalism without migrants

In this part of the chapter the exploration of cosmo-multiculturalism is extended. The usage of multiculturalism is problematised to refer to the cosmopolitan experience. I focus my discussion on Cabramatta,[58] arguing that for cosmopolitan subjects the Cabramatta ethnic-eating scene is perceived as culturally enriching because of its imagined authenticity. Again, what is missing from these constructions of Cabramatta are intercultural interactions in which both the eater and the feeder experience themselves as subjects. In so doing, I want to reassert normatively the importance of recentring the concept of multiculturalism around the processes of migrant home-building and intercultural interaction. It is by going back to this reality of home-building and interaction, and the spaces where it is enacted, like western Sydney, that debates about multiculturalism can regain their significance.

cosmo-multiculturalism, ethnic 'authenticity' and power

In setting up the dichotomy between a multiculturalism of availability and a multiculturalism of inhabitance, it should be made clear that the practices associated with cosmo-multiculturalism do not in themselves preclude the possibility of conceiving within it spaces of migrant home-building or intercultural interaction. For example, cosmo-multiculturalism can and does delineate a homely reality for many people who feel at home precisely in the class-accessible realm of the adventurous, the different, and, paradoxically, the anything-but-home (that is, the traditional home) modes of culinary consumption. It is an undeniable fact that cosmo-multiculturalists derive a homely feeling from 'the five Thais in our street'. Furthermore, cosmo-multicultural eating has provided new opportunities for *some* migrant cooks to express themselves in ways that earlier generations of eaters would not have appreciated. Many such cooks expressed delight at the changes and the possibilities available to them in the 'new eating scene'. As one Italian cook put it: 'Now people have anything we put on the table that is fresh and well-cooked. Before, Australians had a very limited taste'.[59] Others who enjoy working in the cosmo-multicultural scene because of the creative freedom it allows them find some aspects of the 'eating experience' too demanding:

> Some people ask me: 'Where does this dish come from?' I feel like telling them *elmeh elmak* (I know as much as you do about this topic), you think I asked my mother about the origin of every dish she cooked me! But they really want a story about the food you know.
>
> *Interviewer*: Do you tell them a story?
>
> Sometimes I say that this is special to the region I come from in North Lebanon and tell them that it is made differently in Beirut. That makes them happy. But sometimes I just say I don't know. *Alla wakilak ka'enneh maktab syehah* (honestly as if I am a tourist bureau).

In general, therefore, cosmo-multicultural practices can offer homely spaces for its practitioners. The point is, however, that the *dominant* cosmo-multicultural discourse does not encompass the totality of this reality. It represents a specific consumer-oriented version emphasising the 'we have…'-type discourse without taking into account any of the reality of the ethnic producer. Some eaters are well aware of this. As a student from Erskineville has put it when asked if she liked ethnic food: 'It's nice… I guess I enjoy it; I enjoy eating most ethnic food; that's what I mean by it's nice — it's nice for me, though it may not be nice for them (ethnics)'.

The following statement made by an English migrant about what she likes about living in Australia, is an ideal-type example of the role of availability in the cosmo-multicultural discourse:

> I love the climate and the differences: if you want to go to the mountains and wear wellies and a sweater, you can; and if you want to wear a T-shirt all year round you can.
>
> Something else about Sydney in particular that I like is that you can have any type of food you want. I love food — curries and Greek food and Indian — and you can have a bit of all these cultures just by walking up the road. To be

able to sit in a restaurant and have Indian food and hear Indian music and have Indians cook for you is great.⁶⁰

The association of an availability of diversity in climate and the availability of diversity in food reveals a clear perception of ethnicity as an object of experience rather than an experiential subject. This is further reinforced with the English-specific 'have Indians cook for you', which reveals a subconscious colonial imaginary of power underlying this experience of availability.

From this perspective, cosmo-multiculturalism reveals itself as being continuous with one of the main multicultural themes of the dominant culture since the 1970s: the theme of cultural enrichment. In this discourse, multiculturalism is seen as a transcendence of a past where (white) Australians could not appreciate the value of the ethnic cultural forms that surrounded them and perceived them negatively. Multiculturalism on the other hand represents a new era where ethnic cultures are not only not perceived negatively, but actually valued. Embracing such ethnic cultures was seen as 'enriching'. Despite the positive 'anti-racist' nature of this discourse, it is deeply Anglo-centric in positioning Anglo subjects in the role of the appreciators enriched by what are constructed as ethnic objects with no *raison d'être* other than to enrich the Anglo-subject.⁶¹ The author bell hooks has succinctly expressed the imaginary ethnicity presupposed by this discourse of availability: within commodity culture, ethnicity becomes spice, seasoning that can liven up the dull dish that is mainstream culture.⁶² This is clearly one of the major ways in which cosmo-multiculturalism perceives its ethnic others. As one interviewee put it:

> I think it would be pretty sad if we were still all living on the stodgy sort of English food that our parents have been brought up on. I'm really glad to have seen different changes as different cultures have come in. Like the variety of breads that came in when Italians came to Australia...

Cosmo-multiculturalism reconstructs, therefore, the same logic of appreciation present in the multiculturalism of enrichment, but it does so along different lines. First, its central subject, 'the appreciator' is no longer just Anglo (white) but mainly a cosmopolitan person, that is, someone who has accumulated that specific kind of 'classiness' we have called 'cosmopolitan capital'. Such a subject is very likely to be Anglo, but can also be anyone who has enough 'class' to become an appreciator of otherness. Second, and as we have seen in the previous section, in introducing the class criteria, cosmo-multiculturalism creates a further division between the cosmo-multicultural appreciators and a working class constructed as non-multicultural by virtue of its presumed inability to appreciate 'diversity' and ethnic cultures.

The main difference, however, between the multiculturalism of enrichment and cosmo-multiculturalism is in the latter's peculiar conception of its 'ethnic object'. Nowhere is this clearer than in the cosmo-multicultural conception of ethnic 'authenticity'. This authenticity is, first of all, like all constructions of ethnic 'authenticity', a mode of essentialising ethnic cultural forms. In the culinary domain it is primarily an opposition to what is perceived as the 'westernisation' of ethnic food. For example, on the Chinese food front, its main enemy is sweet and sour cooking, seen as a culinary aberration, a deformation of the purity of Chinese cultural forms to cater for the sweet-addicted western palate. Asked if she would like to see changes to the ethnic food scene, one inner-city interviewee responded in a way that was typical of most inner-city responses to this question:

> Yeah, I'd like it to expand, I mean, you tend to find your average…you still tend to find a lot of western Chinese restaurants in small country towns and I find western Chinese food really quite bad sometimes and not really true to Asian cooking. So I'd like to see truer representations of it, which you find in cities like Sydney but so the average person can get a better idea that it's not just sweet and sour pork and stuff like that.
>
> *I*: What do you exactly mean by western Chinese food?
>
> The things that you don't really find when you go overseas; things like sweet and sour pork and the way we typically get it here, which is a lot of colouring. I think it's quite stylised for westerners, and we tend to overuse meat, whereas, if you actually go and visit those countries, the meat use is a lot more limited and it's not a true representation of what that food is like.

But cosmo-multiculturalism does not only see authenticity in the taste, it also sees it in the presentation. Any food, even when 'authentically' cooked, loses at least some of its authenticity if it is prepared with an Anglo customer in mind. Cosmo-multiculturalism expresses a clear liking for ethnic cultural products that appear to exist in themselves and for themselves. The experience is one of entering a restaurant that is not aiming to satisfy western needs but an ethnic clientele. It is in such settings, where there are no attempts at social translation on the part of the restaurant owners to cater for a non-ethnic clientele, that real authenticity can be experienced.

cabra-multiculturalism

This is why Cabramatta has been constructed as a cosmo-multicultural haven. There, Vietnamese restaurants are open for Vietnamese people. It is by entering this self-contained arrangement that the cosmo-multiculturalists experience authenticity. This is how a visitor to Cabramatta described her eating experience:

> two weeks ago we decided to go to Cabramatta for lunch, because a friend of ours is going to live in Laos and we took her there for her birthday, and it was so good going up there; we went to this restaurant and we were the only Caucasians in the restaurant and we didn't know what to order, and everything was in Vietnamese and nobody spoke much English so we were just pointing to what other people had and we ordered that. It was such a good experience; people were just sitting around and pointing at us and laughing because we didn't know how to eat it. And they gave us some scissors and we didn't know what to do with the scissors.
> Much more interesting and much more fun.

The experience portrayed above is a familiar touristic experience. But it is not the experience of any tourist. It is the experience of an adventurous tourist who has gone to those exotic spaces which were not supposed to be part of the touristic circuit, and dared. The language of cosmo-multiculturalism is full of accounts of daring, some of which tell of unsuccessful attempts to master certain dishes. Here is one such account:

at home in the entrails of the west

> I am interested in food, I'm interested in cooking, I'm interested in different flavours, I'm interested in trying something new. The one thing I've never been able to come at (which was while I was overseas) is the sheep's eyes. That kind of tossed me, I couldn't come at that.

Daring is the essence of the cosmo-multicultural 'kick', as it were, and it is brilliantly expressed in this account of eating in Cabramatta by a lawyer who is a resident of Enmore:

> Cabramatta is the only place worth eating at. It is the only place *where you are not expected*, where the restaurant owner does not smile to welcome you. He doesn't want you there. He thinks you're a nuisance. When I go to a restaurant like this I know I am going to eat well. I know I will be eating the real thing. I look inside the restaurant and try to locate the owner and as soon as I see that look of disdain on his face I'm in [laughing]. I love it.

But, here we need to stop and ask ourselves what kind of 'authenticity' and what kind of 'daring' is being constructed in these accounts? Undoubtedly, cosmo-multicultural experiences such as the above are played out as a game of mastery. But it is experienced not as mastery over ethnic people as such. There is nothing more anathema to the aesthetic sense of cosmo-multiculturalism than the idea of an explicitly subjugated ethnic otherness. It is precisely such an otherness that becomes open to corruption by the West. It is such an ethnic otherness that cooks sweet and sour pork. As such, cosmo-multiculturalism does not only see westernised ethnic food as a culinary aberration, it also sees it as a social aberration whereby dominated ethnics are forced to change their cultural practices to service the dominant culture. Cosmo-multiculturalism, on the other hand, values a 'mastery' over — in the sense of a capacity to consume — ethnic cultural experiences, rather than a mastery over ethnic people. Ethnic cultural phenomena are valuable to master precisely when the ethnics who produce them are perceived to have done so free from western coercion. A claim such as 'I went to a Lebanese restaurant last night and I ate raw liver' is a claim of cosmo-multicultural mastery of the raw liver which allows the maker of the claim to accumulate cosmo-multicultural capital commensurate with the difficulty of the situation she or he has mastered. For it to happen, there needs to be an ethnic Lebanese 'feeder' who has not been westernised and 'subjugated' into thinking that raw liver is not something to be eaten. Some cosmo-multiculturalists go as far as seeing in their desire for authenticity a desire for liberating ethnics from colonial servitude by allowing them to cook for themselves rather than cook for others. As an interviewee, a professional from Newtown, stated:

> I'd like to see the removal of non-ethnic recipes from ethnic restaurants, so things like sweet and sour from Chinese, for example. I'd like to see more representation of the history and culture behind some of the foods, rather than just the experience of eating, so for example an explanation of how tofu is connected with religious and cultural aspects of Asian countries. I would also like to see perhaps a lot less meat in traditionally non-meat cultures such as Indian and Japanese, so that instead of presenting us with Australianised food they actually present the real food, and I'd like to see it divorced from the concept of multiculturalism a little more and presented as a community activity by ethnic communities feeding themselves rather than as something that Australians can cash in on. Exploited labour as making food for us.

Here, the interviewee clearly associates multiculturalism with the multiculturalism of enrichment and takes a critical stand towards it. He does not want ethnics to cook for Australians. He wants them to cook for themselves as 'a community activity'. But, clearly, this is only explicitly the message. For he wants them to 'cook-for-themselves-in-community' *for him*. Here we come face to face with the perversity, in Lacan's sense, of the cosmo-multicultural desire for ethnic otherness. Clearly, cosmo-multiculturalists have a preference for otherness appearing in the wild, as it were.[63] They do not value otherness which is too readily available. Nor do they value it when it directly aims at seducing them as a consumers. They value it when it appears as narcissistically available to itself. But at the same time this is not entirely true. For it is not the case that the cosmo-multiculturalists do not want this ethnic otherness to seduce them. They want it to seduce

at home in the entrails of the west

them by appearing as if it is not trying to seduce them. It is precisely that ethnic otherness which appears as existing for itself that they want to exist for them. And they are quite happy to unequivocally state how they like their ethnics.[64] This is precisely where the perversity of the desire lies. Cosmo-multiculturalists want an ethnic otherness available to them as something that is not readily available to them.

Thus a romantic colonial image of the 'natives' engaging in communal cooking clearly underlies the culinary fantasy in the preceding interview. As the interviewee sees it, such a communality will mean that the people concerned will withdraw from the multicultural circle of servility which constructs ethnic cultures as available to an Anglo consumer. But, in the apparent desire to liberate them is the desire to make them available to himself. He wants them to be free for him to enjoy their freedom!

Cosmo-multiculturalism does not delve, however, into the very conditions of possibility of such a mode of appreciation. While it continues to perceive ethnic cultures as a mere object aimed at enriching the central 'cosmo-multicultural subject', it aims to construct this ethnic object as if it existed outside the relations of power which constitute it as an object. For why do the communally cooking natives not spear the explorers instead of inviting them for a meal to enrich them? Why do the Cabramatta restaurant owners not throw the daring cosmo-multicultural adventurers out of their establishments if they are as annoyed by their presence as they appear to be? What is it that *stops* them from doing so? To answer these questions is to reveal the relations of power that already underlie cosmo-multicultural consumption. But it is also to undermine that experience. For the mystification of the relation of power that makes the ethnic other ultimately available is necessary to maintain the illusion of daring and discovery.

Michael Symons notes that despite its long historical presence in Australia, Chinese food 'was gracelessly snubbed until their [Chinese] numbers had fallen to a "safe" low'.[65] It is fundamentally this sense of safety, the sense that the 'natives won't (and can't) spear you', that underlies the cosmo-multiculturalist capacity for 'daring' and 'appreciation'. Here lies one of the crucial bases for the difference between the cosmo-multicultural appreciator and the 'racist, working-

141

class westie'. An Italian–Australian resident of Cabramatta interviewed seems at one level to be the prototype of this 'racist':

> I'm bloody craving for a decent meal you know, and all these bloody trendies come here and say what a great time they're having and we who live here can't even have a decent piece of steak any more.

Many cosmo-multiculturalists we spoke to liked to perceive the difference between statements such as the above and their sense of appreciation of otherness as a difference between decent and indecent people. Yet, quite clearly, this decency is dependent on an experience of power and safety. A 'safe low' is not, as Michael Symons implies, an objective thing. People's conception of what is a safe low depends on their own sense of empowerment, which is clearly class-related. In terms of power relations, the opposite of the appreciation of otherness is not the lack of appreciation but the idea of being force-fed, of losing the power to be appreciative or non-appreciative. It is precisely this sense of being force-fed which is the basis of such an outburst. It is a class-derived subjective feeling which cosmo-multiculturalism reinterprets in voluntaristic moral terms. Again, this moral framework is crucial in mystifying the relation of power which makes the ethnic other experienced as safely enjoyable and appreciable.

The cosmo-multiculturalists coming from the city to Cabramatta like to imagine themselves to be on a safari, tasting culture as it exists in the wild. Essential to their experience is a failure to perceive the colonial history and the relations of power which constitute the very condition of the availability of this 'tamed wilderness' for them. They are more like visitors to a zoo who like to think they are on a wild tour of an African jungle.

Cosmo-multiculturalism, therefore, is far from being a moral high point offering an egalitarian and non-racist conception of the ethnic other and it is not the ideal prototype of multiculturalism it claims to be. There is, however, another kind of mystification involved in the cosmo-multicultural quest for 'wild authentic' experiences within which the 'multiculturalism' of the cosmopolitan experience is problematised. This lies in what we have seen as the valorisation of a conception of the ethnic subject as a narcissistic other turned on itself.

As already pointed out, in continuity with the multiculturalism of enrichment, cosmo-multiculturalism perceives ethnicity more as an object of appreciation than as a subject in its own right. Cosmo-multiculturalism takes this trend even further. It conceives of a multiculturalism from which migrants are totally absent. Only ethnic culinary experiences and ethnic flavours are present. In the cosmo-multicultural imaginary ethnic subjects *have* to be totally absent from the cosmo-multicultural transaction. That they be concerned with cooking for themselves and dealing with each other rather than in dealing with and cooking for westerners is a crucial part of what constitutes their 'authenticity'. To do otherwise, to be involved in attracting a westerner to their restaurant, is to undermine the cosmo-multicultural experience. Ethnics might be subjects in their relation to other ethnics, but they must not show any initiative as far as the cosmo-multicultural transaction is concerned. It is because of this that the presence of Cabramatta as a cosmo-multicultural space within Western Sydney does not contradict the image of western Sydney as a place lacking cosmo-multiculturalism. In this geographical imaginary, ethnic subjects are totally absent. None are supposed to have taken the initiative to attract cosmo-multicultural customers to Cabramatta.

Cabramatta is not cosmo-multicultural by design. No western Sydney ethnic feeding subject constructed it as cosmo-multicultural.[66] A person from Glebe flatly declared: 'I used to go to Cabramatta before anyone knew it existed'.[67] Cabramatta, like any good 'Third World' tourist spot outside of the common touristic circuit, was 'discovered' by the adventurers of the centre playing the colonial explorer game. Indeed, the language of the 'explorer' pervades most of the cosmo-multicultural descriptions of eating there. What this assumes is an ethnic otherness which plays no active role in seeking an encounter with the explorer for the explorer has to discover it. This is why the migrants, as subjects of the cosmo-multicultural experience, remain peculiarly outside the picture.

Such an absence of migrant subjects is further reinforced by the cosmo-multicultural dislike of 'westernised' ethnic food. Sweet and sour cooking might well be a culinary aberration, but there are other ways to see it than as the product of the subjection of Chinese culture to western influence. It also embodies, for example, the Chinese people's usage of their cultural creations to embody forms of dialogue, negotiations and interactions with other cultures. Here, cosmo-multiculturalism enters into direct conflict with the multiculturalism of intercultural interaction. But, perhaps more importantly, it enters into conflict with many of the practices on which it is based.

In our discussion with restaurant owners in Cabramatta it was evident that, not only do they actively seek a non-Vietnamese clientele, but they have an excellent grasp of their expectations. They engaged in very sophisticated strategies of deploying 'exotic' and 'authentic' settings to attract cosmo-multicultural clients. As one restaurant owner revealed through his son, who was interpreting, many of the restaurant owners know that the absence of signs in English is a good way to attract Anglo customers![68]

Clearly such knowledge would be impossible to incorporate into the cosmo-multicultural fantasy of authenticity.[69] The latter cannot reproduce itself, as it likes to perceive itself with a full knowledge that authenticity is actively constructed by the migrant subjects themselves. It has to maintain the reality of a multiculturalism without migrant wills as a condition of its own survival.

for a multiculturalism of inhabitance

In Sydney a vacuous journalistic rave declares multiculturalism 'a myth'.[70] Interestingly, the journalist constructed his arguments around the politics of SBS television and the cosmo-multicultural enjoyment of its programs, as well as around tensions in the so-called multicultural industry. The inner-city of reality the journalist is drawing on to construct his argument is obvious. Multiculturalism is declared a myth as if it was some kind of void superstructure empty of any ordinary reality lived by Australian citizens, and certainly without any reference to the migrant Australians that constitute Australia into a multicultural reality. As if by magic, years of intercultural interaction that form the core of the Australian multicultural experience are eluded in order to declare multiculturalism 'a myth'. It is this kind of pontification that is promoted by the dominance of a cosmo-multiculturalist 'multiculturalism without migrants'.

In a seminal analysis, Alfred Sohn-Rethel links abstract modes of thinking to the dominance of the commodity form. His thesis was, as he put it, that 'the formal analysis of the commodity holds the key not only to the critique of political economy, but also to the historical explanation of the abstract conceptual mode of thinking'.[71] His conclusion is well summarised by Slavoj Zizek: 'Before thought could arrive at pure abstraction, the abstraction was already at work in the social effectivity of the market'.[72]

If this general argument is applied to cosmo-multiculturalism in particular it could be argued that the very possibility of thinking such an abstraction as a multiculturalism without migrants, this plurality of cultures without a plurality of people from different cultures, lies in a subjectivity dominated by the presence and circulation of cultural otherness as a commodity, as abstract ethnic value.

This is why cosmo-multiculturalism cannot be understood without an analysis of its structuring by the circuit of touristic capital and the dominance within it of the production of ethnic products as forms of exoticisms for the international market. A capitalism where, as Lawrence Grossberg has put it, 'it is no longer a matter of capitalism having to work with and across differences…it is difference which is now in the service of capital'.[73]

The nature of producing cosmo-multicultural food involves ethnicity detaching itself from its 'ethnic' producers (this is probably one of the most liberating effects of the phenomenon). Despite the cosmo-multicultural quest for authenticity, we have a Scottish manager owning a Tuscan restaurant, an American managing a Vietnamese one, and so on. The role of the Scottish manager is not to produce a Scottish–Tuscan cuisine but to offer and stage Tuscan authenticity for the cosmo-multicultural clientele.

It would be facile, throughout this chapter, to take this critique of cosmo-multiculturalism as a critique of cosmo-multicultural practices as such. As argued right from the start, this is not what the critique aims to do. To say that a specific kind of practice entertains certain illusions about itself and that it is based on power relations does not invalidate it, for such illusions are part and parcel of all cultural practices. What this critique has aimed to do is more to deconstruct the relation between cosmopolitanism and multiculturalism that is present in the way cosmo-multiculturalism presents itself. Instead, the aim has been to valorise a multiculturalism grounded in the reality of migrant home-building and intercultural interaction presented in the first part of the chapter.

There can be no objective intellectual criteria for such a valorisation. It is a purely political choice in the context of an environment where the concept of multiculturalism is increasingly coming under attack. For it seems that what is in fact being constantly attacked is precisely the fetishised reality of a multiculturalism without migrants. Cosmo-multiculturalism not only belongs to this reality, but the dominance of its categories is also instrumental in reinforcing this reality.

It seems, however, that it can convincingly be argued from a normative perspective that any reality worthy of the title of multiculturalism in Australia has to involve a certain degree of homely forms of intercultural interaction in which both the eater and the feeder experience themselves as subjects. What characterises the multiculturalism articulated to the culinary practices and interactions described here is precisely that it is a multiculturalism that provides this homely space for the migrant by interpellating him or her as a subject: a dominated subject sometimes, but a subject nevertheless. If we direct our gaze to the multicultural reality lived in western Sydney, a far better understanding of what is at stake in debating the multiculturalism of Australia can be achieved.

notes

1 This part of the chapter is based on a research project I conducted on the spatiality of homesickness in Marrickville. The project was initially separate from my restaurant-based research explored in parts II and III of this chapter. The research with the Lebanese of Marrickville spilled out as I became increasingly interested in the Lebanese in the Parramatta region, particularly around Harris Park and the Our Lady of Lebanon church. This is where my own parents lived. I began to meet some of the people who interested me and to take ethnographic notes at my parents' place. This is when my interest in ethnic food sharpened and I decided to focus my Parramatta research on Lebanese food-centred modes of homesickness and home-building. The group interviewed was made of connected families and some of their friends, which sometimes took me away from Parramatta and closer to Blacktown. Most of them had migrated to Australia in the 1950s and 1960s, but some as far back as 1942. The males are securely employed: more than half were self-employed, a third worked in government

institutions and the remainder were employed by private firms. They are mainly, but not exclusively, Christians. Most of the interviews conducted were household interviews, often with the whole family sitting on the sofa and contributing to the story-telling. It was usually the women who did most of the talking with men interjecting and 'correcting' from time to time. (Both the research assistant and I witnessed a number of riotous situations as differences in opinion, sometimes a disagreement about a date, got completely out of hand.) Thirty-two such interviews were conducted. Because the interviews took a historical perspective, with the interviewees telling their story, they were exceptionally long. One lasted three hours and twenty-six minutes!

2 The inclusion of some Arabic throughout the text is meant primarily for Arab-speaking readers who would appreciate the expression in its original form given the layers of meanings it is capable of expressing and that are sometimes lost in translation.

3 See for example, Mary Kalantzis & Bill Cope, 'Multiculturalism and education policy' in Gillian Bottomley & Marie de Lepervanche, *Ethnicity, Class and Gender in Australia*, Allen & Unwin, Sydney, 1984.

4 Emile Benveniste, *Indo-European Language and Society*, Faber & Faber, London, 1973, pp. 239–251.

5 While I realise that this definition of home is stated as if it is an a priori certainty, in fact it is the result of both my empirical investigation and my extensive reading in the substantial literature already available on the subject. In particular, I would like to recognise the important influence of the highly stimulating issue of the journal *new formations*, no. 17, Summer 1992, titled 'The question of home'.

6 If I get up at night, my feet can take me to the toilet or to the fridge without my having to really wake up and think where to go. Home is a space of maximal bodily knowledge.

7 Witness the traumatic event of losing one's house keys to see how the event brings to the fore the anxiety associated with losing the capacity of spatial and practical control over the home.

8 Pierre Bourdieu, *Language and Symbolic Power*, Polity Press, Cambridge, 1991.

9 This is empirically true for both men and women. The point is important to make for in the case of the migrant home, both men and women who bury themselves at home and do not succeed in opening up to the host society are frequently pathologised and their houses considered unhomely.

10 For a critical interaction with such literature see the very stimulating article

by Sneja Gunew, 'Home and Away: Nostalgia in Australian (Migrant) Writing' in Paul Foss (ed.), *Island in the Stream: Myths of place in Australian Culture*, Pluto Press, Sydney, 1988. But see, for instance, Fran Bartkowski, 'Travellers vs. ethnics: Discourses of displacement', in *Discourse*, vol. 15, no. 3, Spring 1993, pp. 158–176, where the travellers as well as the ethnics happen to write excellent literary narratives of their experience of displacement.

11 What is good for Edward Said ('Reflections on exile', *Granta: After the Revolution*, vol. 13, pp. 159–72) or Salman Rushdie (*Imaginary Homelands*, Granta–Viking, London, 1991) is taken as if it represents a universal condition. The point is not that Said and Rushdie's experience of nostalgia is unimportant in explaining other forms of nostalgia but that the sociological specificity of its subject is simply ignored. Interestingly, Said and Rushdie also deploy their own nostalgia to make a life for themselves in the West where they are actually living.

12 See for example, Marjana Lozanovksa, 'Abjection and architecture: the migrant house in multicultural Australia', in Louise C. Johnson (ed.), *Suburban Dreaming*, Deakin University Press, Geelong, 1994.

13 See Gunew, p. 38.

14 It is important to note that for international migrants such spaces of homely feelings are only national spaces (Lebanese, Greek, Vietnamese, etc.) in Australia. That is, if we take an example of a Lebanese woman from one village who marries someone from the same village, she will experience homesickness when she moves to her husband's house. The spatially yearned-for 'back home' in this context is her old home. If they both move from the village to Beirut searching for work, she will also experience homesickness, but in this case the yearned-for 'back home' becomes the village. It is only when she migrates to Australia that 'back home' becomes Lebanon. In all these cases, the sphere of actual experience is much more limited than the spatial category (house, village, city, nation) used to refer to it.

15 *El-Telegraph*, 12 February 1986.

16 Kristeva's notion of the semiotic can be helpful here in characterising the affective potential of such homely songs (see Julia Kristeva, *The Revolution in Poetic Language*, (trans. Margaret Waller), Columbia University Press, New York, 1984).

17 While capturing an important aspect of the process, these descriptions are clearly romanticised. This is because such articles aim at more than just describing, they aim at the construction of migrant eateries as a desirable object of consumption for non-migrants.

at home in the entrails of the west

18 *Sydney Morning Herald*, 26 January 1993, Good Living, p. 22.

19 *Sydney Morning Herald*, 23 May 1972, p. 8.

20 I do not want to leave the impression that these practices of travelling back home in order to engage in home-building in the present leave people entirely satisfied. There is a whole dialectic of lack which, as one woman put it, leaves a bitter taste after each event of this sort. It takes you back home, but not quite, and you are left feeling a lack. Despite its importance, but given that it is a generalised existential condition well analysed in psychoanalysis, I have chosen not to concern myself with this dialectic here.

21 *Sun-Herald*, 15 January 1950, Feature.

22 ibid.

23 As I pointed out in the first part of the chapter, it also includes a sense of operating in a space where the governing law is one's own law.

24 In this structure, as intimated, the fathering and mothering subject do not have to be male and female respectively, although they are generally so within patriarchal families. Borrowing from psychoanalysis, this is a model I am aiming to develop further in a forthcoming work on migrant home-building. In this sense, mothering and fathering subjects are defined through their different relation to the Law.

25 For the research, six restaurants from each area were chosen: two up-market, two down-market, and two in-between (decided largely on the basis of menu prices, and in the case of the Glebe–Newtown area on the basis of intimate knowledge of what is available). It was initially decided to interview the owners, the staff (cooks, waiting staff) and the patrons of these restaurants. Only the owners and the staff were successfully interviewed. Many only for a few minutes, though enough to obtain sufficiently informative material for the research purposes. The interviews were unstructured but were directed at obtaining from the interviewees their conception of good food and good service and an enquiry into their fantasies of ideal restaurants. City restaurant staff were asked to comment on how they viewed the restaurants in Western Sydney and vice versa. These supply-side interviews were later supplemented with interviews of owners and staff of Lebanese restaurants in the three areas, and then further supplemented with four interviews in the Cabramatta area and two in Mosman. In total, fifty-two interviews were conducted.

26 As noted, part of the research plan was to interview restaurant patrons in the restaurants chosen in the three areas. However, while talking to restaurant owners and staff was not difficult, this was not the case with restaurant patrons. It proved hard to find an appropriate way to approach people at a restaurant to request an interview without annoying them on their night out

or annoying the restaurant owners. As a result, we abandoned the idea of interviewing the patrons and aimed at finding any person from the three defined areas willing to be interviewed on the topic of ethnic eating. Initially we divided the eating population into three classes according to educational and economic background: those who possessed high economic and educational capital; those who possessed high educational capital but were low on economic capital; and those who were low on both (measured in terms of educational background and income or profession, or in terms of self-classification as rich, middle-class or poor). As the research proceeded, this was fine-tuned with the notion of cosmopolitan capital developed in the chapter. Initially, what were dubbed the eaters' interviews were done randomly. These interviews were generally unstructured, though they all included three areas of discussion/investigation: the interviewees' history of ethnic eating and ethnic food preferences; their conception of the relation between ethnic food and multiculturalism; and finally, the changes they would like to see happening to the ethnic eating scene.

Early in the research it became clear that not many of the low in both the economic and educational capital category were being successfully interviewed in the Penrith and Parramatta areas. It was also felt that more high in both capitals was also needed from all the regions. An ad-hoc decision was made to direct efforts to obtaining interviews from these two groups. This was finally done by finding research assistants with suitable contacts. Nevertheless, the Parramatta area ended up being underrepresented. No methodical gender differentiation was made as no relevant gender-based differences in the responses was captured in the first set of interviews.

27 Ian Cook & Philip Crang, 'The world on a plate: culinary culture, displacement and geographical knowledges' in *Journal of Material Culture*, vol. 1, no. 2, 1996, p. 131.

28 Arjun Appadurai, 'Disjuncture and difference in the global cultural economy', *Theory, Culture and Society*, vol. 7, 1989, pp. 295–313; and Iain Chambers, *Border Dialogues*, Routledge, London, 1990.

29 Cook & Crang, p. 137.

30 Michael Symons, *One Continuous Picnic: A History of Eating in Australia*, Duck Press, Adelaide, 1982, p. 223.

31 ibid., p. 225.

32 For a more detailed analysis see Ghassan Hage, 'Republicanism, multiculturalism, zoology' in *Communal/Plural* vol. 2, 1993.

33 Committee to Advise on Australia's Immigration Policies, *Immigration: A Commitment to Australia*, AGPS, Canberra, June 1988. Quite tellingly, Fitzgerald saw cosmopolitanism as an alternative label to multiculturalism

at home in the entrails of the west

which he saw as a divisive concept.

34 *Sydney Morning Herald*, 14 June 1976, p. 12.

35 Interview, inner-Sydney waitress, 9 October 1995.

36 *Sydney Morning Herald*, 8 October 1994, Good Weekend, p. 95.

37 ibid.

38 *Sydney Morning Herald*, 25 June 1985, Good Living p. 2.

39 *Sydney Morning Herald*, 19 May 1987, Good Living p. 1.

40 Interview, manager of inner-city restaurant, 1995.

41 *Sydney Morning Herald*, 10 July 1986, p. 9.

42 Symbolic violence is a concept used by Pierre Bourdieu to denote processes by which certain values (such as the only good food is light food), which are essentially arbitrary and produced by a specific section of society, usually the cultural elite, end up being seen as natural and relatively unquestioned norms. See Pierre Bourdieu, *Language and Symbolic Violence*, Polity Press, Cambridge, 1991.

43 *Sydney Morning Herald*, 17 February 1987, Good Living pp. 1, 10.

44 An example of such a figure in Australia is the well-known Leo Schofield whose published reviews of restaurants have had an important impact on their fortunes.

45 *Sydney Morning Herald*, 16 March 1984, p. 3.

46 *Sydney Morning Herald*, 21 October 1986, Good Living p. 1.

47 Michel Foucault, *The Order of Things*, Tavistock, London, 1970, p. xv.

48 Pierre Bourdieu, *Distinction: A Social Critique of the Judgement of Taste*, Routledge & Kegan Paul, London, 1984, p.6.

49 Interview, March 1995.

50 At the 1993 Census, a larger proportion of people from western Sydney left school at 15 years or younger than for the rest of Sydney. That is, 23.1% of students in the Greater West left at 15 years compared to 17.6% for the rest of Sydney. Proportionally larger numbers of people from western Sydney are employed as tradepeople, clerks and labourers when compared with the rest of Sydney. For example, 15.4% of those in the Greater West are tradespeople compared with 11.3% for the rest of Sydney, whereas 8.9% of those in western Sydney are managers and administrators while the figure for the rest of Sydney is 12.2% (WESTIR, *Social Indicators of Western Sydney*, vol. 5, no. 1, September 1993).

51 We have compared a range of restaurants (categorised as expensive, middle-range and cheap) in Penrith, Parramatta and the Newtown–Glebe area.

52 This is not the case with the majority of the patrons who on the whole do not have the inter-city comparative knowledge to make such statements but who base their judgment on a comparison of what is available to them in their city or neighbourhood.

53 Bourdieu, 1984.

54 *Bulletin*, 12 March, 1996, pp. 46–7.

55 Bourdieu, 1984, p. 5.

56 Dianne Powell, *Out West: Perceptions of Sydney's western suburbs*, Allen & Unwin, Sydney, 1993, p. 7.

57 *Sydney Morning Herald*, 13 November 1993, Spectrum, p. 10A.

58 As the importance of the Cabramatta region for the culinary imaginary of inner-city eaters became a more pronounced aspect of the research findings, it was decided to conduct a series of interviews with restaurant owners and customers there. We conducted six Cabramatta eater interviews. This gave us a total of sixty-three eater interviews for the overall project.

59 Interview, March 1995.

60 Liz Thompson, *From Somewhere Else: People From Other Countries Who Have Made Australia Home*, Simon & Schuster, East Roseville, 1993, p. 132.

61 Ghassan Hage, 'Locating multiculturalism's other: a critique of practical tolerance', *new formations*, vol. 24, Winter 1996, pp.19–34.

62 bell hooks, *Black Looks: Race and Representation*, Turnaround, London, 1992, p. 29.

63 'Go primitive tonight and put dinner on a skewer or two. See what happens when the taboos of civilisation are broken and instinct takes over' begins a *Sydney Morning Herald* Good Living (12 October 1996) article on various international modes of skewering food. It goes on:
'Give cutlery a rest, hide the polished silver and put away the steak knives. It's time to return to primitive swords, to spear our food on sticks, to cook over naked flames and to burn away the veneer of civilisation in the hot coals of tonight's family dinner.
Since primitive man — or, far more likely, primitive woman — first rubbed two sticks together to create fire, he or she has been skewering food with any remaining sticks of wood and cooking it on top.'
Beside exemplifying the way skewered food is invited to metonymically convey an adventurous eating experience, this draws attention to the important role of culinary cosmo-journalists in the *construction* of this experience.

64 The interview passage quoted was a response to a direct request to state what kind of changes the interviewee would like to see happening on the Australian culinary scene. Thus, the response to this question with an 'I want', 'I would like to see' language might appear unexceptional. Yet it is important to note that not all respondents were capable or felt empowered to answer this question. A number of people, mainly from working-class backgrounds, either could not express themselves or did not feel comfortable with an expectation of being able to state how they want the Australian ethnic culinary field arranged. The capacity to do so was definitely a cosmo-multicultural class-specific conception of people's power.

65 Symons, p. 224.

66 Let us remember the interviewee quoted in the previous section claiming that the inhabitants of Cabramatta were idiots who did not know what they had.

67 Interview, 24 April 1996.

68 For an article which looks at the mode of deployment of authenticity and other strategies in Chinese restaurants, and also reviews some of the key American literature on this topic, see Shun Lu & Gary Alan Fine, 'The presentation of ethnic authenticity: Chinese food as social accomplishment', *Sociological Quarterly*, vol. 36, no. 3, 1995, pp. 535–53.

69 However, one can easily see another form of cosmo-multiculturalism being strategically playful in relation to such a phenomenon.

70 Paul Sheehan, 'The multicultural myth', *Sydney Morning Herald*, 25 May 1996, Spectrum, pp.1s, 4s.

71 Alfred Sohn-Retel, *Intellectual and Manual Labour*, Macmillan, London, 1978, p. 33.

72 Slavoj Zizek, *The Sublime Object of Ideology*, Verso, London, 1989, p.17.

73 Lawrence Grossberg, 'The space of culture, the power of space' in Iain Chambers & Lidia Curti (eds), *The Post-Colonial Question: Common Skies, Divided Horizons*, Routledge, London, 1995, p. 184.

acknowledgement

I would like to thank the many research assistants who in the last four years have worked directly or indirectly on this project: Ashley Carruthers, Nahed Chehad, Susanne Fraser, Nada Kerbage, Julie Langsworth, Justine Lloyd, Phil Mar, Clive Morgan, Ian Shapter. I would also like to thank the many others who have worked on transcribing the interviews.

5. 'icon house':

towards a suburban topophilia

helen grace

> That people could come into the world in a place they could not at first even name and had never known before; and that out of a nameless and unknown place they could grow and move around in it until its name they knew and called with love, and call it home, and put roots there and love others there; so that whenever they left this place they would sing homesick songs about it and write poems of yearning for it, like a lover...'[1]

> And will the troglodyte with his cave, the Australian with his clay hut or the Indian with his own hearth ever accomplish a June insurrection or a Paris Commune.[2]

This chapter speculates on the suburban space of the display home village, a site which has not received very much serious attention in Australian studies of suburbia. This may be because it is seen as an inauthentic manifestation of the idea of home, a commercialisation of homeliness, an unreal space incapable of yielding knowledge of any kind. My particular focus is a place called HomeWorld, the 'largest display centre in Australia',[3] situated in the aptly named suburb of Prospect in western Sydney.[4] This concentration of names (home, world, prospect) neatly condenses the hopes and dreams of home-seekers in the broad spaces of western Sydney and beyond. In this consideration of HomeWorld, I argue that the display village is the site of projection and indeed enactment of ideas of home, ideas which are themselves partly utopian, even if their realisation is reduced ultimately by the economic limitation of individual dreams. These dreams are spatially realised in the display home 'village' which I call a 'dreamscape' in order to suggest that the imagination is highly active in producing individual meaning and value in these sites and that we must read beyond their surfaces. I also argue that the display home reveals an aesthetic overarticulation of the feminine and a spatial absence of the masculine, which is a manifestation of women's power, rather than powerlessness, in the symbolic construction of home.

'icon house'

If there is a home for these speculations, it might be located in an imaginary place between the two epigrams with which this chapter began. The first refers to a spatial reverie which acknowledges a longing we might simply call sentimental or even nostalgic ('homesickness'[5]) and the second to the unrealised dreams of a utopian political desire. The images invoked by these two epigrams in turn identify the separate spheres of the domestic or private, and the public — home and world — which define the boundaries of the space in which I am working here.[6] What becomes immediately obvious is that the domestic is never a separate sphere but constantly intersects with the public sphere, creating its very conditions of possibility and its ethical purpose. This image of intersection or, more accurately interchange, is a useful way of thinking about the relation between home and world, the private and public, the local and the global.

To explore the meaning of HomeWorld and its location in the western suburbs of Sydney, I want to begin by looking at what at first might appear to be a very different dream of domestic bliss. At the end of the nineteenth century and beginning of the twentieth century, reformist ideals of the garden city or suburb received considerable support in many countries, including Australia. These schemes promised the spatial realisation of homely ideals for individuals and families, as well as the possibility of shaping populations through the rational planning of urban spaces by governments. Later in this chapter I will consider the contemporary re-emergence of garden city architecture in what is now being called 'new urbanist' or 'neo-traditionalist' architectural and planning discourse. But I begin with a historical example — the Sokol housing settlement, established in the suburbs of Moscow in the 1920s — which allows me to consider some important debates on domestic space and reveals most starkly the utopian dreaming that underlies such schemes. I want to look at this scheme to introduce three main themes in relation to domestic space and the imagination of the ideal home in Australia.

First, consideration of the Sokol housing settlement allows me to explore a notion of residual utopianism as continuing to exist in the desires for an ideal living space now articulated in the space of the display home village. I argue that individual solutions emerge to enable the pursuit of this ideal at a moment of disenchantment with the

155

home/world

Sokol — utopian remains

HomeWorld — utopia privatised

collective dream or a realisation of its impossibility.[7] Second, I use the Sokol example to emphasise the intensity of a parallel historical experience occurring after the First World War, one of extreme displacement and disorientation. Despite clear national–historical differences between Russia and Australia, the experience determines the nature of the different housing solutions which are subsequently developed in each place. Third, the debate over the uses of domestic space, especially in attempts to collectivise domestic labour, provides a stark reminder of the everyday intersections of public and private. Spatially, it might be said that the focus of these concerns is the kitchen and the bathroom — the heart and circulatory system of the house, the sites of women's most intensive labour and the very spaces which were the most contentious in the Soviet communal house.[8]

These three themes provide the framework for this chapter. I look first at utopian dreaming as revealed in the socialist garden suburb and in the plans for urban development in Australia after the First World War. I then turn to examine the tensions that emerged after both the First and Second World War in Australia as people became frustrated by the lack of adequate accommodation. The beginning of project homes and the development of display villages are traced to these historical moments as 'speculative builders' began to find ways of responding to these needs and desires. Though these developments emerged as effective selling tactics of commercial interests, the physical setting of the display village did not look unlike the garden suburb or city. I am interested in the echoes of the same kind of urban dreaming in both the commercial and government schemes, as well as the differences to be found there too. Finally I explore the gendering of spaces within the contemporary display home. Suburban developments, whether they have been sponsored by government or commercial interests, have typically been analysed by feminist scholars as oppressive of women. The domestic interiors of HomeWorld suggest that a more complex analysis is needed.

I utopian dreaming

the socialist garden suburb

Not far beyond Moscow's Garden Ring — the series of boulevards which delineate the city centre — and just before Leningradsky Prospect divides into two highways heading north by north-west out of the metropolis, lies a unique settlement of single-family dwelling wooden houses, surrounded by trees and gardens and complete with picket fences. The streets are named after nineteenth-century realist and symbolist artists: Ulitsa Levitana, Ulitsa Surikova, Ulitsa Vrubelya. This remarkable settlement, a remnant of utopian housing plans is a rare and unexpected example of Soviet *gorod sad* (garden city) architecture. The settlement was established by the Sokol Housing Association[9] in 1923 at a time of fierce polemic about the nature of socialist housing and city redevelopment.[10]

Markovnikov, the architect of the Sokol scheme, had participated in a number of experimental housing projects in the early 1920s, involving single-family dwellings, favoured as a model of workers' housing by supporters of the garden-city concept. On the other side of this polemic and much better known, the communal house was proposed, in which the socialisation of 'domestic concerns' was a key element: 'What is a socialist home? It is a home free of all domestic concerns, whether individual or collective'. In one of the more revolutionary aspects of the reorganisation of everyday life, kitchens and bathrooms were collectivised, producing, by the late 1920s, a particular technical problem:

> We have now arrived at a moment of disenchantment with the so-called 'commune' that deprives the worker of living space in favor of corridors and heated passages. The pseudo-commune that allows the worker to do no more than sleep at home, the pseudo-commune that deprives him of both living space and personal convenience (the lines that form outside bathrooms and cloakrooms and in the canteen) is beginning to provoke mass unrest.[11]

The main protagonists in this debate about socialist housing and city redevelopment were the more western-oriented modernists or urbanists (the Constructivists) and the more organicist 'de-urbanists' (the Rationalists). The latter believed that the architect needs to take into account the biological and physiological aspects of perception in devising forms and structures.[12]

Between 1919 and 1923 a new city plan for Moscow was devised by Zholtovsky and Shchusev (who were classicists rather than de-

'icon house'

urbanists). In their New Moscow plan, they envisaged surrounding the city with a ring of green spaces between which garden suburbs for the workers would be built. The plan was barely realised because of the civil war in particular, and the heated architectural polemics of the time.

For Ginsburg, one of the most prominent of the Constructivists (though later a de-urbanist[13]), socialist housing solutions did not lie in the scaled down 'manor house' model of the detached dwelling, which represented the ideals of the 'sentimental and individualistic bourgeoisie'.[14] The garden-city idea was seen as 'catastrophic' by El Lissitsky: 'These Utopians have simply quickened the corpse of eighteenth century Moscow and revived the old ring concept. Such ridiculous fantasies are born and will die in the archives.'[15]

While this prediction proved to be more or less correct, most of the plans of the Constructivists also shared this fate when a 1930 decision of the Party Central Committee brought an end to the utopian schemes of both the urbanists and the de-urbanists[16] and architecture developed its better-known monumental Stalinist style. The *Great Soviet Encyclopedia* of 1932 had the final word on the garden-city movement, the worst possible insult which could be directed at it: it was of course 'petit-bourgeois'.[17]

'the Australian with his clay hut'

Engels' 1872 speculations about housing locates home ownership in the space of the pre-industrial — the sentimental, the petit-bourgeois — and, indeed, the primitive. When he refers to 'the Australian with his clay hut' in the second of my epigrams, he does not of course have in mind a white Australian suburban dweller, but an Aboriginal Australian. In almost all references to Australia in the work of European social and political theorists (Marx, Engels, Freud, Weber, Levi-Strauss), the whole country remains an entirely ethnographic and unsettled territory, useful as a site for speculating on the possibilities of ideal societies, in spite of its primitivist limitations. We will hold onto this shadow of European thought in considering the present and the local because it has strong resonances in western Sydney, and in Australia, today. This example also reveals how dependent European political theory is on those colonial localities beyond the international

159

sphere of 'real' historical consciousness — places where the laws of history and historical materialism do not apply, allowing the theatre of European politics to enact its dramas as exemplary narratives to be emulated everywhere. And so it is Engels who brings me back to Australia and particularly to western Sydney — spaces which are imagined culturally, politically and historically as *tabula rasa*, places where revolution could, ostensibly, never happen because of the limited cultural development of people who have an attachment to small ideas of home.

everyman's 'instinctive desire'

If this space beyond history is regarded as primitive or petit-bourgeois in the terms of Engels' imagining, the implication of its being designated 'sentimental'[18] is that it is also frequently characterised as feminine.[19] Later the ambivalences of this femininity will be seen in the formulation of the terms of housing need in Australia earlier in the twentieth century. It is perhaps surprising to discover that the 'natural' preference for home ownership and for the single dwelling turns out to be, above all, what men want. In introducing the 1927–8 *Commonwealth Housing Act*, the conservative prime minister Earl Page argues that social stability and individual contentment are only possible through 'the satisfaction of the *intense desire* of the individual to own and live in *his* own home' (my emphasis), and Charles Morgan, a Labor Party member for the western suburbs seat of Reid, went even further in identifying the urge to home ownership: 'Every man has *an instinctive desire* to own his own home and this instinct should be fostered in the interests of the nation'[20] (my emphasis).

These projections of everyman's instinctive desire for home ownership are the culmination of a long history of spatial practices of bodily reform. The view that a certain relation to space itself has the capacity to reform or indeed to produce the modern citizen is implicit in prison, barracks, workhouse and hospital design from the late eighteenth century. In early nineteenth-century philanthropic schemes such as Robert Owen's model village in Scotland, The Institution for the Formation of Character at New Lanark, opened in 1816,[21] attention to ideas of communality and bodily discipline provided a model for later nineteenth-century 'model housing' projects in Europe which began to consider the spatial requirements of the working classes. In debate around the 1834 Amendments to the English Poor Law, a strict economy of space applied, with the establishment of specific allowances by the Poor Law Board: paupers in good health required 300 cubic feet each (8.5 cubic metres); the sick, 500 cubic feet (14 cubic metres) and criminals 1000 cubic feet (28 cubic metres).[22] From here, the optimum size of rooms in model housing could begin to be devised, as well as the correct division of space between the preparation of food and toilet facilities, living and sleeping quarters, sexual and generational segregation within sleeping quarters (the separation of children from adults, and men and women in lodging house accommodation). Exposure to the elements — light, air, warmth — under controlled circumstances[23] became the means by which romantic ideals of the benefits of nature were domesticated. Later this would become anti-urban in Ebenezer Howard's 'garden city' idea,[24] which gave rise to a whole movement far more realisable in the New World than the Old.

Australian suburban solutions in turn-of-the-century land subdivisions[25] established the ideal of the quarter-acre block, now increasingly seen as part of the problem of urban sprawl — or a 'waste of space'. This perception of space as a non-renewable resource, something like oil or minerals, has entered contemporary planning discourse and in particular marks the limit of the concept of western Sydney as an infinite space of expansion.[26]

In referring to garden-city ideas of urban redevelopment, it is worth remembering that Ebenezer Howard's inspiration was a socialist novel, Edward Bellamy's utopian *Looking Backward*,[27] in which a young American, seeking relief from insomnia through a hypnotist, wakes up to find himself in the year 2000; the world has been transformed and a new civilisation has arrived in which monopoly capitalism has been replaced by the benevolent state ownership of industry and services; conflict has disappeared and service to the community rather than self-interest is the dominant spirit. Howard reads the novel and immediately begins to imagine his own ideal future, one in which housing and its arrangement becomes the solution. This dream of the possibility of a rational city, a community separate from the larger unmanageable city is an old one, forming the basis of Fourier's Phalanstère — the idea of a self-managing commune. It is an ideal shared both by the garden-city planners and by the more modernist utopians like Le Corbusier. In the more banal forms of this utopianism and by the time it reaches the western suburbs of Sydney, communal dreams have been replaced by family values.[28]

But, like all utopias, failure rather than success is the more common outcome. In 1931 an ambitious plan by Australian-Made Motor Cars and Aeroplanes Ltd to build Austral City, a model industrial community near the western suburb of St Marys, came to grief in the depressed economy of the early 1930s.[29] This early plan to introduce a 'motor car manufacturing industry' in Australia argued that the establishment of such an industry invariably resulted in new, large communities of citizens and highly profitable businesses and cited the growth of the American auto industry, with asset and profit figures for the Ford Motor Company, Dodge Brothers and Studebaker. Imagined international markets were projected ('New Zealand, Fiji, Dutch East Indies, British Malaya, Philippines, Indo China, Siam, India, South Africa, China and Japan'[30]), and it was argued that Australia, with its vast mineral resources, was the 'natural manufacturing centre for the whole of the East' because it was, by steam, many days closer to its potential markets than other manufacturing nations.

The Austral City plan provided for an art-deco-style factory building which would not merely be a functional building but a 'thing of beauty' in itself, complementing the mission-style architecture of the civic centre, arranged in radial fashion around a circular park, with provision made for residential housing, churches, a social hall, a shopping centre, recreation facilities, irrigated land for growing fruit and vegetables, the installation of a water service, electric light, and power and sewerage for a self-contained city — 'all the requirements of a modern city laid out in accordance with town planning principles'[31] (that is, garden-city principles).

Sixty years later, another ambitious plan to bring the garden city to western Sydney was attempted, reviving earlier ideals of community; in an ironic coincidence, the plan overlapped the site of the earlier failed development. The proposed new development at St Marys was designed for major property developers Lendlease, by leading American architects and townplanners, Andres Duany & Elizabeth Plater-Zyberk, the internationally prominent proponents of 'new urbanism' or, as they prefer to call it, 'neo-traditionalism'. The development is characterised by 'pedestrian-friendly' living and an emphasis on what we might call *topophilia*, a love of place. The general principle is eloquently articulated in Duany's words: 'Things are not safe anywhere in a city unless the streets are loved … and it's only the places that are loved that retain their value'.[32]

The philosophy of new urbanism represents, on one level, an aesthetic–architectural engagement with the perceived social evils of urbanism, a belief that the reformation of space can reduce, or at least isolate, the undesirable features of urban expansion.[33] A desire for 'urban consolidation' has been a feature of governmental policy debate in Australia since the late 1970s, influenced at that time by rising oil prices and the need for extensive investment in infrastructure to solve the social problems of earlier urban development.[34] As a result, substantial consolidation had already begun[35] and this debate and its effects provided the climate in which the desire for an 'architecture of community' (as opposed to 'social engineering') could emerge. A competing architectural view would see the overwhelming size of the city as a positive quality, and one which might encourage technological (or more capital-intensive) solutions.[36]

II displacement and disorientation

'house famine'

As noted earlier, my second reason for using the example of the Sokol settlement is because of the parallels which can be drawn between the intensity of post-war experience in both places. The Sokol settlement elaborates a particular ideal relation to space at a time of intense displacement, such as also happened in Australia after the First World War. Within that moment a certain imaginary was formed which produced the terms of debates about housing provision in Australia up to the present. In both places, a dream of semi-rural self-sufficiency existed, one which was shaped by the particular histories of each national experience: in one place the ideal of the suburb of single dwellings remained an isolated example; in the other it became the norm.

In a quite striking example, a returned serviceman and professional who had served with the AIF throughout the war refers to a 'house famine' which greeted him on his return to Sydney. Although increased housing construction was occurring by 1920, this had little impact on 'the undoubted overcrowding which had resulted from the comparatively little building done during the war and the tendency to crowd people into tenements, flats and houses sublet to families'.[37] In Australia the intensity of housing desire in post-war periods was a direct response to shortage and homelessness which have been acute at a number of moments: after both wars and during the Depression, when widespread evictions occurred.[38]

Our present concerns with housing and the search for homeliness might also be said to relate to a post-war experience: in general, in the sense of the end of the Cold War, but very particularly for Vietnamese, Laotians, Cambodians, Lebanese, Bosnians and Turkish refugees as well as Fijian Indians, Pacific Islanders displaced by massive economic shifts in the Pacific Basin, or Hong Kong Chinese nervous about July 1997.[39] The post-war experiences which formed an Anglo sub-urban consciousness are now forming another kind of Australian sub-urban life, which manifests itself in particular transformations of landscape and interior space.

Another 'house famine' occurred in Sydney at the end of the Second World War and, like many famines in history, it might be said that it was artificially produced. The 1948 *Landlord and Tenant (Amendment) Act* extended wartime legislation which protected tenants and introduced rent control mechanisms; investors responded by not investing in housing and, because evictions were difficult to obtain, by allowing properties to fall into disrepair or by selling them. Aided by public housing policies which encouraged owning rather than renting, owner occupancy rose from 39.7 per cent in 1947 to 71.8 per cent by 1966.[40] The 'naturalness' of home ownership was thus achieved.

'house hunger'

> Of all the people who knew his obsession, who knew it and admired it and even profited by it, little Julie Maide had been the only one who understood that Roger's huge talent

for architecture was really his own wistful homelessness turned into something presentable. Of the brilliant admiring people who knew him now, she was the only one who had known Roger's house-hunger when it was so ingenuous that it did not wear its acceptable disguise of talent.[41]

As well as producing orphans and homelessness, war provides a sphere for pure research and unlimited funds for materials experimentation which find more profitable civilian uses at the cessation of conflict. Troops have to be housed and the prefabrication experiments find their way into civilian housing schemes in peacetime. In the United States, during the Second World War, leading architects such as Frank Lloyd Wright, Walter Gropius and Richard Neytra were commissioned by the government to design defence housing communities. Their projects were among the first in the United States to feature elements of European modern design — flat roofs, large windows, site plans harmonising with the landscape.

The largest private builder of housing communities in the eastern United States was Levitt & Sons, who, before the war, specialised in custom-built houses in affluent New York suburbs. The firm's wartime experience constructing defence houses was then applied in the building of private housing, or the Levittown concept, a lower-cost, less utopian version of the garden-city model, sold through project or display home developments. The moulded plywood chairs, tables and screens introduced by Charles and Ray Eames in 1946, and later reproduced in lower-cost versions, ideal for the modern project home, grew out of wartime designs for molded plywood stretchers and leg splints developed for the United States Navy.[42]

In Australia, the Commonwealth Housing Commission, established in 1943 within the Ministry of Post-War Reconstruction, set up the Commonwealth Experimental Building Station, which explored alternative housing construction, such as mudbrick or rammed earth construction, wheaten-straw houses and ideas for water storage tanks as well as insulating materials using wool. Steel and concrete houses and methods of prefabrication were successfully attempted.[43] This idealism and experimentation did not, however, prevent the situation in which post-war migrants were inadeqately housed for many years in the temporary quarters for war workers built by the Commonwealth Housing Commission during the war.

Radical architects formed the Modern Architectural Research Society (MARS), led by Walter Bunning, a Commonwealth Housing Commissioner and an early advocate of innovative housing and solar design.[44] House and garden magazines were one of the key sites for the dissemination of these new ideas, and regularly carried articles about leading international architects, such as Frank Lloyd Wright.[45] They also carried fictional stories about a longing for home ('house-hunger'), such as the story which begins this section: an orphaned child adopted by a childless couple takes refuge from a loveless family life by building cubby houses; when he grows up, he goes to an Ivy League college and becomes a leading architect, a lonely figure until he realises that his childhood sweetheart has always loved him.[46]

In spite of the promotion of modern architecture and interior decoration, a more amateur, do-it-yourself approach also becomes popular for economic reasons.[47] A tension exists throughout the period between the professionalisation advocated by architects and the necessary improvisation of the owner builders. This is manifest in the usual way, in that a process of professionalisation displaces the diversity of vernacular use, instituting its own normative practices and values: from the height of assumed authority in aesthetic matters, the vernacular and the improvised are declared to be inferior and in poor taste. An early article by Robin Boyd describes Australian house-building as being in a 'rut' because the builders are 'amateurs'. Help is at hand, however, as the Royal Victorian Institute of Architects has responded to the need to beautify the Australian 'ugliness'[48] by introducing a new service of making available architect-designed houseplans which might be purchased by prospective owner-builders and dreamers of home.[49] This follows a practice which *Australian Home Beautiful* introduced from the mid-1940s of presenting a regular column in which readers were invited to submit their own plans for aesthetic critique by a resident architect.[50]

Remnants of this tension between the architect and the builder or, more accurately, between mental and manual labour, exists in current project home design, which specifically employs contract draughtspeople rather

'icon house'

than architects — the same people that architects use to visualise and draw up their own plans.[51] Elements of design are determined by market research, which identifies preferences and market trends.[52]

This suburban DIY story is a feature of the Australian narrative of the project home which begins in 1932. In that year, according to the industry's own account, Albert Jennings took out a £700 overdraft and, using the designs of a young architect, Edgar Gurney, hired six men, built nine homes costing £895, and made a £1000 profit. The Jennings narrative ends in 1995, when the Jennings Group went into receivership[53] after losing heavily on debt-funded investments in the commercial property market, which crashed in 1990–91.

The purpose of starting the operation was, to quote Jennings: 'to build houses that were good enough and cheap enough to sell against the many mortgage sales taking place in those depression years'.[54] This 'good enough and cheap enough' dictum must be understood in the context of its emergence — the loss of home during the Depression. This narrative of loss continues to determine the nature of housing provided in the home and land packaging industry, and helps to explain the very quality of domestic space provided, the dimensions of rooms, the connections between rooms, the cost minimisation for plumbing and servicing, and so on. Notwithstanding the assumption of cheapness, the features of Hillcrest, in Caulfield, a suburb of Melbourne, Victoria, the first of the Jennings estates were not completely spartan; they included hot water to six points, tiled bathrooms and kitchens, French-polished joinery, chrome-plated swivel taps, a solid brick fence and a tree on the nature strip.

One of the original purposes of the display home — a simulacrum of the idea of home — was to provide local utility companies with the opportunity to display their appliances. If we regard the rapid expansion of domestic commodity consumption as having occurred primarily after the Second World War, then it is worth noting that the display home phenomenon, arising as it did out of the shortages of the Depression and the immediate post-war period, had helped put a consuming desire into circulation before the technical and economic possibility of its realisation could be put in place.[55]

For reasons to do with the specific nature of post-war public housing policies in New South Wales, the first display-home village in Sydney, located in Carlingford in the north-west, was not built until 1961[56] but since then the display home — initially small pockets of houses in new release areas, constructed by individual 'speculative' builders — has become a widespread feature of outer urban landscapes.

III at homeworld

dreamscapes

HomeWorld II is one of a number of display-home villages dedicated to the selling and celebration of the idea of home, and because of the availability of larger pockets of land on the edges of the city, almost all these project home selling points are located in western or south-western Sydney.[57] The original HomeWorld, also in Prospect, was opened in 1986 with the intent of turning it into an actual living environment after all the homes were sold. Today there are no longer any indications that the small quarter of houses, built around curving roads like any other suburb, was once a display-home village.

The same fate has just overtaken HomeWorld II, established in 1990 and closed in September 1996. Although the houses are said to become 'tired'[58] and require new decor and new trim, the time-span of about six years seems to be the life cycle, not only of the display home but also of the village in which it is located. Beyond this time frame, the spaces cannot maintain the appearance of a dreamscape, since they become worn, lived in — too homely perhaps. They shift from representing the idea of home to becoming actual homes. The dream of an ideal space becomes the reality of houses which are lived in; the interior decoration, chosen according to an interpretation of market taste, is removed and replaced by ordinary things, objects which are selected — or select themselves — according to economy rather than aesthetics, or according to an unpredictable combination of the two.

In this sense, the display-home village comes to life in a way that it can never do when it is fulfilling its purpose as a point of sale. There is a troubling presence in the display home, an emptiness at its heart, which is produced by the static, frozen neatness of its arrangement and the sadness of a space designed for familial occupation yet finding itself unoccupied. It is a quintessentially melancholic space, having links with

'icon house'

Organic origins, cosmological suburbanism
Created by I.H.J. Advertising Pty Ltd. © Homeworld III Pty Ltd. 1996

other such spaces, like the theme park at the end of the day, the fairground or circus once the show is over and the sideshows and all the animals packed up to move onto the next town. The display-home village is always moving onto the next town, which means it is constantly engaged in the contradiction of setting up an ideal space, which when consumed as such, leads to its destruction. And so the caravans and coloured flags move on and are set up somewhere else, along another margin, a kind of frontier of the surburban dream, a circus, a sideshow, a mundane carnival, part of an everyday dreaming. These are not, then, landscapes so much as dreamscapes for an endless dreaming. In the latest version of the HomeWorld theme, the latest episode of this popular and long-running serial, New HomeWorld at Kellyville promises to be bigger and better. There will be 127 homes and, if HomeWorld II could claim to be the biggest display-home village in the southern hemisphere, the New HomeWorld is aiming for global distinction.

The project home concept is one which, although centred on groups of houses specially built for display purposes, spreads beyond the 'village', determining the look of all the new houses in the surrounding areas. This is particularly apparent around the display-home development at Cecil Park, west of Fairfield, where acres of new housing in endless variations of the designs at the display home site, are being built, in an area of extraordinary social — and architectural — diversity. Project homes in a range of sizes, depending on the needs and resources of the purchasers, have sprung up, around mosques, Buddhist temples, a Serbian cultural centre, theme parks (Australia's Wonderland), service stations, garden centres.

If it seems inappropriate to speak of houses 'springing' up in the context of a highly planned activity, determined at every step by restrictions — local government regulations, building codes, bank interest rates — which seem to preclude the possibility of describing these activities in organic terms, there is nonetheless a propensity to use the metaphor of new life to understand both the rapidity of change and the naturalness of urban development. This is made explicit in the first of the advertisements for New HomeWorld. An egg with the tiled eaves of a new house bursting through its shell is used as the central image announcing the new concept, and prospective seekers of home are invited to 'Come and see the beginning of a whole New HomeWorld'. In this way, the fact that the village is incomplete (it is only in its infancy) does not prevent it from functioning immediately. Houses can still be bought and sold, since they will be built afresh on the purchasers' own land.

New HomeWorld's very incompleteness enhances the possibilities of imagining the dream home and simulates home life itself, an always incomplete, provisional process. The homes which are completed will stand alongside empty blocks of land and new building sites. If incompleteness in this sense can be thought of as a kind of real virtuality, computer simulation also brings the world of virtual reality to the idea of home and to the home construction industry. The expense of building actual houses is replaced with software that creates virtual model homes, infinitely increasing the choices — the menu items — which may be available.[59] In this context, the organic image of the egg serves to anchor the dream in a world of reality and a sphere of

'icon house'

reproduction, a cycle of life which is not simply suburban but cosmological.

Although the idea of home and suburbia which has been the subject of much intellectual activity in Australia since the 1950s is assumed to be quintessentially Anglo-Australian, as many as half the sales of homes through the HomeWorld II site are to Asian buyers,[60] either settled here or investing in Australian property. The architecture of the houses might be called 'international–domestic' style, providing a kind of generic western idea of the use of home space, one which imagines a two-generational nuclear family unit, even though this might not apply to the single-parent families or extended multi-generational families who live in the houses.

The houses are given names, which suggest aspirations or dreams which are a long way from the real lives of the purchasers: the Regency Royale, the Ascot Grove, the Brittany, the Killara series, the Cremorne series, the Forrest Lodge, the Seaview. The name of the house refers to another time, another place, a better suburb, a better location, a better view, an Anglo or European imaginary. The new migrant, whose cultural background is beyond this experience, encounters a desirable foreignness which will be adapted by the use of furniture never seen in the display homes, by food, clothing, religious ornamentation, subtle changes which will transform the living spaces, subverting the connotations of the naming. These details are, on the whole, worn in the interior spaces of the houses and are not yet reflected in external architectural details or styles. Some architectural register of population change occurs in the building of places of worship, for example in mosques and temples, but domestic architecture does not yet declare these shifts.

The home theme continues in other consumption possibilities close to HomeWorld II. The local shopping centre is Homebase, a group of furnishing and home supply shops which includes a McDonald's and other fast food stores. The complex also includes a huge Ikea store, a model of conveyer-belt consumption which also applies in moving through HomeWorld II. The one-way traffic direction of this marketing concept means that the consumer is processed in a particular way, directed through the store according to a carefully worked out plan of consumption habits. There is little room in this model for what

171

Margaret Crawford describes as the Gruen Transfer,[61] a principle which applies in shopping malls in which the consumer is converted from being a shopper with a specific purpose and focus, walking briskly towards a particular destination, into an impulse shopper, with a more meandering gait, and a less focused purpose, a kind of sleepwalking.

The uni-direction of the prospective purchaser's walk through HomeWorld also has a specific purpose. It suggests a path of social advancement, an upward mobility, beginning with the house at the bottom end of the market, its lower ceilings, its smaller rooms and overall space, its cheaper cost, moving up through higher ceilings and more bedrooms to the deluxe models, with two storeys, spa-baths, walk-in wardrobes, en-suite bathrooms, centralised vacuum cleaning with outlets in each room, and two and even three garages. The reality is harsher than this and the purchasers are aware of their economic constraints but the dreaming has no limits.

'icon house'

If the problem of the popularity of the project home blurs the borders of the display-home village, so that it appears to spill into the surrounding suburbs, a new marketing concept attempts to recentre the site and also to deal with the perception of decentredness, which may be a disorienting aspect of life in the postmodern metropolis.[62] In the newest configuration of the display-home model, one of the largest of the home-building firms, Pioneer Homes, is using the concept of the 'icon house'. In this marketing concept, they have developed a model village in which a central house — the icon house — is surrounded by a small group of exhibition houses. The icon house is used as the place where all the business of mixing and matching house styles, colours, fittings and so on is done, finance arranged and contracts signed. Once these transactions are finished for the day, it is hoped that the icon house can be used as a 'community house' for functions and meetings by local groups. Because the icon house is set up as a house rather than a hall, it has an inbuilt 'homeliness' absent from older kinds of public space. As such, we might suggest that it constitutes a newer form of public space, ambivalently located between public and private. A sense of communality is in this case being produced around the idea of homeliness. This tendency might be called the spatial production of community since it draws on the same material as New Urbanism's 'architecture of community'.

What is emerging in the improvisational attempts to build homes in cities and to build them with(in) communities is a newer form of civic life markedly different from the classical forms which it has taken. In these newer models, governmentality is increasingly privatised, although this tendency has not been as formalised in Australia as it has been in the United States.[63]

the real and the fake home

> there is ground for taking the house as a tool for analysis of the human soul.[64]

> What are the contradictions of camp and kitsch, the proliferation of consumption as a form of magical labor, the over-articulation of the discourse of the feminine here, but the contradictions of a sign in crisis?[65]

The materiality of homeliness is not easily locatable. It belongs primarily in the sphere of experience and memory and its value cannot be specified or quantified but it can be evoked in spaces which are thought to be homely. The display home is a space which imagines the possibility of successfully simulating homeliness, and the unoccupied absence which resides at its heart is the very ground on which this possibility is realised. In discussions of suburban Australia, the emphasis has been on the more quantifiable aspects of domestic life, the historical, economic, political and sociological details of that experience.[66] More recently, particularly in architectural and aesthetic theory,[67] and to some extent in anthropology and cross-cultural studies,[68] attention has been given to what might be called the spatial experience of the house — or the incorporation of perception, memory and experience.[69]

The domestic interior has long had a capacity to be seen in iconic terms: it is a place where objects become icons — photographs on a mantelpiece, things to which deep sentimental value is attached as well as devotional items themselves. One of the richest speculations on the meaning of interior space is Bachelard's *Poetics of Space*, and I would like to draw on it in walking through the display home, in order to suggest the possibilities of reverie even in reading such a site, a space usually thought to be beyond the possibilities of such imaginings.

The houses of Bachelard's reverie are old houses, houses which possess the sediment of history, while the display home is a new house, one unmarked by personal association. It is, in this sense, a blank space on which the occupiers write their own histories, inventing a past as well as a future. In any case, in Bachelard's reverie, the meaning of the house is not to be explained in terms of its history, the politics and economy of urban planning and consolidation, or in the sociological account of its use, since: 'Space that has been seized upon by the imagination cannot remain indifferent space subject to the measures and estimates of the surveyor. It has been lived in, not in its positivity, but with all the partiality of the imagination.'[70]

Bachelard employs a phenomenological poetics, concentrating less on the materials of causality and prosaics and more on the materials of poetry. For Bachelard, space has a resonance, a quality of reverberation produced by the poetic image, which has the capacity to make the distant past resound with an echo, the intensity and duration of which is hard to predict. Bachelard's concern in *Poetics of Space* is with what he calls *felicitous space*, with eulogised space, and he prefers to call his investigations *topophilia*, since 'they seek to determine the human value of the sorts of space that may be grasped, that may be defended against adverse forces, the space we love'.[71]

The display home is resistant to this kind of analysis because it is a space of simulated memory and yet such an approach is able to recognise the value of the *idea* of space in which the display home also partakes. This is all the more so if we refuse to accept the opposition between 'the real' and simulation, between authenticity and inauthenticity (which we must do as soon as we allow imagination to enter our deliberations). Bachelard's approach is, however, more on the side of a particular authenticity and one which must also be allowed in thinking of the value of the spaces with which I am dealing — an authenticity of knowing the self:

> Not only our memories, but the things we have forgotten are 'housed'. Our soul is an abode. And by remembering 'houses' and 'rooms' we learn to 'abide' within ourselves.[72]

'icon house'

There is also a certain romanticism in Bachelard's evocations, particularly of 'the "wax" civilization', a little reverie on domestic labour, harder to imagine for those who actually perform it:

> From one object in a room to another, housewifely care weaves the ties that unite a very ancient past to the new epoch. The housewife awakens furniture that is asleep.[73]

And yet HomeWorld in its name mirrors Bachelard's contrast of house and universe, a contrast which is clearly operative in the space itself. Bachelard's spatial reverie is evoked wherever there are dreams of the French provincial countryside; these are not New World spaces, though they may also be dreamed here.

Although Bachelard's work provides a preliminary framework in thinking about the display home, Susan Stewart's work can also help in understanding the fine detail which is to be observed in these spaces. Her book, *On Longing*, a critical discussion of the miniature, the gigantic, the grotesque, the souvenir, arises from within the New World's attempts to come to terms with spaces which do not carry (for the newcomers) the sediment of history. In considering the space of the display home, Stewart's work is especially useful because her concerns have a place for the value of the inauthentic:

> If authority is invested in domains such as the marketplace, the university, or the state, it is necessary that exaggeration, fantasy, and fictiveness in general be socially placed within the domains of anti- or nonauthority: the feminine, the childish, the mad, and the senile, for example. In formulating the loci of authority and exaggeration in this way, we necessarily and nostalgically must partake in the lost paradise of the body and the myths of the margin, the outside. Exaggeration always reveals the cheap romance that is reality, but then it must move on.[74]

The 'fake' home is such a reality and its magic consists in the infinite capacity which people have to transform its exaggerated promises into meaningful living spaces, while also savouring its cheap romance. And so we move to the manifestation of dreamscape in the prosaics of display-home space.

175

IV 'the lost paradise of the body'

As already cited, Stewart has written of the over-articulation of the discourse of the feminine in referring to the camp and the kitsch and if we can, with due respect for them, suggest that indeed these two styles are also operative in the display home, then it is hardly surprising that we should find a particular decorative intensity here. But paradoxically, what we might call the 'feminisation of space' in the display home is also accompanied by the desexualisation of the family. The ideal home is a place of impossible innocence, like the framed illustrations of pastel-coloured fairy stories on the walls of children's rooms. 'Family values' must eliminate all those signs of the possibility of its own reproduction in the context of an increasingly obsessive attention to the protection of children from strangers, trusted caregivers, incestuous parents and even other children.[75] This desexualisation of the family is figured in a number of details: the centrality of the girl's room, the marital bedspread, the gender-neutrality of the nursery and frequently the absence of the boy's room. If the use of sex in advertising can be seen as one of the main features of commodity marketing, sexlessness is one of the features of display in the project home.[76]

the centrality of the girl's room

In the display home, the girl's room features strongly and is signified by an excessiveness of furnishings: frills, flounces, obsessive details and ornamentation, a fussiness thought to be feminine. It may have virginal bedcoverings, white or the softest pastel colours, lace, embroidery, broderie anglaise, appliqué; paintings and prints on the walls will feature softness in subject matter (pets, flowers, idealised images of girl children), suggesting overall innocence and purity. Considerable attention to detail is paid in this bedroom and it may sometimes be a more noticeable feature of the house than the 'master' bedroom itself, though of course, never as large. The girl's room becomes a space for imagining the possibilities of a future femininity which will be supportive rather than challenging, ordered rather than disruptive. The decoration of this space is designed to appeal to the parental (or potentially parental) shopper rather than to the girl child: the young couple imagining a happy family, domestic order and homely peace. It is of course a reality which rarely exists; the daughter will not necessarily be neater and tidier than the son and she will not necessarily be less disruptive. Her delinquency (if it comes to that) will perhaps be more traumatic, especially for the mother.

The door[77] to the girl's room is open in the display home, but in the 'real' home it is more likely to be shut firmly in the face of the mother. The girl will reside permanently there, playing loud music, or watching television, playing video games, surfing the Net looking for sex and sticking posters of rock musicians on the walls, lifting the paint in the process. Clothes will be scattered everywhere in the room except in the drawers; remnants of food and drink will be found on all flat surfaces, covered in mould, or ants or cockroaches; ashtrays will be full; cigarette butts will be scattered around, especially if there are non-smoking restrictions in the rest of the house. Of course the display home cannot be expected to suggest these possibilities, and indeed there may be some real homes where they do not occur, but these are very rare situations, as rare as the discovery of lost tribes in remote jungles.

the marital bedspread

In the enchanted landscape of the display home, the marital bedspread deliberately and ostentatiously covers over the activities of the bed, detracting from them in a way which also seeks to suggest order and good taste. It must be thick enough to cover the wrinkles of blankets, sheets and pillows, and large enough to entirely cover the bed, including especially its legs or coasters (like tablecloths in Victorian times, designed to cover the legs of tables because it was considered impolite to reveal them). But the bedspread itself is a strange object with its own history. It is frequently padded or quilted. In the past this has provided a space on which personal narratives might be written, narratives of economy and industry, narratives of loss and longing, narratives of family and home. In recent feminist art-historical research, the importance of the quilt has been reinstated and a revival has seen the production of commemorative quilts as historical narratives and these have become major artworks.[78]

In the display home the bedspread retains only a residual connection with the tradition of quilting. It is more likely to be an industrially produced object, made from synthetic ('man-made') fabrics unknown to the earlier quilting traditions. It is designed to be impervious to the stresses and strains of family life (such as the children jumping on the bed with their shoes on). One of the modern forms of the quilt was the more generic chenille bedspread, representing a particular industrial technique, and signifying a certain homeliness. But the bedspread today is of a stiffer substance, making it somewhat more unhomely in its feel and texture. Instead, it suggests the kind of synthetic material and pattern one expects to find out of this world, in space stations for example. This type of bedspread does not suggest sensuality but rather practicality, since within the display home it must withstand the onslaught of hordes of potential buyers and their sticky-fingered children.

More specialised bedroom displays in furniture salesrooms and manchester shops display more fully the practical and sensual possibilities of bedlinen, in the use of natural materials, particularly cotton and linen, the use of extra pillows, suggesting a life for the bed other than sleeping, an increased use of larger, 'European'-style pillows which suggest luxury and a distinction not to be found in the 'standard' pillow. In display homes, standard pillows are used, but occasionally a number of small 'scatter cushions' may be placed on the bed for ornamental purposes rather than for comfort and this also has the effect of breaking up the overwhelming immensity of the bedspread, especially if the bed is king- or queen-sized.

Because of the particular marketing needs of the display home — the necessity to minimise the threatening suggestion of familial sexual activity — the 'master' bedroom cannot be seen as an intimate space. As already discussed, it is the bedspread itself which succeeds in preventing any sense of intimacy from appearing in this space, by virtue of the loudness of its patterning or the discomfort of its texture when touched. This is again the space of exaggeration as Stewart understands it and as Bachelard writes: 'One might say that immensity is a philosophical category of daydream. Daydream undoubtedly feeds on all kinds of sights, but through a sort of natural inclination, it contemplates grandeur.'[79]

The marital bedspread possesses what we might call, after Bachelard, an 'intimate immensity', bearing in mind the dream of grandeur which

'icon house'

the 'master' bedroom evokes in its scale, its walk-in robe, its en-suite bathroom; this is the territory of television soap rather than suburbia, 'Dynasty' rather than 'Doonside'.

Although I have suggested that the display home is a dreamscape, the sense of reverie which is suggested by this observation is not experienced as intensely in those spaces where sleep and dreaming occur. Rather it is in the spaces of wakefulness and familial activity, the kitchen, the 'living' room, the 'family' room, where daydreaming is more possible. In general the bed itself is less imposing than the bedspread, and the constraints of a certain taste in interior design exclude more imposing beds, such as wondrously baroque expanses of swirling white fibreglass bedheads with built-in mirrors and stereo systems. Expressiveness is limited to the bedspread, and the potential buyer whose taste runs to such beds will not find them here. The display home presents generic choice and the particularity of consumption occurs beyond its confines.

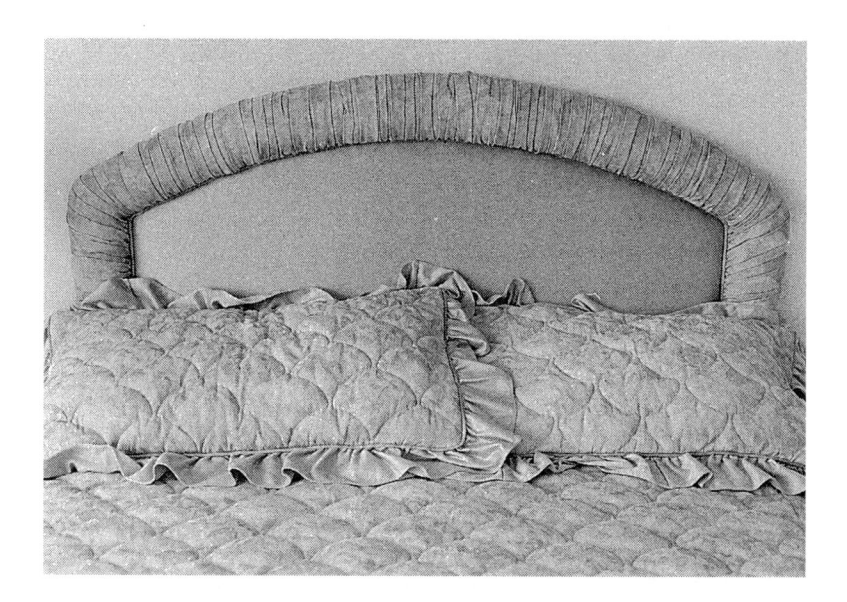

The marital bedspread — desexualising space

home/world

The genderless nursery — the 'fanciful cravings' of pregnancy

'icon house'

the nursery

If the 'master' bedroom's reproductive function is masked by the bedspread, the outcome of its activities is represented by displacement onto the nursery, another fantasy space offering considerable scope for decorative excess. The nursery is rarely seen as a gendered space within the display home, so that this most fundamental aspect of the child's life, the first question asked of its identity ('is it a boy or a girl?') remains unanswerable in these rooms. Instead, the display-home nursery is more interested in the crib or bassinet and its coverings, which is the most obvious content of the room especially in the absence of its expected contents. This creates a sense of neurotic intensity, indeed a barrenness within the space, a sense of the anxiety of infertility. Where has the baby gone? Who has taken the baby? Will there ever be a baby? Of course the space can only represent expectant hopes, and marketing departments must be careful in dealing with the complexity of the couple's desires for children. The neutered space leaves room for individual projections of desire, just as the girl's room projects an ideal femininity and the generic master bedroom leaves space for the baroque imaginary bed.

The nursery is a quiet, still space with delicate wallpaper and even greater softness than the girl's room; unlike the other bedrooms, there is a potential for reverie in this space, all the more so because of the absence of the detail of gender. It evokes the rich possibilities of the beginning of life, before the reality of the baby's demanding presence descends into the space, bringing with it endless changing, washing, feeding and, most especially, constantly disrupted sleep.

But the intensity of the space of the nursery can also be related to another dimension of longing and imagination. In Stewart's discussion of longing, she identifies two meanings of the word, one which refers to 'yearning desire' and the other to 'the fanciful cravings incident to women during pregnancy'. It is this second meaning which, she argues:

> takes us closer to an imagined location of origin, be it the transcendent with its seeming proximity to the immortal or the rural/agrarian with its seeming proximity to the earth; for it is in pregnancy that we see the articulation of the threshold between nature and culture, the place of margin

between the biological 'reality' of splitting cells and the cultural 'reality' of the beginning of the symbolic.[80]

In the display home, a space which is geographically located between the rural and the urban, projecting a future in which purchasers are able to imagine an escape from reality into an ideal, transcendent private world, the nursery and remembered places of childhood remain sites of 'fanciful cravings', evocative rooms where nostalgia clings to the walls.

the absence of the boy's room

In some display homes, the boy's room may be particularly prominent, signified again by the bedspread, or a bed in the shape of a racing car, a train, a rocket. More commonly, there is no recognisable boy's room within the house. The four bedrooms in display homes will be marked clearly as 'master' bedroom, girl's room, nursery, while the fourth bedroom will be a more neutral space, hard to fix in terms of gender. It may have soft furnishings and wallpaper which is heavier and deeper in tone, but this could equally suggest occupation by another adult, a grandparent or a guest.

This gender ambiguity underlines the problem of masculinity in the space of the display home. It is as if the boy will be required to conduct his activities outside as a means of maintaining order within. It might also suggest that he will be required to leave as soon as possible, vacating his room so that it becomes the longed-for 'spare' room, a breathing space within the stages of family life, allowing for a parental imagining of other possible uses (guests, grandparents, an exchange student, a boarder, a storage space).

The ambiguity of the space suggests a containment which parallels the projections of ideal femininity determining the furnishings of the girl's room. If femininity has to be actively produced within the space of the girl's room, then masculinity must be actively reduced or minimised in the boy's room. A similar scenario of occupation can be imagined for the boy's room as was earlier imagined for the girl's room. However, in this scenario, the volume is turned up. There is an electric guitar or a drum-kit. The room is cluttered and disordered. Or the opposite is also possible. It is quieter: the door will still be closed in the face of the parent but inside, long hours might be spent in a darkened room, in front of a computer screen playing games. Another world beyond the space of the house itself might be entered, a virtual world of fantastic characters, nothing like the parents, the sister, the neighbours. The boy may indeed eliminate himself from the space, may simply cease to be there, even though he is physically occupying the room.

kitchen and bathroom utopias

As indicated, the spaces of reverie in the display home are more likely to be the waking rather than the sleeping spaces. In part this possibility is produced by the very fact that the house is a display home. Its *not-lived-in-ness* places it in a state of suspended animation which the real home never possesses, so the neatness and order and peace which it convincingly simulates provides an ideal dreamscape. To relax on the new sofa and look at the (always) spacious 'living' room, uncluttered by toys, newspapers scattered everywhere, clothes waiting to be put away; to walk through the kitchen and caress the granite benchtop cleared of dishes, abandoned knives covered in butter and vegemite, half-eaten apples, saucepans soaking, crumbs everywhere — these are the pleasures of daydreaming. In the sphere of revolutionary politics, the truly utopian dream of the collectivisation of housework — the Soviet projection of 'a home free of all domestic concerns' — attempted unsuccessfully to respond to this fantasy that domestic labour might magically disappear simply by turning domestic labourers into industrial workers and eliminating domestic spaces in which individual kitchens were the focus.

It is the kitchen which occupies the central place in the display home, and on floorplans this is easy to see in a spatial sense. Although the kitchen may not be in the middle of the house — it also needs to oversee the backyard — the house's activities are arranged around it. The kitchen is the control room of the house and is one of its most technologically complex and capital-intensive spaces — like the control room in the Starship Enterprise, especially in the case of the 'ultra-modern' style (for those who prefer a more feudal image of power relations, the 'country-style' or 'French provincial' kitchen evokes the domestic order of an *ancien regime*).

It is the place from which activity is directed and discipline and control exercised. In some cases, a bay-window layout provides an overseer's panoramic view of the backyard and the 'family room' simultaneously. This allows for parental surveillance of the other occupants. One might be tempted to invoke the frequently overused idea of panopticism here — the mother's line of vision as a panoptic gaze. But it is perhaps more useful at this point to mention Foucault's emphasis on the productivity of power: children have an infinite capacity to evade supervision and to fall into the pool or to injure themselves just as the mother's back is turned to answer the phone.[81]

If the mechanics of sexual reproduction are concealed as I have suggested by the marital bedspread and the arrangement of bedrooms, the kitchen's place in bodily reproduction is more centrally acknowledged by emphasising the mechanics of food production and consumption and the mother's assumed role in this. At the end of this cycle, toilets and bathrooms compete with the kitchen as technological fantasy spaces of the house. Recently, the spa bath has become a new feature of the display home, competing with the now largely defunct waterbed as one of the more excessive details of domestic design — features which exist primarily to signify luxury. Occasionally there will be two spa baths in the one house, one in a bathroom exclusively for the parents and another for more general use. The spa bath appropriates a more social space — the bath house — and privatises it, appropriating it for heterosexual family use. If the master bedroom of a family home must conceal its sensual activities, the fittings of the bathroom and toilets become the site where a formal sensuality is permitted to manifest itself, in the luscious curves of toilet bowls, baths and handbasins, the smoothness of finish in glazed surfaces.

the veneer of the father

There is, however, a contradictory aspect to the over-articulation of the feminine in the display home. We began by referring to the problem of domestic labour in a revolutionary context and the sense in which the activities of the kitchen and the bathroom could be defined as secondary in the face of a need to collectivise and industrialise a society. We saw that in the Australian context, on the other hand, the values of an idealised feminine domesticity were invoked as much by men as

'icon house'

THE MASTERTON HOMES STORY

Masterton Homes began from humble beginnings in 1962 after its founder, Jim Masterton, recognised the unique advantages of prefabrication in home building as he pre-assembled frames and trusses on the front lawn of his modest home.

Like all businesses, Masterton Homes began in a small way, but has grown to be one of the largest contract home builders in NSW. One of the secrets of Jim Masterton's success is that so many of the components of his homes are made by companies within the Masterton Group.

Jim Masterton purchased Superior Frames and Trusses in 1985. This company has since grown to be one of the largest Frame and Truss manufacturing plants in Australia.

In 1986, Jim purchased the Knebel Kitchen company. Knebel Kitchens are exclusive to Masterton, so you can be sure you're getting the kitchen of your dreams.

In 1988, Jim Masterton began manufacturing Aluminium Windows and Doors as well as Vanity tops in a new factory in Moorebank. In 1990, consumer trends turned towards Marble Bench Tops and Vanities which meant moving Fantasy Marble & Glass to even larger premises.

Masterton Homes has constructed just over 17,000 new homes to date and has always been seen as "THE INNOVATOR – NOT THE IMITATOR" and accordingly is seen to be the leading force in the cottage building industry.

Masterton have won more awards than any other builder – 34 awards in 1989-1992 alone. Jim Masterton also won the prestigious "Liverpool Businessman of the Year" award in 1989.

Masterton Homes Exhibition Village at Warwick Farm is forever changing with 18 homes on display 7 days a week. Why not visit us and discover for yourself "the Mastery of Masterton".

The veneer of the father

Reproduced Courtesy of Masteron Homes

185

women in the establishment of the single dwelling home as a housing norm and the basis of urban development. Alternative possibilities (multi-unit options such as terrace houses, now called 'town-houses', or flats) were not considered until after the Second World War, by which time the ideal had become established as a persistent dream which is realised, more or less, in the display-home village.

One of the most noticeable aspects of the display home is that there is a problem of masculinity in these spaces; it is as if the picket fence is built from the inside, rather than the reverse and men are kept out as much as women are kept in.[82] If masculinity is figured within the house, it is frequently in terms of a quite marginal front room — a 'study' — spatially separate from the family. It might appear that masculinity does not fit within the home, as if its furnishings prove too heavy and the activities of masculinity too disruptive to maintain order within this realm. These activities are relegated to outside: the garage, the garden shed, the barbecue area.

More particularly, it is masculinity which oversees the concept of the display home itself. At this level, patriarchy functions as a kind of veneer, a sign in search of a referent. The television advertisements for AV Jennings Homes feature an old man — the original Jennings, now dead — declaring 'It makes me a very proud old builder'. In the 1994–95 catalogue for Masterton Homes, a 1950s layout style is employed to suggest the ideal of the Australian dream ('Masterton Homes — Making it easier to achieve the great Australian dream'). But the narrative of the company would be incomplete without a story of origins, a master builder, a story of 'humble beginnings' and hard work. Again, the figure of the patriarch is presented, in this case in a photograph of the builder, looking benevolent, with a young girl who, hyperfeminine in her frilly dress, white shoes, pink ribbon, grasps his arm above the wrist. A granddaughter perhaps. The patriarch must give rise to more than one generation.

The most pointed manifestation of the phenomenon I am describing is condensed in a display feature in one of the Masterton homes at HomeWorld II. A life-sized cardboard cut-out figure of radio talk-show host John Laws is propped in the corner of a living room declaring via a voice balloon, 'Discover the mastery of Masterton'. The irony is that

'icon house'

these are not spaces where men's mastery has a place, hence the necessity to create an appearance of control which is absent in practice.

On the surface, the display home is clad with this veneer of patriarchy: the image of the master builder remains the sign of that which was said to be man's 'instinctive desire' as home ownership became a mass phenomenon. As already argued, in these earlier phases it was the house 'famine' observed by the returned soldier, or the house 'hunger' experienced by the orphan, which gave shape to an ideal space. But within the lived experience of the spaces themselves it is the discourse of the feminine which remains dominant, while the masculine production of domestic meaning and value has not increased.[83]

The display home is both an ideal place, a dreamscape and a space of anxiety, a contradictory site in which femininity is dominant in an ambivalent sense and masculinity is awkwardly displaced, disturbing the easy assumptions which have been made about gender relations. It is an enchanted space in a complex landscape of the everyday and my reading of it attempts to understand some of the issues at stake when we think about the technical provision of housing, issues which are no longer simply reducible to questions of public versus private. I am also suggesting that the display home is a place in which meaning is made and imagination is at play. A well-known theorist of the everyday reminds us of some of the reasons for taking seriously the value of the meanings produced here:

> The everyday is a kind of screen, in both senses of the word: it both shows and hides; it reveals both what has and has not changed … It is what Hegel called 'the prose of the world', nothing more modest. Before Marx, labor was considered unworthy of study as before psychoanalysis and Freud, sex was considered unworthy of study. I think the same can be said of the everyday. As Hegel said, what is the most familiar is not for all that the best known. The *unrecognized*, that is, the everyday, still has some surprises in store for us. Indeed as I was first rethinking the everyday, the surrealists were already attempting to conjure up ways to bring the extraordinary out of the ordinary.[84]

notes

1 William Goyen, 'House of breath', cited in Gaston Bachelard, *The Poetics of Space*, Beacon Press, Boston, 1969, p. 58.

2 Engels, *The Housing Question*, Progress Publishers, Moscow, 1975, p. 25.

3 Home '93', Blacktown TAFE Advanced Certificate of Management Students Research Project, 1993, p. 2.

4 For an account of the emergence of western Sydney as a distinct area, the result of specific post-war policy and planning decisions, see chapter 2.

5 On the ambivalences of nostalgia and 'homesickness', see chapter 4.

6 For a more philosophically developed discussion of the significance of this separation of private and public, see chapter 3.

7 In Australia of course, the revolution is always a disappointing affair. Robert Freestone refers, for example, to the 'incomplete revolution' which garden suburb thought and experiment achieved in Australia; R. Freestone, 'The Great Lever of Social Reform: The Garden Suburb 1900–30' in M. Kelly (ed.), *Sydney: City of Suburbs,* University of New South Wales Press, Kensington, 1987, p. 73.

8 In an ironic return of the repressed, a new kitchen–bathroom renovation shop recently opened in Moscow, called *Svetlyi Put* (Radiant Path), named after a still very popular 1940 Stalinist musical comedy (directed by Grigory Alexandrov, starring Liubov Orlova with music by Dunaevsky) about the values of socialism, collectivism and epic industrial labour. For the best and most richly resonant account of communal living, see S. Boym, *Common Places: Mythologies of Everyday Life in Russia*, Harvard University Press, Cambridge, Mass., 1994.

9 A collective of artists and intellectuals whose descendents still live there. I am grateful to Dr Alla Petrikovskaya, Academy of Sciences, Moscow, for drawing my attention to the settlement and encouraging me to visit it.

10 Selim Khan-Magomedov, *Pioneers of Soviet Architecture: The Search for New Solutions in the 1920s and 1930s,* Rizzoli, New York, 1987, p. 345.

11 'For a new socialist resettlement of mankind', *Sovremennaya Arkhitektura*, nos 1–2, 1930, reproduced in Anatole Kopp, *Town and Revolution: Soviet Architecture and City Planning 1917–1935*, Thames & Hudson, London, 1970, p. 248.

12 N.V. Dokuchaev, 'The rationalist group of modern Soviet architects' in W. Rosenberg (ed.), *Bolshevik Visions: First Phase of the Cultural Revolution in Soviet Russia,* part 2, *Creating Soviet Cultural Forms: Art, Architecture, Music, Film, and the New Tasks of Education,* University of Michigan Press,

'icon house'

Ann Arbor, 1990, p. 175.

13 Vladimir Paperny, *Kultura 'Dva'* (Moscow, 1996) (1st edn, Ardis Publishers, Ann Arbor, Michigan, 1985). An excerpt entitled 'Movement — Immobility' appears in translation in A. Efimova & L. Manovich (eds), *Tekstura: Russian Essays on Visual Culture*, University of Chicago Press, 1993.

14 M. Ginsburg, 'The prerequisites of the new style' in Rosenberg, p. 169.

15 A. Tarkhanov & S. Kavtaradze, *Stalinist Architecture*, Laurence King, London, 1992, p. 80.

16 Tasks relating to the transformation of the way of life: 'Decree of the Party Central Committee', *Pravda*, 29 May, 1930, reproduced in Kopp p. 259.

17 Cited in S. Buder, *Visionaries and Planners: The Garden City Movement and the Modern Community*, Oxford University Press, Oxford, 1990, p. 140.

18 Ginsburg, in Rosenberg, p. 169.

19 T. Rowse, 'Heaven and a Hills Hoist: Australian critics on suburbia', *Meanjin*, vol 37, 1978, p. 12. See also A. Gilbert 'The roots of anti-suburbanism in Australia' in S. Goldberg & F. Smith, *Australian Cultural History*, Cambridge University Press, Melbourne, 1988.

20 Carolyn Allport, 'Castles of security: The New South Wales Housing Commission and Home Ownership 1941–61' in M Kelly (ed.) *Sydney: City of Suburbs*, University of New South Wales Press, 1987, pp. 96–7.

21 Robert Owen, 'An address to the Inhabitants of New Lanark' in A. Fried & R. Sanders (eds), *Socialist Thought: A Documentary History*, Doubleday Anchor, 1964, p. 154.

22 Cited in E. Gauldie, *Cruel Habitations: A History of Working-Class Housing 1780–1918*, Allen & Unwin, London, 1974, p. 92. In the twentieth century, the quantification of breathing space reached new heights in the Soviet communal apartment, in which it was established that a minimum living space of 10 square metres per person and 13 square metres per family were required. S. Boym *Common Places: Mythologies of Everyday Life in Russia*, Harvard University Press, Cambridge, Mass., 1994, p. 124.

23 In one ingenious scheme proposed to reduce infant mortality it was suggested that infants and children from the slums and 'crowded quarters' should be loaded onto barges during the hot season and towed out to sea to be exposed to the fresh ocean breezes. P.E. Muskett, *An Australian Appeal: The Evil, the Cause, the Remedy*, Sydney, c. 1892. From an advertisement contained in P.E. Muskett, *The Art of Living in Australia,* Eyre & Spottiswoode, Sydney, 1893, facsimile ed., Kangaroo Press, 1987).

24 Ebenezer Howard, *Tomorrow: A Peaceful Path to Real Reform.* Rev. and

home/world

republished as *Garden Cities of Tomorrow* (London, 1902). Howard had trouble finding a publisher for the first edition and was finally assisted, as it happens, by George Eastman, the managing director of Kodak. Dulgad MacFadyen, *Sir Ebenezer Howard and the Town Planning Movement*, Manchester University Press, Manchester, 1970, p. 22.

25 The most comprehensive account of these developments is Robert Freestone's *Model Communities: The Garden City Movement in Australia* Nelson, Melbourne, 1989.

26 'There will only be about four years supply of land left in the older release areas of the western corridor after 2000', Lendlease Presentation on ADI Site Plan, University of Western Sydney, Nepean, 14 October, 1996.

27 Edward Bellamy, *Looking Backward: 2000–1887*, Ticknor & Co, Boston, 1887.

28 In a promotional tour of Australia by Charles Reade, from the British Garden Cities and Town Planning Association in 1914, a 'one family, one house' message was being presented (Freestone, in Kelly, p. 57).

29 R. Freestone, *Model Communities: The Garden City Movement in Australia*, Nelson, Melbourne, 1989, p. 160.

30 'Austral City: An Australian Motor Enterprise', *Building*, 12 January, 1931, p. 60.

31 ibid., p. 64.

32 Anne Susskind, 'Visiting architect warns about the garages that could eat Sydney', *Sydney Morning Herald*, 13 September, 1995, p. 9. See also chapter 2 on 'feral suburbia'. For more detail on New Urbanism, including a selection of New Urbanist projects in the USA, see Peter Katz, *The New Urbanism: Toward an Architecture of Community*, McGraw-Hill, New York, 1994, (afterword by Vincent Scully). For Australian responses to the concept see Natalie O'Brien, 'Failure in the suburbs and an end to rubber-stamped houses' and Chris Johnson, 'Ten commandments: a better way to live' *Weekend Australian*, 26 October, 1996, Property section, pp. 6–7.

33 The Lendlease promotional package on the St Marys development identifies the problems of suburban sprawl, pollution, transport congestion and unemployment, which it will 'assist the NSW State Government' to reduce by building a new community on the Australian Defence Industries site.

34 M. Edwards, Response from the National Housing Strategy, in *Consolidating for People: The impact of urban consolidation on the planning and provision of human services: Western Sydney Regional Organisation of Councils (WSROC)Proceedings of Seminar*, 16 November, 1990, p. 32. See also C. Edmondson, *Urban Consolidation and Social*

Justice: Final Report, workshop proceedings and resource manual, WSROC, March 1992.

35 There were much higher rates of growth in multi-unit housing than in detached dwellings in western Sydney. See A. Gooding, *Background to the Study and its Findings in Consolidating for People: Proceedings of Seminar*, p. 22.

36 D. Jones-Evans, 'Vision of a modern city: bigger, denser, networked', *Sydney Morning Herald* 26 April, 1995.

37 J.S. Purdy, *Metropolitan Health Officers Report*, Department of Public Health Annual Report, NSWPP, Sydney, 1920. Also cited in P. Spearritt, *Sydney Since the Twenties*, Hale & Iremonger, Sydney, 1978, p. 14.

38 N. Wheatley, 'Meeting them at the door: radicalism, militancy, and the Sydney anti-eviction campaign of 1931' in J. Roe (ed.), *Twentieth Century Sydney: Studies in Urban and Social History*, Hale & Iremonger, Sydney History Group, 1980.

39 The most impressive recent presentation of this is Clara Law's film, *A Floating Life*, 1996, which has been called 'the best Chinese diaspora film ever' (J. Hoberman, *Village Voice*, 18 September 1996). In particular, Dion Beebe's evocative cinematography produces a sense of the colour of the western suburbs — and of the domestic interior — which conveys the experience of the display home better than any other description.

40 Terry Kass, 'Cheaper than rent: aspects of the growth of owner-occupation in Sydney 1911–66' in M. Kelly (ed.), *Sydney: City of Suburbs*, University of New South Wales Press, Kensington, 1987.

41 'Life sized dream', *Australian House & Garden* February, 1949.

42 'World War II & the American Dream: How Wartime Building Changed a Nation' exhibition, National Building Museum Washington, 11 November 1994–31 December 1995. Exhibition design by Michael Sorkin Studio and Design Writing Research. Information taken from electronic version of pamphlet distributed on the exhibit. On Levittown see B. M. Kelly, *Expanding the American Dream: Building and Rebuilding Levittown*, State University of New York Press, New York, 1993.

43 C. Allport, 'The unrealised promise: plans for Sydney housing in the forties', in J. Roe (ed.), *Twentieth Century Sydney: Studies in Urban and Social History*, Hale & Iremonger, Sydney History Group, 1980.

44 W. Bunning, *Homes in the Sun: The Past, Present and Future of Australian Housing*, W.J. Nesbit, Sydney,1945. (Foreword by Dr H.C. Coombs).

45 'A century of modern architecture, part 1', *Australian Home Beautiful*, August 1946, pp. 21–3.

home/world

46 'Life sized dream', *Australian House & Garden* February 1949, pp. 62ff. The story, like much of the material, is syndicated from an American edition of the magazine.

47 In 1952–53 half of the new houses in New South Wales were being built by owner-builders. C. Allport, 'Castles of security: The New South Wales Housing Commission and home ownership 1941–61, in M. Kelly (ed.), *Sydney: City of Suburbs*, University of New South Wales Press, Kensington, 1987, p. 111.

48 Robin Boyd, *The Australian Ugliness*, Penguin Books, Ringwood, 1960.

49 Robin Boyd, 'Planning for better living', *Australian House & Garden,* July 1949, pp. 22–3.

50 'Considering the plan', *Australian Home Beautiful,* 1945.

51 For a recent exchange of views similar to the late 1940s and early 1950s territorial–professional disputes, see P. Ward, *Weekend Australian*, Property section, 5 October 1996, and letters in response (*Weekend Australian*, Property section, 26 October, 1996, p. 9.) It is claimed by one correspondent that 80% of home plans submitted to local councils are put together by building designers rather than architects.

52 Interview with Allam & Meriden Classic Homes, sales & marketing manager, 21 November 1995; interview with Pioneer Homes sales & marketing manager.

53 'Receiver for Jennings: $258m debts', *Sydney Morning Herald,* November, 1995. The land and home building operations were sold to Long Homes.

54 Cited in 'Home '93' p. 4. For more detail see D. Garden, *Builders to the Nation: The AV Jennings Story*, Melbourne University Press, Melbourne, 1992.

55 In the late 1940s, the concept of the 'packet mortgage' — a scheme for including the cost of a refrigerator, vacuum cleaner, washing machine, floor polisher and sewing machine in the overall mortgage — was promoted. See 'The anti-drudgery plan', *Australian House and Garden* January, 1949, p. 15. The article is addressed to the husband rather than the wife, since it involves economic decisions which were then thought to belong to the realm of the husband. A spatial argument is used to justify the extra loan amount — the provision of a washing machine reduces the amount of space needed for a laundry, thus reducing the overall cost of the house. Laundries remain small spaces in display homes.

56 'Home '93', p. 4.

57 The main display-home villages in Sydney are located at Prospect (HomeWorld II, with approximately 94 homes,) Cecil Hills (The Masters,

'icon house'

Elizabeth Park, 94 homes), Narellan (Mt Annan II, 35 homes), Parklea (Parklea Homemarket, 30 homes), Casula (Housing World Casula, 60 homes), Camden (Harrington Park, 26 homes) and Holsworthy (Wattle Grove, 11 homes). New HomeWorld (which will eventually have 124 homes) is at Kellyville.

58 S. Molitorisz, 'Buyers feel right at home in display villages', *Sydney Morning Herald*, 12 December, 1994, p. 7.

59 A. M. Moodie, 'Dream homes to become virtual reality', *Weekend Australian*, 8–9 April, 1995, p. 13. D. Vrana 'Virtually home', *Los Angeles Times*, 23 September, 1996, p. D1.

60 S. Molitorisz, *Sydney Morning Herald*, p. 7. The builders who display homes at the site are responsible for 70% of all new home starts in NSW, worth three-quarters of a billion dollars annually. The price range of houses is low, beginning at around $50 000, so the 'good enough, cheap enough' dictum still applies.

61 Margaret Crawford, ' The world in a shopping mall' in Michael Sorkin (ed.), *Variations on a Theme Park: The New American City and the End of Public Space*, Hill & Wang, New York, 1992.

62 Mike Davis' *City of Quartz*, (Verso, London, 1990) is one of the best known accounts of this decentredness of urban form.

63 See in particular E. McKenzie, *Privatopia: Homeowner Associations and the Rise of Residential Private Government*, Yale University Press, Princeton, NJ, 1994.

64 Gaston Bachelard, *The Poetics of Space*, Beacon Press, Boston, 1969, p. xxxiii.

65 Susan Stewart, *On Longing: Narratives of the Miniature, the Gigantic, the Souvenir, the Collection,* Duke University Press, 1993, p. 171.

66 Here I have in mind the excellent mapping of suburban space which it is necessary to use, rather like a street directory, in driving around this territory (even though the spaces which are my concern are, on the whole, off the edges of the maps supplied here); M. Kelly (ed.), *Nineteenth Century Sydney: Essays in Urban History*, Sydney University Press/Sydney History Group, 1978; P. Spearritt, *Sydney Since the Twenties*, Hale & Iremonger, Sydney, 1978; J. Roe, (ed.), *Twentieth Century Sydney: Studies in Urban and Social History*, Hale & Iremonger/Sydney History Group, 1980; G. Wotherspoon (ed.), *Sydney's Transport: Studies in Urban History*, Hale & Iremonger/Sydney History Group, 1983; M. Kelly (ed.), *Sydney: City of Suburbs*, University of New South Wales Press, Kensington, 1987.

67 B. Hillier & J. Hanson, *The Social Logic of Space*, Cambridge University Press, Cambridge, 1984.

68 S. Kent (ed.), *Domestic Architecture and the Use of Space: An Interdisciplinary Cross-Cultural Study*, Cambridge University Press, Cambridge, 1993; J. Fox (ed.), *Inside Austronesian Houses: Perspectives on Domestic Designs for Living*, National Library of Australia, Canberra, 1993.

69 In particular K. Dovey, 'Model houses and housing ideology in Australia', *Housing Studies*, vol. 7, no. 3, pp. 177–188. See also B. Colomina, 'The split wall: domestic voyeurism' in B. Colomina (ed.), *Sexuality & Space*, Princeton Architectural Press, New York, 1992. Colomina's discussion of the organisation of the interior in the houses of Loos and Le Corbusier is finely nuanced. Although my concern is with the space of more anonymous houses, those which are not 'authored' by high modernist architects, Colomina's approach is useful because she is also dealing in a sense with empty spaces (even if they are lived in).

70 Bouchard, op. cit., p. xxxii.

71 ibid., p. xxxi.

72 ibid., p. xxxiii.

73 ibid., p. 68.

74 Stewart, p. xiii.

75 J. Cashmore, 'When child's play goes wrong', *Sydney Morning Herald*, 9 December, 1996, p. 11.

76 'The exclusion of sexuality is itself sexual' (Mark Wigley, 'Untitled: The Housing of Gender', in B. Colomina (ed.), *Sexuality & Space*, Princeton Architectural Press, New York, 1992). In the 1993 Australian Perspecta exhibition, a group of artists installed works in one of the display homes at HomeWorld II. The works were uncanny presences within the house, and one artist in particular chose to comment ironically on the pretence of asexuality within the girl's bedroom (see work by Eugenia Raskopoulos in 'Sweet Dreams', curated by Suhanya Raffel & Isobel Johnston, 'Australian Perspecta', 1993, satellite exhibition, The Balmoral (Clarendon Homes), HomeWorld II, 16 October–21 November 1993).

77 'But how many daydreams we should have to analyse under the simple heading of Doors! for the door is an entire cosmos of the Half-open', Bachelard, p. 222.

78 For example, the commemorative quilt hung in Parliament House Canberra, designed by Kay Lawrence and executed by embroiderers' guilds in each state. For a general account of domestic craft, see Jennifer Isaacs, *The*

'icon house'

Gentle Arts: 200 Years of Australian Women's domestic & Decorative Arts, Landsdowne Press, Sydney, 1987. For a more critical account of the place of craft, and especially embroidery, see Roszika Parker, *The Subversive Stitch: Embroidery and the making of the feminine*, The Women's Press, London, 1984. On quilts, see C. L. Safford & R. Bishop, *America's Quilts and Coverlets*, Dutton, New York, 1972.

79 Bachelard, p. 183.

80 Stewart, p. x.

81 M. Foucault, *Discipline and Punish: The Birth of the Prison*, Penguin Books, London, 1977.

82 On the philosophical problem of inside and outside, Bachelard is again useful. He calls the oppositional relation between the two terms 'this geometrical cancerization of the linguistic tissue of contemporary philosophy'(p. 213). The final chapter of *The Poetics of Space* is indeed 'The dialectics of outside and inside': 'Outside and inside form a dialectic of division, the obvious geometry of which blinds us as soon as we bring it into play in metaphorical domains. It has the sharpness of the dialectics of *yes* and *no*, which decides everything. Unless one is careful it is made into the basis of images that govern all thoughts of positive and negative ... Philosophers, when confronted with outside and inside, think in terms of being and non-being' (p. 211-12). If outside, the space of being, is thought to be masculine, then inside, the space of non-being is feminine. As we have seen however, this dividing line collapses from the inside; in the interior space of the display home it is the masculine which is the space of non-being.

83 D. Ironmonger, (ed.), *Household Work: Productive Activities, Women and Incomes in the Household Economy*, Allen & Unwin, Sydney, 1989.

84 H. Lefebvre, 'Toward a leftist cultural politics: remarks occasioned by the centenary of Marx's death' in C. Nelson & L. Grossberg, *Marxism and the Interpretation of Culture*, University of Illinois Press, 1988, p. 78.

Acknowledgement

Photographs by author unless otherwise indicated.

index

ABC television 33
Aboriginal Family Resettlement Scheme 10
Aboriginal peoples 1–2, 6, 7–11, 28(n22)
Aborigines' Welfare Board 8–10
Adorno, Theodore 15, 24, 82, 95–6(n37 & 38)
aged people, Aboriginal 10–11
alienation 78–9
Allen, Woody 76
Anglo-Australians, food and 111–24
anonymity 79
Antigone (Sophocles) 70–5, 77, 79, 80–3, 93(n16)
Appadurai, Arjun 120
Arcadia 44, 51
architects 165–6
artists and cities 76–7
Ashton, Nigel 61
Ashton, Paul 38
assimilation 8–9, 114–15
Aussie battler 68, 92
Austral City 162
Australian bush 85–7
Australian Home Beautiful (magazine) 166
Australian landscapes 89–91
Australian Ugliness (Boyd) 18, 90
authenticity
  ethnic food and 125–6, 134–8
  homes and display homes 172–5
AV Jennings 167, 186

Bachelard, Gaston 173–5, 178, 195(n82)
Banks, Joseph 85–6
bathrooms, display homes 184
Baudelaire, Charles 20, 76
Bauman, Zygmont 23–4
bedspreads, dreamscapes and 178–9

Bellamy, Edward 161
Benjamin, Walter 20–1
Bentham, Jeremy 39
Benveniste, Emile 101
Blacktown 1, 2, 6, 44
Blainey, Geoffrey 133
Blue Mountains LGA 6
Bourdieu, Pierre 13, 14, 102–3, 128, 129–30, 151(n42)
Boyd, Robin 12, 18, 90
boys rooms, display homes 182–3
Britain, urban planning and 36–7, 161
bureaucracy 78–9

Cabramatta 134, 138–44
Campbelltown 44
Carlingford 168
Cartwright, Rev. Robert 1
Caulfield 167
Cecil Park 170
Chambers, Iain 120
Chinese food 113, 137–8, 141–4
cinema 81, 95(n36)
cities
  anonymity, alienation and impersonality 78–80
  culture and 70–6, 78–80
  development of and human reason (Sophocles) 70–5
  European origins of 66, 69–70
  food and 108–11
  Hegel's views 70–5
  home and 81–4
  modernity 20–4, 37, 63(n11), 66, 69, 78–80
  nature and 77–8, 84–5
  Plato (city as centre of culture) 75–6
  postmodernity and 20–4
  suburbia and 26, 84–92

196

index

City of Sydney Strategic Plan 39
Clarke, George 38–9, 41–2, 52
class
   cosmo-multiculturalism and 100, 124–34
   housing and 36, 159–61, 189(n23)
   Western Sydney and 11, 18, 24–5, 33, 35, 67, 88–9
communal housing 155, 157–9
communality 108, 111–12, 160
community
   home and 103
   houses, in display villages 172–3
Community (DURD publication) 7
Condition of Postmodernity (Harvey) 22–4
Cook, Ian 119–20
cookbooks 120
cooks, demand for 123–4
cosmo-multiculturalism 99, 118
   authentic food and 134–8
      Cabramatta 138–44
   class and 124–34
   culinary 118–24
   power relations and 139–46
cosmo-vegetarians 125–6
cosmopolitan capital 124–5
cosmopolitanism 121, 150–1(n33)
   see also cosmo-multiculturalism
County of Cumberland Council 41
County of Cumberland Planning Scheme 25
   green belt and urban village concept 43–5, 60–1
   historical roots of 35, 41–2
   hopes of authors 42–3
   newspaper supplement 52–3
   public exhibition 52–7
   public submissions to 57–8
   school projects and 54–7

   selling the concept 52–7
   Sydney's growth overriding 60–2
   whole area concept 46–7
Cox, Philip 31, 32, 35, 44
Crang, Philip 119–20
Crawford, Margaret 172
Creative Cultures 7
cultural diversity 121, 131, 133
   Cabramatta 142–4
   tourism and 126–9, 145
   urban planners and 17–19
culture
   cities and 70–7
   impersonality and bureaucracy 78–80
   migrants and food 111–18
   Sydney and 67, 69, 77, 84, 121
   tourism and 126–9, 142–6
   Western Sydney's lack 84–92, 126–9

Daley, M. T. 7
Daruk Aboriginal Medical Service 10
Dawkins, John 13
de Certeau, Michel 37–8, 60
democracy and planning 37, 57–62
Derrida, Jacques 93(n16)
developers 7, 33
Dharuk Local Aboriginal Land Council 10
Dharuk people 2, 8
Dialectic of Enlightenment (Adorno & Horkheimer) 95–6(n37 & 38)
difference, urban planners and 17–19
Directorate of Aboriginal Welfare 10
disease
   Aboriginal peoples and 8
   cities and 36, 189(n23)
display home villages 26–7, 154, 167–70
   domestic history and 174–5

197

femininity of 176–84
genderless spaces in 180–2, 194(n76)
icon house 172–3
male absence in 182–3
masculine overview of 184–7
styles 170–2
Dixon family 9
domestic labour 157, 183
Donald, James 36–7
dormitory suburbs 44
dreams, of home 57–62, 154, 163–4
  display homes 168–72
    interiors of 176–84
Drysdale, Russel 87, 90
Duany, Andres 162–3
DURD 7

eating habits 118–24
education
  Aboriginal people 9–10
  Western Sydney residents 127, 151(n50)
El Safi, Wadih 107
El Telegraph (newspaper) 107
employment, planning and 43–4
Engels, Fredrich 154, 159–60
ethnic food 26, 99, 111–18
  authenticity 134–8
  class and 124–34
  commodification and 135–6, 144–6
  power relations and 115–18
  restaurants 118–24
  western culture and 136–8
  see also cosmo-multiculturalism
Eyre, John 85–6

Fairfield 6
familiarity, home and 102
family

and the universal 72–5
construction of in display homes 176–84
modernity and 79
femininity
  display homes and 176–84
  home ownership and 160–1
feminist theory
  critique of Hegel 93(n18)
  home and 94(n41)
  postmodernism and the city 21–4
  suburbia and 17–18
feral suburbia 31–3, 35
Fishman, R. 95(n35)
Fitzgerald Inquiry (1988) 121, 150–1(n33)
flaneur 20
Flesh and Stone (Sennett) 96(n40)
Floating Life (film; Law) 191(n39)
Forrest Gump (film) 81, 95(n36)
Foucault, Michel 124, 184
Fourier, Charles 161
Freestone, Robert 188(n7)
Fulop, Liz 12

garden cities 27, 158, 161, 188(n7)
gardens 89–91
Gastronomy, Symposium of 124
gaze 112–13, 129–30
gender, display homes representations
of 176–84, 194(n76)
Gilgai Centre 11
Gilligan, Carol 96(n41)
Ginsburg, M. 159
girls rooms, display homes 176–7
Greater West, defined 4–7
  see also Western Sydney
Greater Western Sydney Economic Development Board 7
green belts 43, 45, 54, 60–1

index

Gropius, Walter 165
Grossberg, Lawrence 145
Gruen Transfer 172
Gurney, Edgar 167

Habermas, Jurgen 76
habitus 102–3
Harvey, David 21–4, 25
Hawkesbury LGA 6
health
   Aborginal peoples and 8, 10
   cities and 36, 161, 189(n23)
Hegel
   discussion of *Antigone* by 69–75, 83, 93(n16), 96(n41)
   study of the ordinary and 187
Hewson, John 68
Hillcrest estate, Caulfield 167
home 74, 80–4, 87–8, 96(n41), 99
   and home building, nature of 101–4
   display villages and 154, 174–5
   dominant culture, migrants and 111–18
   food and 100, 108–11, 111–18
   history and 174
   migrants and 100–1, 104–8
   real and fake 173–5
home ownership
   desire for 58–9, 64(n31), 160–1, 164, 191(n39)
   do it yourself and architects 166–7, 192(n47 & 51)
   urban planning and 58–60, 159
Homebase shopping centre 171
homemaking 82–3
HomeWorld (I and II) 154, 155, 156, 168–72, 175
hooks, bell 136
Horkheimer, Max 82, 95–6(n37 & 38)

Horne, Donald 17, 19, 87
house and garden magazines 166
house building
   builders and architects 166–7, 192(n47 & 51)
housing
   Aboriginal peoples and 8–10
   construction material and style 164–8
   display homes 26–7
   ethnic differences and 17–19
   garden suburbs 27, 158
   post war shortage 163–4
   Soviet planning 26–7, 155–9
Housing Commission of NSW 3, 9–10
housing estates 167
Housing Question, The (Engels) 154, 159–60
Howard, Ebenezer 161, 189–90(n24)
Humphries, Barry 16

'icon house', display villages 172–3
Ideas for Australian Cities (Stretton) 17, 67
image, of Western Sydney 2, 4, 7, 11–12, 31–3
see also othering
immigration
   home ownership and 58–9, 64(n31)
   multiculturalism and 121
income, culinary choices and 125–6
individualism 79, 81
Indo-European Language and Society (Benveniste) 101–2
infrastructure provision 7
inner city
   decay 36, 44, 49, 189(n23)
   restaurants 118–19, 122, 124–6

199

separateness from the west 126–34
intellectuals
  postmodernism and 23–4
  suburbia 16–19
intimations, home building and 104–8
Irigaray, Luce 93(n18)
Irish migrants 97(n45)
isolation 78–9

Jennings, Albert 167

Kay-Shuttleworth, James 36
Keating, Paul 68
Kellyville 169
kitchen spaces, display homes 179, 183–4
Kohen, Jim 2
Kristeva, Julia 107, 148(n16)

law
  and nature 71–5, 81
  cities and impersonality 78–9
Law, Clara 191(n39)
Lawson, Henry 86–7
Le Corbusier 162
Lebanese migrants 100–1, 105–8, 146(n1)
  food and 108–11, 114–16
Lefebvre, Henri 25, 187
Lendlease 61, 162–3, 190(n33)
longing, display homes and 176–82
Looking Backward (Bellamy) 161
'Lost in Space' (ABC television program) 33
Lovelock family 9
Lucky Country (Horne) 17, 19, 87

McGillivray, Alec 17
McLeod family 9

Macquarie, Governor 1–2
Margan, Frank 121
Marxism and postmodernism 23–4
masculinity, display homes and 182–3, 184–7
Massey, Doreen 22–4
Masterton Homes 185–6
media
  representations of Western Sydney 2–4, 7, 11–12, 31–3
migrants
  dominant culture, food and 111–18
  food, multiculturalism and 100–1, 108–11, 132
  home building 100, 104–8
  restaurants and 124–38
    Cabramatta 138–44
modernity
  city and 20–4, 37, 66, 69
  culture and loss 78–80, 83–4
  Western Sydney and 84
Morgan, Charles 160
Morris family 9
Morris, Meaghan 19, 22–3
Moscow 155–9
multiculturalism
  food and 26, 99–101, 111–18
  immigration 121
  Western Sydney 131–2
  see also cosmo-multiculturalism; migrants
Mundara Youth Refuge 10
Murrawina Child Care Centre 10

National Tourism Industry Training Committee 124
nationalism 86
Native Institution, Parramatta 1
nature
  and human reason 71–5

index

and the city 77–8, 89–91
Australian experience of 84–91
Western Sydney and absence of 84–8
NESB people 6
  housing and 17–19
  see also migrants; multiculturalism
New Lanark 160
New Towns, English 43
new urbanism 61–2, 162–3, 173, 190(n32)
Neytra, Richard 165
Non English Speaking Background people
  see NESB people
North Shore, contrast with the 'west' 31, 32, 35, 44
nostalgia, migrants and 104–6, 147–8(n10)
Nugent, Maria 28(n22)
nursery, dreams and 180–1

O'Farrell, Patrick 97(n45)
Odyssey (Homer) 82, 96(n38)
Olympic bid 121
On Longing (Stewart) 175, 176
opportunity, home and 103–4
Orientalism (Said) 68
othering
  ethnic food and 140–2
  of Western Sydney 11–12, 67–8, 88, 126–9
Out West: perceptions of Sydney's Suburbs (Powell) 2, 4, 11–12, 32–3, 67, 131
Owen, Robert 160

Page, Earl 160
Parramatta 1, 2, 6
particularity 80

Penrith 33–4, 44
Phaedrus (Plato) 75–6
Phenomenology of the Spirit (Hegel) 69–75, 93(n16)
Phillip, Governor Arthur 46–7
Pignolet, Josephine 124
Pioneer Homes 172
Pittuma Resource Centre 11
Plater-Zyberk, Elizabeth 162–3
Plato 75–7
Poetics of Space (Bachelard) 173–5, 178, 195(n82)
polis 75
Politics and Poetics of Transgression (Stallybrass and White) 11–12
Post-War Reconstruction, Ministry of 41–2
Postmodern Geographies (Soja) 21–4, 25
postmodernism, city and 21–4
Powell, Diane 2, 4, 11–12, 13, 15, 18, 31–3, 67, 131
power relations
  cities and 22–3, 115–18
  ethnic food and 134, 139–46
Practice of Everyday Life (de Certeau) 37–8
'problem' suburbs 14, 31–3
Production of Space (Lefebvre) 25
project homes 168–72
  icon house and 172–3
Prospect 154, 168
public housing 164–7
public sphere and the domestic 76, 96(n41), 155
public transport 7

quilts 177–8, 194–5(n78)

Rabinow, Paul 37
racism 9, 114–18, 131

201

reason and nature 71–5
reflexivity 14, 66
Regarding Henry (film) 81, 95(n36)
religion and modernity 79–80
representation 14–15
  cities 36–7, 66–7
Republic (Plato) 75
restaurants 118–24, 149–50(n25 & 26)
  authenticity and 134–8
  Cabramatta 138–44
Reynolds, Henry 97(n42–4)
Richmond 44
Riverstone 44
Rowse, Tim 16–17
Royal Commission for Greater Sydney 41
Rushdie, Salman 109, 148(n11)

Said, Edward 68, 148(n11)
satellite towns 44, 61
SBS television 144
scholars, Western Sydney and 13–14
security, home and 102
Sennett, Richard 96(n40)
shopping malls 171–2
Smithers, Carmel 122
social body 36
social disadvantage 33, 35
social reform, urban planning and 36–8, 41–2
social research, Western Sydney and 11–16
Sohn-Rethel, Afred 144–5
Soja, Edward 21–2
Sokol housing settlement 155–9, 163
Sophocles 70–5
space
  County of Cumberland as a 46–7
  ethics of 66–7, 96–7(n42)
  home and 103, 173–5, 187

personal and planning 57–62, 160–1, 189(n22)
postmodern theory and 21–4
social relations and 11, 18, 24–5, 33–5
urban planning and representation 36–8
Western Sydney as separate 89, 126–9, 132
St Marys 43, 44, 61, 162–3, 190(n33)
Stallybrass, P. 11–12
State Planning Authority 61
state, site of reason 73–5, 96(n39)
stereotypes, negative 2–4
  see also image, of Western Sydney; 'westies'
Stewart, Susan 175, 176, 178, 181
Stretton, Hugh 17, 67
student population, Western Sydney 6
subjectivity
  and objectivity 71–5, 76
  Western Sydney denied 84–92
suburbia 95(n35)
  critiques of 12, 16–19, 26
  planning and 31
  praise for 17, 67
  wasteland status 87–9
surveillance
  new urbanism and 173
  urban planning and 36–7
Sydney
  County of Cumberland plan 42–62
  culture and 67, 69, 77, 84
  planning and 39–41
Sydney Morning Herald (newspaper)
  Aboriginal housing in the West 9
  County of Cumberland plan supplement 52–3
  eating habits and 123, 152(n63)

index

immigrants and 111
Western Sydney, 'problems' and 31–3
Sydney Region Outline Plan 61
symbolic violence 123–4, 151(n42)
Symons, Michael 120–1, 141–2

tenants 164
Terra Nullius 85, 97(n42–4)
theory, multiplicity of 15, 24
Time Out (London magazine) 119–20
tourism 126–8, 145
  Cabramatta and 142–4
truths 15–16
2WS radio 7, 33

universal and the particular 71–5
University of Western Sydney 6, 7, 12–13
Urban and Regional Development, Federal Department of (DURD) 7
urban consolidation 163
urban design 31
urban development 33, 39
urban planning 6–7, 23, 25
  Clarke's approach in Sydney 38–41, 52
  County of Cumberland Scheme 42–62
  history of, in Europe 36–8
  home ownership and 57–60
  housing styles 165–6, 171, 191(n42 & 43)
  migrants and 58–60, 64(n31), 171
  public rationalism v private dreams 57–62
  Soviet Union 26–7, 155–9
  utopian and garden city ideas 155–63, 189(n23)
  view from above 39, 41, 46–52, 60

urban renewal 39
urban sprawl 31, 33, 35, 44, 50, 61–2, 161
urban squalor 44, 49, 189(n23)
urbanisation 69
utopian planning 155–9, 160–2, 189(n23)
  see also garden cities

vegetarianism, culinary choice and 125–6
Vietnamese restaurants 138–44
village communities 43–4
'Voice of Lebanon' 107

Ward, Russel 86
Watson, Sophie 17–18
Weber, Max 78–9
Weir, Peter 3, 4
Western Sydney
  Aboriginal peoples 1–2, 6, 7–11, 28(n22)
  as the other 11–12, 67–8, 88, 126–9
  changing perceptions of 91–2
  cosmo-multiculturalism and 126–34
  defining 3–4
  display homes and 154–5, 162–3, 168–71
  economic significance 6
  locating the 'west' 11–16
  mapping and geography of 4–7, 27(n12)
  media depiction of 2–4, 7, 31–3
  multiculturalism 131–2
  population 6
  'problems' 11, 14
  scholars and 13–14
  social research and 11–16
  subjectivity denied 84–92

Western Sydney Area Assistance Scheme (WSAAS) 7
Western Sydney Regional Organisation of Councils (WSROC) 7, 12
'westies' 4, 7, 66, 67, 68, 84, 89, 91–2
WESTIR 4
Whatever Happened to Green Valley (film; Weir) 3, 3
Whelan, Paul 4
White, A. 11–12
Whiteley, Brett 90
Whitlam government 7
whole area planning 46–7
Willey, Keith 2
Windsor 44
women and suburbia 17–19
    see also femininity
Wright, Frank Lloyd 165, 166

Zizek, Slavoj 145
zoning 54